A TIMBER FRAMER'S WORKSHOP

Joinery, Design & Construction of
Traditional Timber Frames

Fox Maple Press

Parlor of a reproduction of Jefferd's Tavern, originally built, circa 1760, York, Maine. Reproduction built in Brownfield, Maine, 1979.

A Timber Framer's Workshop

Joinery, Design & Construction of Traditional Timber Frames

By Steve Chappell

A Corn Hill Book
Fox Maple Press, Inc. West Brownfield, Maine

A note about this Revised Edition:

The lion's share of this book was first written between 1983 to 1990 from information gleaned from my experiences building frames and teaching about timber framing dating from the period of my first encounter with timber framing in 1970. The book was first developed and used primarily as the instruction manual for my students. It was expanded in equal measure to knowledge learned about the craft of timber framing, and was ultimately published for general distribution in this form in 1998—a work-in-process for a good 15 years or more. Back in 1983, and even up through the 1990's, there were virtually no testing results or information available that dealt directly with the design and strength of pegged joinery. Most of the information I used to express design values were extrapolated from other realms of engineering and applied to timber frame joinery where corollaries existed. Testing results were available for bolted joints, so this was all one could draw from. In the past several years, things have changed. Thanks in large part to Ben Brungraber and Joseph Miller, among others, in conjunction with the Timber Framers Guild (TFG) and the Timber Framing Engineering Council (TFEC), scientific testing has been taking place for the past few years and some of the results have recently been published which address four basic failure modes of pegged joinery. This is extremely important work, for if uniform standards of design are to gain widespread acceptance by every building department, the process must follow a strict and rigid protocol of scientific testing. This is what Brungraber, Miller and others are doing in conjunction with the TFEC. Their work is to be applauded.

This revision is intended, in part, to be an update to include some of the more recent developments in the engineering of joined structures. Along the way, I could not help adding additional photos and elaborating on subjects where I felt it was necessary, while keeping it to the same page length. In once again reliving this part of my life while sorting through photos, I couldn't help but look back in great appreciation upon the people who made the early journey in timber framing with me. In particular I would like to thank Don Morrison, for his steady pace and deep seated sense of perfection and grace. Mike Sandman, for being the best timber framer in America, a title not merely bestowed, but earned. Curtis Milton, for his ability to see the opposite side of every issue, therefore never overlooking anything. Richard Gardner, for his steadfast ability to get the job done under the most abstract of circumstances, heat, snow, tornados, hurricanes, you name it, and we've been through them all, but always with the same perfect results. And last but not least, Tim Bickford, who just may be the real prodigy. The missing among them, however, is Michael Peterson, my first partner and compatriot in the early days. Mike's life was tragically cut short in a logging accident in 1980 helping a friend clear a woodlot, but his presence lives on with me still to this day in memory, and as a blessing at every raising.

I would also like to thank John Wolbeck, P.E., Department Chair for Science, Engineering, and Architecture, SUNY Orange Community College, for his many suggestions and help in creating a standard notation throughout this revision. John has devoted considerable time helping to edit and streamline the threads of connection as only a college professor could do.   —Steve Chappell, June 1, 2011

All photographs and illustrations by Steve Chappell, with the exception of those appearing on the following pages: illustrations on pages 49-74, by Alan Amioka. Additional Photographs and illustration credits: page 1, Maine Public Broadcasting; page 17, John Mitchell; page 58, Don Morrison; page 71 Agrafiotis; page 253, Ben Young; back cover center and page 47 by Anne Gummerson; page 123 & 208 top left by Dan Welden. Several photos that appear were taken by unknown persons with the author's own camera.

Front cover clockwise from top left: Principal rafter to king post assembly, spring 2005 Fox Maple TF workshop; half dovetailed & wedged tie beam to post assembly, Gagetown, NB Canada TF workshop 2004; checking teasel tenon on post top in English tying joint assembly, spring 2006 Fox Maple TF workshop; Red oak hammerbeam frame, Weston, CT, 2008; King post truss in the library at Fox Maple, cut in the spring 1997 TF workshop; Raising the scissor truss at the Head-of-Jeddore NS, Canada, summer 1995 TF workshop; Shouldered tusk tenon to tie beam assembly, Grand Junction, Iowa TF workshop 2004. Center photo: Raising the first bent in the Winter 2005 workshop in Costa Rica.

The intention of this book is to provide a general overview of the basic system of traditional timber framing and was initially designed to be the companion work manual for the hands-on workshops conducted by Fox Maple School of Traditional Building. The structural engineering formulas, guidelines and theories expressed in this book are intended to be guidelines only, and should not be relied upon as the sole basis for designing, engineering and constructing timber frames. It is the express advice of the author and publisher that anyone who is not specifically trained in mechanical and structural engineering seek professional assistance from a licensed engineer, in addition to following all state and local building code requirements, before attempting to design or build a timber frame structure.

Library of Congress Cataloging-in-Publication Data:
Chappell, Steve
A Timber Framer's Workshop: Joinery, Design & Construction of Traditional Timber Frames
/ Steve Chappell.
    Includes bibliographical references and index
    ISBN-10: 0-188926-00-X   ISBN-13: 978-1-889269-00-9
1. Framing (Building). 2. Timber joints. 3. Wooden-frame buildings
TH2301.C428 2001

694'.2—dc22

Printed in the United States of America
Tenth printing, June 2011

10 9 8 7 6 5 4 3 2 1

Fox Maple Press
P.O. Box 249
65 Corn Hill Road
Brownfield, Maine 04010
www.foxmaple.com
207-935-3720

"When we build, let us think that we build forever.
Let it not be for present delight nor for present use alone.
Let it be such work as our descendents will thank us for;
and let us think, as we lay stone on stone, that a time is to
come when those stones will be held sacred because our
hands have touched them, and that men will say, as they
look upon the labor and wrought substance of them,
'See! This our father did for us.'"

—John Ruskin

A Barn for Noah Blake

That was a jolly crew from Fox-Maple Post and Beam
  which built this barn
    or house if it so becomes;
masters of the past
  creating the frame of the progenitor;
no artificial stays,
trunnels, oak,
    pounded with a beetle,
braces, oak,
pine, mortised, tenoned,
summer beams, massive,
  dovetailed in the girts,
rafters, twelve in twelve,
  isosceles,
rising to the sky and pointing,
  without steel of the spike,
    only wood
  fashioned by man
    but grown by nature
      which is God
  whoever your God may be —

    Allah
    Buddha
    Christ
    His Father
    Krishnu
    or
    None

      which, too, is the Deity
      in the vacuum
      of this life.

Dedication to a frame raising at the topping of the tree ceremony
by Carlton Abbott, Summer 1982

This book is dedicated to the memory of my father, J.B. Chappell, a carpenter and cabinetmaker of 40 years, who taught me that level was level, plumb was plumb, and that the thumb would heal. But greatest of all, he bestowed upon me his sense and conviction that the greatest reward we could ever receive from our work was in the knowing and feeling—in our heart of hearts—that we performed it to the best of our abilities, and without compromise.

Contents

Contents

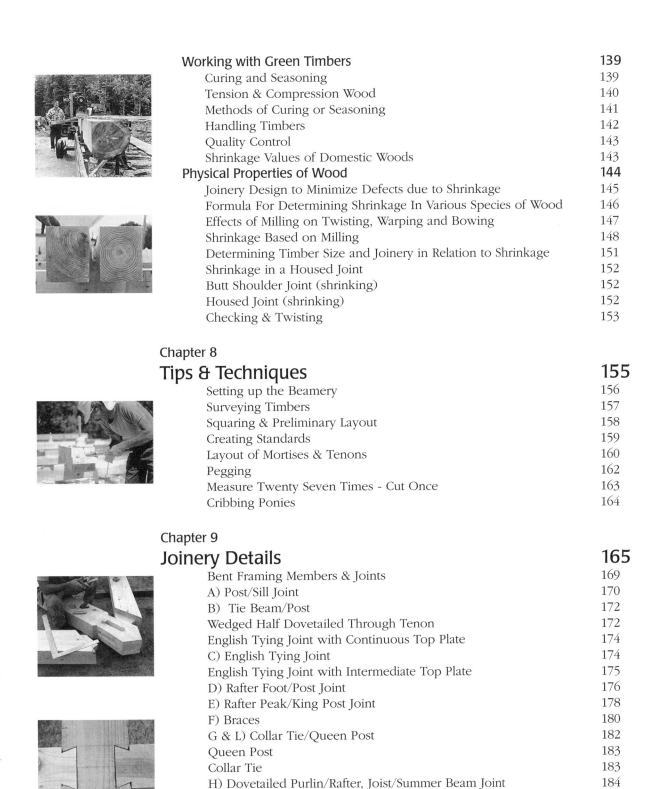

Contents

Preface

It's difficult to present a book such as this without giving a little insight as to how it came about—how I was led to be in the position of making timber framing my life's work.

I spent most of the summer of 1970 hitchhiking around the country with a backpack and little money. I covered most of the Western and Rocky Mountain states and one day found myself heading south on Route 1 on the northern coast of California, just south of Fort Bragg. It was a cold and foggy day, with a surreal sense about it. The mist clung eerily to the craggy shoreline and the surf pounded the cliffs in thunderous claps—giving me the sense that it may be the beginning of creation. Few cars were traveling the highway, so I walked on in this surreal world with no anticipation. Finally, a pickup careens around a corner, slows, and pulls into a turnoff about 200 yards up the road. A woman steps out of the driver's seat. She's in her sixties, and has pure silver hair flowing bright and shiny to her waist. She speaks, in a thick German accent, and says she is going to Albion. I can have a ride if I don't mind sitting in the back. Fifty miles on Rte. 1 is like a thousand on I-80, so I take it, anticipating a cold and miserable ride.

I endure the ride under the cover of my sleeping bag. We get to Mendocino and she pulls over at a gas station. We introduce, her name is Sabina. She says she has a farm down the road and I am welcome to stay the night if I wish. The offer sounds great, so we head down the road to her farm. The farm's a few miles up Navarro Ridge Road, just south of Albion. The incline is steep and before long we rise above the fog, stretching below to the horizon like a sea, and it's 75 degrees and sunny. I realize it's still early in the afternoon. We stop in front of a large, sculpted metal gate. Atop the gate a piece of heavy sheet metal has been cut out with a torch, like a stencil, with the words, *'La Terra Santa'*.

I jump out, open the gate, and walk ahead of the truck. It opens to a large field, with a large barn, and a small farmhouse—both are weathered and appear to be built in the early 20s—old for the local standards. There's a group of people bent over an antique sickle mower, banging it with a hammer. It's being pulled by a 1949 Ford pickup. They are in the process of harvesting oats, but the mower doesn't seem to work. A couple of people pick up hand scythes and sickles and begin cutting the oats by hand. The others soon give up on the mower and join them with more hand scythes. They work until dusk to finish cutting the acre or two crop. Another group begins threshing some of the mown oats by beating the seed heads with sticks over a large canvas tarp. My presence is felt, and one of the threshers motions to a pile of sticks. I take it as an invitation, or request, to join in. I begin beating alongside the others. No one seems to care who I am or what I'm doing there. I work on, beating, removing the threshed stalks, pile on another fresh armful, and on and on. By nightfall, we've threshed maybe a half bushel. A small amount for so much effort.

The next day I get up early and find my first opportunity to explore the surrounding land. The first thing that strikes me are the huge redwood stumps spread about the property. They range from 6 to 12 feet in diameter, and stand nearly 30 feet tall. They were not stumps left by logging, but evidently a horrendous storm that blew them down 50, 100, or even 200 years prior. Many are scorched by flame, the result of the intermittent fires that sweep through this area every 50 years or so. Some stand alone and bare, others are concealed in clumps of bay laurel, appearing as trees unto themselves. I head down a trail and in passing one of the clumps I notice a small trail leading inside. I crouch through the opening and find myself in a small hollow. I stand up. What I see is the first inkling that I have stumbled onto a very special place, *La Terra Santa*. Rising before me is a giant redwood trunk, towering thirty feet above and nearly 12 feet in diameter, and completely concealed from the outside by the shroud of bay laurels.

Preface

Over countless years of nature's storms and fires the trunk has become completely hollowed, and it has now been transformed into a house. At the base is a natural arch shaped opening into the hollowed shaft, and fitted to it seamlessly, is a door of redwood and oak, with handmade wooden latch and hinges. At various places up the trunk's shaft a number of natural, irregular shaped openings, are fitted with windows—some with stained glass, others clear. All are meticulously fitted and married to the natural shape of the openings. Atop is a roof of redwood shakes, shaped to contour with the uneven sides of the broken off trunk. I stand silent for several moments, then hear a sound from within. I knock on the door, a voice greets me to enter. I crouch through the low door and am greeted by a man in his early thirties, he introduces himself as John the Carpenter. No doubt, I think in my mind.

The stump had been scorched deeply by fire, but the inner surfaces were meticulously scraped down to the natural redwood surface. At three or four places up the shaft small lofts had been joined into the sides so as to appear that they actually grew, or remained, naturally as part of the tree. Some are large enough to set up chairs, one is a sleeping loft, others are merely steps that become part of the winding stair that traces its way up 15 or 20 feet. For a moment, I think I may be in the home of Bilbo Baggins. It is the mental picture that my mind created when I read the *Hobbit*.

John gives me some insight as to the nature of the community, and about his work on the trunk. It took him nearly 2 summers to bring it to this stage, but his work is ongoing. He invites me to continue down the main path, for there are more equally unique buildings along the way. I continue down the trail and find a half dozen more buildings, mostly small, but all wrought, molded and sculpted from the materials at hand. Most incorporated, or were built around, an already existing natural element. A few years later I would recognize several of these houses, as well as the wrought gate, on the back cover jacket, in the book, *Hand Made Houses*.

My father was a cabinetmaker and carpenter of some esteem. I'd grown up seeing him build and work on some truly exciting projects. I had been exposed to fine carpentry, but I had never seen anything like the work and craftsmanship in these buildings tucked away in the redwoods.

Before noon, I settled down in a sunny spot to ponder my next move. Should I head out, or what? I don't have a chance to think too much when a woman approaches. She tells me a group of men are working to retrieve some redwood logs from a ravine, and they might need some help pulling them out. She points the way, and I head down the path. I arrive at a fairly large ravine to find 5 or 6 men halfway down heaving on a large redwood log with ropes. I move down to offer a hand. It's readily accepted. The log is actually a quarter section of a 20 foot long redwood log that had been split to make it a manageable size to move. It seems that 100 years earlier, when they first logged this area, many of the logs fell in places that were too difficult to retrieve. With so many logs available, they just left the 'mavericks'. Every ravine on the 200 acre property was littered with these mavericks, lain for nearly 100 years, but still as prime and sound as the day they were felled.

We muckle the first section to the level landing and continue work dragging up the remaining three quarters. This takes the rest of the day. Someone asks if I'll be around the next day to help haul some more. The next day turned into 3 weeks, and the experience was about to alter the course of my life.

I soon find out they are attempting to build a timber frame that uses no nails, only pegs, with mortise and tenons to join the timbers together. They have already hauled up 10 or 15 log quarters of various sizes from another ravine, and a few round logs as well. The next three days are spent finding appropriate logs, under 36 inches in diameter, splitting them with mauls and wedges, oak and steel, and hauling them to the landing. The leader of the group is from Rhode Island, where he grew up playing in an old timber framed barn on his uncle's farm. He has a visual concept of what these barns look like, but he isn't really sure about the joinery, so it is essentially made up as we move along. After a day or two the crew is whittled down to just three of us. There are no framing plans, or drawings of any sort. John the Carpenter, whom I'd met the first day, joins us for most of the project, and I generally follow his lead. The timbers are hewed with axes and adzes to smooth the surfaces, and to highlight any natural characteristics. Much time is spent analyzing the grain pattern and texture for its artistic beauty. Structural qualities were secondary—but it was select, old growth redwood!

The timbers are laid out through a combination of mapping, scribing, and squaring, cut with hand saws, bit braces, chisel and mallet. As a few timbers are completed we stand them up in place to assess our work, and move to the next batch. The design changes in accordance with the grain patterns of the timbers, and on whims. If I had to describe a style it would be *nouveau funk*. The footprint is about 20' x 20', with three principal post and tie beam assemblies. Not true bents. A central post rose from the floor to the peak, and plates were partially lapped over the tie beam. A ridge beam ran the length of the building and joined to the central posts with a mortise and through tenon joint—mortise on ridge, tenon of posts. It was a free-form process with plenty of guesswork. However, we completed the cutting, raised it, pegged it, and dedicated the frame in about three weeks time. My interest grew on a daily basis. When it was completed, I was filled with a sense of accomplishment that I had never felt before. I couldn't believe we actually built it with no nails. A new and amazing concept, and one that would live with me.

I had no idea I would be so closely connected to timber framing nearly 30 years later. Much less, that I would move to Maine and make it my life's work. After the experience, I began to rethink my options of becoming a carpenter. It seemed an appropriate thing to do, given the fact that I grew up with off-drops and hand planes as toys, and a father who I now realize was a craftsman in the purest sense.

I found myself in Colorado the following year building condominiums and custom houses. After six months working for a general contractor, I found an easy supply of work and started my own building company—framing condos and taking subcontracts for trim. Within a month I had 12 guys working for me and couldn't keep up with the work. I was 19 and making lots of money, but recognized that most of the older builders I knew (old being the mid 20's) were burnt out from this pace. I wasn't ready for this, so I decided to fold shop and take up an invitation from a Lakota Indian family—who mysteriously pulled into the door-yard of my cabin in Kittredge, Colorado, out of the blue one day—to help them build an addition to their house on the Rosebud Reservation, in South Dakota.

I arrived in Rosebud in the late summer of 1972, shortly after their annual Sun Dance. The *res* was jumping with feds, and revolution was in the air. I found myself in the midst of it, as I was living with the spiritual leaders of the clan, Al and Diane Running, the daughter and son-in-law of Henry Crow Dog. Crow Dog, one of the sacred elders of the Ogalala tribe, was in his 80's at the time. Diane's brother, Leonard Crow Dog, became known to the rest of the world in April, of 1973, for leading the takeover of the church at Wounded Knee. I worked through the fall salvaging materials from around the reservation to build the small addition to the Running's house, rechinked and repaired the elder Crow Dog's log cabin—all the while absorbing as much of the spirit, wisdom and stories of their sacred past, and current struggles, that Crow Dog, Al, Diane, and their children, evoked and lived.

When the cold winds began to sweep across the plains, I decided it was time to head west to Oregon. As a gift, or perhaps a token of payment for my work on the land, they gave me a medicine stick that was used by Crow Dog in the Sun Dance that summer. By fortune, or bad luck, I left the reservation only several weeks prior to the takeover at Wounded Knee. My experiences on the reservation cannot be conveyed in terms of how it sharpened my focus and tempered my view of how one should live one's life.

Preface

I left Rosebud and headed to Oregon with a mission and renewed hope, but my truck broke down in Wall, South Dakota, a town famous for its drugstore, a mere 80 miles from Rosebud. Four months on the *res* left me near broke, so I had no choice but to get a job to earn the $500 for a new engine. Fortunately, as I trudged into town to find a tow, I passed a building site, so I stopped in. The builder was a man in his sixties, he was working alone building trusses on the deck. I asked if he needed help. He said he had three houses to frame and hired me on the spot. I accepted, but told him I couldn't start for two weeks because I had a date in Oregon to meet my future wife. He agreed. I headed out with my dog and guitar, made the momentous date, and arrived back in Wall on schedule. At $3 an hour it took 3 months to save enough to retrieve my truck, but the time proved to be a priceless experience of building with an ingenious, old-style carpenter and craftsman who preferred hand saws over my Black & Decker worm drive. On another level, it provided a backdrop to the real struggles that the native people of this region faced in day-to-day life.

I finally made it to the Oregon coast in mid winter, settled in, and by and by, started a subcontracting business building houses, condos and doing renovations. I worked for nearly a year, did quite well working by myself, and may have spent the next winter, and perhaps the rest of my life, had a hitchhiker not stumbled onto my building site in Newport, one late summer day. I was working on the roof of a 3 story building, so I saw him approach from a good distance. He weaved his way to the site and asked me for a job. We talked, and I found he had just hitchhiked from Maine. "Maine, where is that," I thought. As we spoke I became more intrigued as he described the old timber frame buildings and barns that dotted the landscape. He'd grown up in a house built in 1820. We spoke for an hour and by the end of the conversation I'd made up my mind—I was moving to Maine.

Three months later, my soon-to-be wife and I packed up our '61 Ford pickup, headed to Maine, and arrived in November, 1973. As I entered the first town in Maine, across the New Hampshire border, I spotted a carpenter working on the façade of an old federal in the center of Kezar Falls. Three miles down the road I turned around and went back to talk to him with the thought looming in my head that if I did, I would probably spend the rest of my life in the town (38 years later, I live in the next town over). After a ten minute chat he offered me a job, which was difficult to turn down, considering I'd made it all the way to Maine. He agreed to a week reprieve so I could find a place to live, and the next week I was disassembling, splicing and repairing a rotted English tying joint on an 1820's timber frame. Freddy, a veteran of the Battle of the Bulge, had been working on, and building, timber frames his whole career. It was all second nature to him, just part of a day's pay. As the local town carpenter he spent most of his time renovating and repairing the oldest buildings in town. I became his apprentice, as it were, and had the opportunity to experience timber framing from one of the few natural links that remained. This was something that could only be found in rural New England at the time, and I was fortunate, or destined, to fall in its lap. This began my true journey as a builder, and my life has been entrenched in the art and craft of timber framing ever since. Some things are just meant to be.

My path began as an exciting venture, and even today, more than 40 years later, I still wait in anticipation for the next frame raising. This book is just a portion of what I can convey of the experiences, adventure, and lessons I have learned in my quest of becoming a craftsman. — Steve Chappell

Introduction

The revival of timber framing over the past 30 years may be one of the most successful attempts ever at reviving an ancient craft and bringing it back into full blossom. Its success, in part, may be due to the fact that it fulfills the requirements of structure in such a pure and direct way, and it naturally inspires and heightens our sense and awareness of craftsmanship. Our reverence for architecture and art stems from an innate human need to see talent expressed. When it is expressed in usable and functional forms, such as buildings that we can live and worship in, we become connected with it in a more intimate way. In an age when technology is expanding at such a rapid pace that today's advances are often obsolete tomorrow, we yearn for things in life that have substance. Timber framing, by its nature—requiring the touch and feel of a craftsman's hand, its use of nearly raw materials, and its substantiality—provides a sense of permanence. There is nothing to hide or mask in a joined frame. The work of the craftsman who handled and fitted the joints remains visible—to feel, touch, and to imagine what his days were like cutting the frame. Timber frames remain alive throughout their life, inviting all who will inhabit or enter its space for many generations to come an opportunity to sense the craftsman who worked the timbers. Who among us has entered an old barn and resisted the temptation to run our palms over the timbers, touch the joints, and in so doing, imagined and felt, in some measure, the presence of the builder within the timbers?

This unique nature of timber framing has inspired many owner-builders to design and build their own timber framed home, and many to enter the trade professionally. Fueled with inspiration, anyone can accomplish just about anything. However, there is hard work involved, and if one is to be successful, a working understanding of the complete system—structural design, joinery, and a basic understanding of the mechanical and physical properties of wood—is required.

Joinery, being the primary element that sets timber framing apart from conventional building systems, is the logical place to begin—but it is only one aspect. This book is designed to unfold as if it were a hands-on workshop. The primary focus is on the fundamental elements of timber framing that will allow the student to gain the understanding and confidence to begin, and successfully complete, a timber framing project on his or her own. This begins with the delivery of the timbers to the site. What do you do with them? What are the characteristics of the wood, what qualities are you looking for, and where is their best placement in the frame? What are the basic structural design considerations? How do you approach the layout and cutting of the joinery? How do you achieve perfect joinery?

In an actual hands-on workshop, I attempt to unravel the mysteries of timber framing—through the process of laying out, cutting and erecting a frame—by providing practical and systematic guidelines that can be applied to any framing situation. Hands-on experience is direct and immediate. You can see, and feel, and heft the timbers. The score line is evident, the cut is actual. Until one has cut a series of joints, assembled the bents, and raised the frame, there is no way to fully understand the process, however there is more to building timber frames than chopping mortises, and the only real mystery is lack of knowledge. Any motivated individual can tackle a frame on their own, and achieve a high level of quality, if they first take the necessary steps to learn and understand the approach, underlying principles, and structural requirements. As a testament to this, the photographs of joinery and frames in this book are, for the most part, the work of students in workshops who had no previous experience.

The intent of this workbook is to outline the fundamental approach, coupled with concepts of structural design and joinery, that will allow beginners to develop a strategy that will make their *first* timber framing project a successful one. I have made no attempt to create a paint-by-numbers book. Timber joinery is a fluid system, limited only by the creativity, knowledge and ability of the designer and builder. Every frame is different, and even when similarities exist, there are elements that need to be adjusted for the particular circumstance. In addition to providing hard-lined details, I have attempted to provide the underlying reasons, structural parameters, and practical engineering concepts that will allow creativity, flexibility, and understanding as to how and why a particular joint or structural system will work. Gaining a broader depth of knowledge of the whole system will open many more doorways to creativity.

This book was initially designed to be a companion to our hands-on workshops. It has evolved in direct relation to my own understanding of the system, and how it can best be presented to students in a structured educational environment. It should be used as a reference, for taking notes, and for familiarizing yourself with the basics of traditional timber frame design and joinery. The structural principles should be studied thoroughly. Test yourself, and make them part of your building vocabulary.

To those of you who come upon this book in a workshop, I expect that it will be worn and tattered, marked upon and scored, and contain much more than mere words on paper in the end. If you are intent, it will become a chronicle of your own timber framing experience. When you open it at a future date—working on your own frame, or relaxing by a winter fire—my hope is that the workshop experience will once again be as clear as the days spent laying out and cutting the workshop frame. These were joyous times, and the friendships that were sparked will remain for all time. To those who happen upon this book in any other way, I can only hope that you will be inspired to someday build your own frame.

The workshop experience is much more than just learning the terms and conditions of joinery and timber framing. It is also an opportunity to work with people from diverse backgrounds and locations, unified in a specific task, who have come together to create something that will remain as an important part of life's many experiences. Friendships will be born and knowledge will be gained from one another as much as it will be imparted through the structured course instruction. And, when your raising day comes, you'll find that you have a ready group of friends who will come to assist, enjoy and celebrate in your hard won efforts. *Vive Jean-Claude!*

Chapter 1
Introduction to Timber Framing

Raising the frame of the Maine Public Broadcasting House, cut in the Fall 1992 Workshop. The frame was donated, and the completed house was auctioned off as a fund raiser for MPB.

Oak German Fachwerk half-timber house built in 1687.

Introduction to Timber Framing

Timber framing is an ancient building form with a widespread and rich history. Evidence of joined timber frames in western cultures date back to 6220 BC in Macedonia, northern Greece. Ruins of more sophisticated timber frames have been found in the south of Germany, dating from the 10th century BC. By the 3rd century AD, the form of timber framing we are familiar with today was beginning to evolve as a common building method for peasant dwellings throughout northern Europe. In Scandinavia, wooden Stave Churches built in the 12th century still survive. By the 11th century, cathedrals with complex, joined timber frame roof systems were being built across the whole of Europe. These seem to defy even today's engineering capabilities, and remain as some of the most remarkable architectural masterpieces in the world. A similar evolution took place in the Far East. The *Five Story-Pagoda* in Japan was built in 607 AD, proving that building with timber, joined and fashioned with hand tools, and only those materials at hand, could not only provide shelter, but beauty and inspiration as well.

The evolution of timber framing over the centuries was a result of trial and error and empirical evidence, coupled with an ever expanding understanding of the scientific principles of structure. From peasant dwellings to cathedrals, the builders and carpenters were people of normal means, but most often of acute talent. Their talent and design capabilities expanded as the manufacture of higher grades of steel and tools were developed. Better cutting tools allowed more elaborate woodworking, and the opportunity for the craftsmen of the day to demonstrate their talents on a much higher level. Wood was a valuable resource a thousand years ago. Though there was plenty of it, the time and effort to transform it from trees to temple was costly and labor intensive. The carpenter who engaged in work with timbers was carefully trained through a required apprenticeship of from 3 to 7 years. He was required to understand every aspect of wood—grain, fiber, texture, taste, smell and long term aging effects. Upon completing his apprenticeship, and journey, he was required to present evidence of his work and talent in order to be accepted into the Guild, and to take on his own apprentices.

The magnificent cathedrals are inspiring, and certainly helped to foster the revival of timber framing, but the grace and beauty of the simple dwellings built by and for the common man also hold a sort of magic. These dwellings feel close and obtainable, and worthy of replication, because of their practical and functional elegance. It's this nature, and the fact that human hands have touched and worked and cajoled the timbers into place, that so many have been inspired to spend the time and effort in apprenticeship, as it were, to learn and revive their craft.

In the following chapter an overview of the joinery, structural design and the mechanics of traditional timber framing will be covered. A primer, of sorts, to a fairly in-depth discussion of the finer elements of traditional timber framing.

This 16th century English cottage in Stratford-upon-Avon, was the house of Anne Hathaway, the wife of William Shakespeare. This may be proof that houses built with timbers, reeds, earth and straw can be truly inspiring. These old dwellings also are a testament to the practicality and durability of natural materials.

Structural Overview

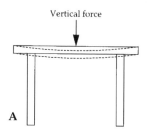

Post & Lintel Framework

The fundamental goal of any framed structure is to transfer the roof and floor loads to the foundation. The earliest timber frame examples relied on post and lintel construction. Post and lintel is a basic structural form consisting of a simple load bearing beam (lintel), supported by posts (columns). Stonehenge (2500BC) is a classic example of a post and lintel framework, and may be one of the early refinements of joinery because the lintels were dovetailed to each other and mortised and tenoned to the uprights. There was also a Woodhenge, built in the same period and proximity to Stonehenge. It has long ago returned to the earth, but presumably it also used dovetails and mortise and tenon joinery.

Post and lintel frameworks are limited in their design scope because they rely on the direct strength of the individual members to support vertical loads, and have little resistance to horizontal forces. To resist horizontal loading, wind or seismic motion, bracing becomes necessary to prevent collapse. This creates a rigid structural framework. In some cases, braces are used to transfer a concentrated load to a post. However, the primary function of braces is simply to keep the frame rigid and square.

The need for more sophisticated buildings brought about the development of more sophisticated joinery. This allowed frameworks and trusses to

An English style barn made up of seven bents. Bents span 36 feet, and are spaced 12 feet, making six equal bays. Both tension braces, those going from corner posts to timber sill beam, and knee braces are used. Warrenton, Virginia, 1986.

Parts of the Frame

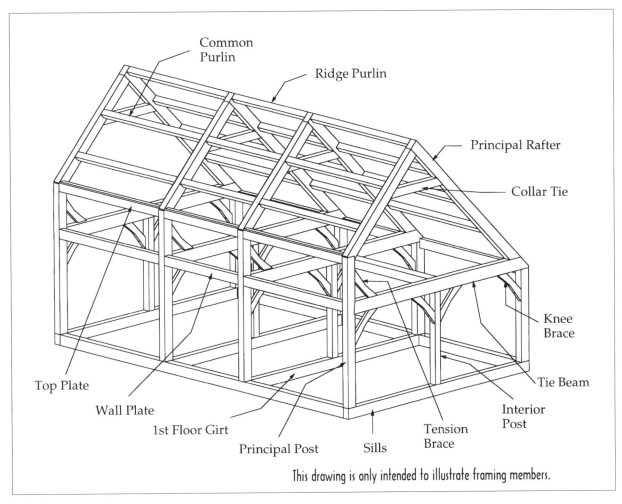

Common Purlin

Ridge Purlin

Principal Rafter

Collar Tie

Knee Brace

Tie Beam

Top Plate

Wall Plate

1st Floor Girt

Principal Post

Sills

Tension Brace

Interior Post

This drawing is only intended to illustrate framing members.

be built that could span greater distances with smaller timbers. Joinery is the one element that allowed timber framing to evolve from ad hoc arrangements of timbers and logs into a true craft. It was the development of joinery that allowed trusses to be built, and the cathedral to rise.

Modern timber framing is a mixture of simple post and lintel framing, truss dynamics and appropriate joinery design. By gaining an understanding of the basic principles of structure, the greatest amount of creativity will result. The object of this workbook is to explore these principles and develop some practical guidelines that can be used in the cutting and raising of a frame. The following is a brief overview of the structural components of a joined timber frame.

This timber frame work is relying on the principles of a simple post & lintel framework to carry roof loads. See page 36.

Framing Members

There are three structural elements that must be analyzed if a sound frame is to be built; 1) Bent design, 2) Beam design (species, dimension, strength), and 3) Joinery design. In many cases, the dimensions of the beams will be dictated more by the type and requirements of the joinery, and less by the span and the load. However, it is generally accepted that the fewer the posts, the larger the beam needed to carry a span.

Timber framing does not rely strictly on simple beams carrying simple loads, but on rigid structural frameworks, known as **bents**.

Principal Framing Members

Bents are a rigid structural framework, and are designed to work as a single unit to transfer loads uniformly throughout the framework to the foundation. Bents are made up of **principal** framing members, to support the primary external loads, and secondary internal members within the framework to distribute internal loads. The principal members in a bent are the **posts, rafters**, and **tie beams**. The secondary members within the bent are the **braces, collar ties, struts** (queen posts are considered struts), and **interior posts**. These are necessary (depending on the bent design) to support and distribute internal loads, and to stiffen the framework to resist lateral movement, or racking. Bents have many of the same characteristics as a truss (and in some cases may be trusses), however, they often rely more on timber size and strength (post & lintel) than the structural dynamics of a truss. Truss dynamics will be discussed in more detail in Chapter 6.

A frame may consist of two or more bents, spaced anywhere from 8 to 16 feet on center. Four bent frames were the most common for house frames in colonial New England. Barn frames often used five to seven bents, and were usually spaced 12 feet on center.

Secondary Connecting Members

The bents are secured to each other with **secondary connecting members—wall plates, top plates, joists, summer beams** and **purlins.** In most cases, the secondary members are subjected only to vertical loading and are sized using formulas to determine design loads for simple load bearing beams.

Setting the connecting top plates within the bents requires spreading the bents, using straps and come-alongs as safeties. In most cases, connecting plates are considered simple load bearing beams and designed to resist vertical loading. Braces are designed strictly to resist horizontal racking, and should not be relied upon to transfer loading. To transfer loads, one needs to use struts, which will be discussed later.

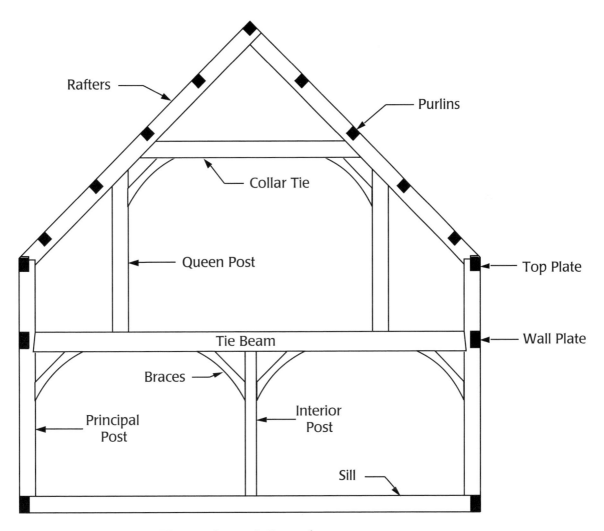

Bent Framing Members

The drawing above illustrates a basic bent framing plan. The principal members are the Posts, Tie Beam and Rafters. The secondary members are the Interior Posts, Queen Posts and Collar Tie. Secondary members are necessary only when bent spans exceed the structural limitations of any of the principal members. Braces are required to make it a rigid structural framework.

Queen posts can join to rafters
or directly to the collar tie.

Braces

The third element of the frame is the bracing. **Knee braces** are required to prevent racking, and as mentioned previously, are not generally relied upon to carry or transfer loads within the frame. In some cases they may carry some portion of the load, but in determining design loads for secondary members, no factor should be allowed for support by braces. To transfer loads within the frame using brace-like members one may use what is known as a **strut**. Struts, technically speaking, are a secondary member within a truss and have specific structural design criteria. The dynamics of braces, bracing and struts will be covered more thoroughly Chapter 4.

Design Considerations
Joinery, Aesthetic, and Timber Quality

Executing joinery accurately to make clean, tight fits and full surface contact interfaces will make stronger joints and also prevent twisting and rotation of timbers as they age. This half-dovetailed & shouldered post detail was cut by a student in the Iowa 2004 workshop.

1) Properly Designed & Executed Joinery. Joinery is perhaps the most important element in the design and construction of a traditional frame. It is the basis upon which the craft is founded. Without properly designed joinery, no frame will stand the test of time. Timber frame joinery, as practiced in Colonial New England, was the culmination of hundreds of years of development. Just as we have standards in modern construction, the standards used in the construction of traditional timber frames were well established and imperative to structural integrity.

In directing workshops, my goal is to provide instruction in the proper design, application and execution of traditional joinery details and techniques. Developing a basic vocabulary of common joinery details will allow beginners to expand their own creativity and talent. It is impossible to cover all of the countless variations that exist in joinery details and building styles in a workshop, or this book, and may not even be necessary. In teaching, my preference is to focus on the essential joinery common to New England in the 18th and early 19th centuries—the reason why these joints were used, how and why they work, their design criteria, structural makeup and appropriate use—in detail. Understanding the underlying principles will allow a greater amount of creativity and flexibility in designing and adapting joinery for any application. Therefore, I will discuss those methods that are the most practical in use, and provide the broadest array of design applications.

2) Proper Beam Design, Aesthetic, and Timber Species. The strength of a timber is related directly to the species, structural grade and its dimensions in relation to the span and load. The requirements of the joinery may often dictate the minimum dimensions of a given timber, but there is also a visual element to take into consideration. Attractive frames rely on a delicate balance and arrangement of timbers. Long spans are neither structurally desirable, nor visually appealing. By joining small members to larger timbers, the eye gracefully follows the flow of the timbers, and the beauty and significance of the larger timbers are magnified.

The eaves-dropper floor joist in this yellow pine frame provides an aesthetic balance by reducing the required depth from top of tie beam to plate, to the depth required for the floor joists.

Over the years I have developed some basic rule-of-thumb guidelines that attempt to reduce long beam spans while increasing the visual impact. By following these guidelines, a natural balance of structure and aesthetic will result. These guidelines will be fully covered in the workshop and elsewhere in this manual.

Common sense and rule-of-thumb calculations are important elements to understand, and may result in adequate timber sizes for most common situations, however, they should be used only as guidelines. Advice on sizing timbers should be sought out if you do not have those capabilities. It is not the primary objective of this manual to discuss the detailed theories of structural engineering. This would require several volumes to thoroughly cover all aspects. A general overview, as it pertains to timber framing, will be covered, and a bibliography for further reference is provided in the appendices for further study.

3) Timber Quality. For both strength and visual appeal, the quality of the timbers used is of utmost importance. Use only solid and sound timbers, with as few defects as possible. Most timbers will arrive at the shop ungraded, or *mill run*. Therefore, it is often up to the framer to survey the timbers for grade, and to identify any structural defects. A few considerations are as follows.

Grain runout. For any horizontal member, or member loaded perpendicular to the grain, the slope of the grain should never exceed a ratio of 1:15 (or 1" in 15" as measured parallel to the side faces of the timber). A reduction in strength is proportional to the ratio of the grain slope to the side face of the timber. Reductions in the strength of the modulus of rupture are as follows, assuming that straight-grain is 100%: 1:25 = 96%; 1:20 = 93%; 1:15 = 89%; 1:10 = 81%; 1:5 = 55%. Grain slope has less effect when the timber is loaded in compression parallel to the grain, as is the case with a post. A grain slope of 1:5 only reduces the strength by 7%, or 93% of a straight-grained timber. Therefore, timbers with grain slope are best used for posts.

Knots and knot clusters. From a structural standpoint, a knot is considered to be the same as a hole in a timber. Reductions are made based on the ratio of the size of the knot to the face of the timber, and its location on the face, relative to the edges (knots in the middle of the face have less effect than those on the edges). This is known as the *Strength Ratio*. The formula to determine the strength ratio is:

SR = $1-(k/h)^2$

SR = strength ratio; k = knot size (diameter);

h = width of the timber face.

If a timber with a 10 inch face has a knot 3 inches in diameter, the resulting SR would be as follows: $1-(3/10)^2 = .91$. In this case the timber is presumed to be 91% as strong as a timber with no knot.

Knots in tension are affected more than those in compression, so all edge knots or localized knot clusters oriented close to or near an edge, should be positioned to be on the compression side of the timber. In a horizontal timber, this would be the top face.

The mechanical and physical properties of wood and tips for surveying timbers is covered in-depth in Chapter 7 of this manual. Considerable time is spent during our workshops surveying the timbers, analyzing their qualities and characteristics, and determining where and why they may find their best use and placement in the frame. This aspect should not be taken lightly. A thorough and comprehensive survey of your timbers prior to laying out and cutting will save many hours in layout and cutting, help to prevent costly mistakes and result in both higher quality joinery and overall aesthetic of the frame. I urge everyone to pay proper diligence to this process.

A properly built timber frame has the potential to stand for many hundreds of years. Choosing the appropriate wood species and grade both deserve careful attention. Assuming that 25% of the cost of a frame is material and 75% labor, it becomes clear that nothing is gained by using inferior timbers.

Though free of knots, this pine timber has grain runout and shake. All timbers must be surveyed carefully to determine their best location in the frame and how any defects will affect joinery, both in the layout and cutting and also how long-term loading and aging will affect these defects.

This detail of a king post, joining to the top chord of a 20' span king post bridge truss, has two struts joining to its sides.

Design Overview

When we think of timber framing, we think of a traditional, long-forgotten craft, based on ancient methods and principles of engineering. It is true that the joinery, the structural criteria, and the fundamental approach that we use today are based on ancient methods and models. However, the structural components of a joined timber frame and the engineering principles at play remain as one of the most commonly used methods of construction to this day.

As a structural system, timber framing relies on a combination of rigid frameworks and individual member strength to carry and redirect specified loads to a rather limited number of points. These same principles are used predominantly in commercial steel construction around the world, and in the steel bridges crossing so many of our rivers. Even the names of the members have remained the same.

The concept is an easy one to understand; the post, or column, supports a horizontal beam designed to carry a specified load. To a reasonable point, increasing beam size (steel or wood) increases the span possible. As spans increase, deflection increases by the cube of the length. Therefore, a point is soon reached when the material reaches its practical maximum limit. At this point, it becomes necessary to add another support. In this way, larger open spaces are possible, which can then be partitioned off as needed. These areas can be adjusted, rearranged and remodeled without regard to the structural integrity of the building—so long as no principal members are removed. This system allows greater flexibility in the living environment, and can be molded to reflect our changing needs.

Conventional residential construction relies on many smaller members to distribute loads uniformly to many more points. In this method, the interior partitions become part of the overall structural design, and by their structural nature, impose limitations when the goal is to design open and flexible living areas.

With this in mind, the first concept to understand when it comes to designing and building timber framed structures is what is known as *Bent Framing*.

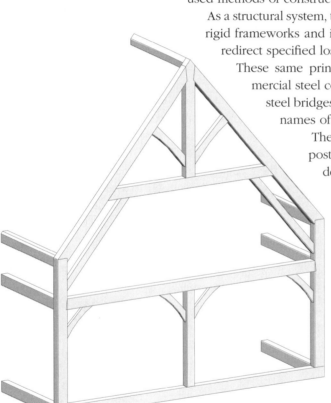

Bents are a combination of simple load bearing beams, structural frameworks, and trusses. In the drawing above, the tie beam is both a simple beam, supported at midpoint, and the lower chord of a truss.

Bent Framing

A bent is the structural framework consisting, at minimum, of two posts, a horizontal tie beam connecting the posts, and two opposing rafters. Additional members may be required, such as collar ties, queen posts and intermediate posts, depending on the size and span of the bent. A typical house frame will consist of three or more of these bents, spaced at intervals of up to 16 feet. The space between the bents is called a *bay*. While bays greater than 16 feet may be obtained, the practical span of a timber is 16 feet (as the length of a load bearing timber increases, the effect of the load on the timber in relation to its length increases by the cube). With this in mind, the practical limit for bent spacings is 16 feet.

Traditional timber frame houses commonly consisted of four bents. Let's say that we were building a 32 foot by 40 foot, four bent cape. Traditionally, the two outer bays would incorporate the primary living area, living room on one end, and kitchen/dining area on the other. The center bay, traditionally known as the *chimney bay*, becomes the functional utility area of the house. This bay is usually narrower than the outer bays, and is where all of the functional and mechanical systems of the house are placed; these being the

This traditional four bent red oak cape represents an efficient use of timber and joinery techniques. Posts, rafters, tie beam and collar tie make up the principal bent frame. English tying joint, continuous top plates and a purlin roof system are used for the connecting members. Don Morrison and Curtis Milton, on the second floor, were the crew for this raising. Leesburg, VA, 1985.

Hammer beam to hammer post joinery, recycled douglas fir.

stairway, chimney, bathroom and hallways. This area is accessible equally to both outer bays, and in most cases, by limiting its width to accommodate only what is functionally necessary (usually 8 to 10 feet), fewer partitions are required, resulting in less wasted living area in the house (see pg. 14).

In this design there would only be the necessity of two interior posts in the house. These would be located at the midpoint of the tie beam (16 feet). Since the stairway and chimney are coming up in this area, the posts generally fall at a point where they do not cause any interruption to the open living area. In this case, if the center bay was 8 feet, the two outer bays would have 16 feet of uninterrupted living area. Depending on the needs of the household, these could be partitioned off to create bedrooms or other private areas. However, this would not be necessary for any structural reasons.

Once an understanding of bent framing is achieved, an enormous amount of creativity and flexibility can be employed in designing a home. The spacing of bays, the length and number of bents, and the design of the bent framing will allow the designer to create modular living areas to fit the needs at hand. From a cost standpoint, the fewer the bents, and wider the bays, the less money it will cost to construct the frame.

Joinery

Fortunately, we have a rich history of timber framing to draw from when we set out to design and build timber framed structures. These range from the simple and unpretentious medieval cottage, to the great cathedrals found throughout Europe and the Orient. The more fluent we become in understanding these traditional examples, the more freedom we can achieve in designing our own timber frames. But first, we must gain an understanding of the system of joinery that makes bent framing possible.

Post joinery for octagonal frame with wedged/half dovetailed through mortise and connecting wall plate mortise.

Most of the joinery found in modern timber framing is based on examples that began to be perfected in the 13th and 14th century across the whole of Europe. These were developed by trial and error (the bad examples have long since crumbled and decayed into the earth) and rudimentary engineering concepts. What these early craftsmen did understand was that the vertical forces acting on the frame had to remain vertical throughout the structure, and ultimately, be diverted to the foundation. The primary reaction to vertical forces is horizontal thrust at the rafter feet. The *tie beam* is the principal member designed to resist thrust, and therefore, one of the most important members in the frame. As such, its effectiveness is directly related to the strength of the joinery. The criteria and design for appropriate tie beam joinery will be covered in detail.

The ability to design a timber frame bent will be enhanced as your vocabulary of joinery increases. While many joints may appear different to the eye, in reality, a consistent theme persists, and all joints are linked intrinsically because they are all merely variations of the simple mortise and tenon. These variations, how they are applied and adapted, rule-of-thumb design considerations, and how they affect load transfer will all be discussed.

Foundations and Decks

In most cases, foundations designed to meet your local and state building codes will suffice for timber frame structures. I would always recommend a 10 inch wall thickness, reinforced with rebar to meet your local building code. In some cases, pilasters may be necessary to accommodate increased point loads where principal posts fall. But if the design is carefully devised, these are more often than not unnecessary.

The floor system above, built upon a standard 10 inch concrete foundation, has joined timber sills and principal floor girts, in-filled with 2 by 10 joists.

First floor decks can range from fully timber framed systems to conventional floor decks. The reality is that most foundations are basements, used for storage and mechanical systems. The cavities between joists will likely be filled with pipes and wiring and ducts of some sort. So, unless the basement is to be used as a living area, a fully timber framed first floor deck is not necessary and can add difficulty and cost to installing systems. And you must remember, the favorite tool of plumbers and electricians are reciprocating saws. So much for your fine work.

However, there is something to be said about joining all of the post feet to timbers. This creates a unified frame that can more easily be moved to another site at some future date. This may seem like an odd thing to consider, but when you build a house to last 500 years, the odds are great that it may be moved a time or two in its life. That, of course, is assuming that it is worthy. And why should it not be?. In my area of Maine I'd guess that nearly 15 percent of the houses older than 200 years have been moved at least once. In the 1880s, the whole town of Cornish, Maine, was moved from the High Road down to the river so as to be closer to the new woolen mill, and work. This included over 50 buildings, all moved on sleds drawn by oxen nearly two miles in one winter. Now, this would have been much more difficult if the frames had not been joined to the sills.

Corner detail of a joined timber sill floor system. In this example the sub-sill is extended 4-1/2" from sill to support stress skin panels.

Understanding this potential, I favor the compromise of joining the sills and principal floor girts with timbers and in-filling the bays with conventional 2 by floor joists. The timber sill reduces the requirements of the foundation by spreading the loads over a greater area of the foundation (allowing for even an 8 inch foundation wall), and the conventional joist system facilitates the installation of mechanical systems.

In this frame the 2 by 10 joists were let-in to mortises in the floor girt. The other ends rested on top of the foundation sub sill, butting to the timber sill, and secured with nails.

The most cost efficient system is to frame a conventional deck using double rim joists and solid or built-up girders in line with the bents. This can save time and expenses, and allows easier installation of wiring and plumbing. In this case, the posts need to be notched around the double 2 by rims and rest directly on the sub-sill. A 10 inch foundation in this system would be the norm.

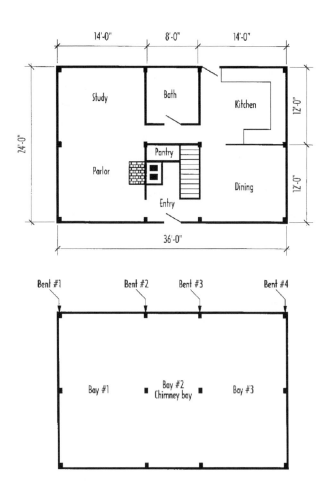

The bays between the bent framing create the living areas. By allowing the frame to naturally reflect and define the living areas, a more comfortable environment will result.

Interior Layout

Bent design and interior post placement are primary considerations when designing the interior floor plan. Working with the timber structure, allowing it to naturally create and define your living areas, will not only make the process easier, but save money as well.

When we examine the traditional timber houses of both the East and the West, we find that there is a common vernacular pattern shared across broad geographic and cultural regions. This may be due to the fact that the first essential of structural design is to use the timbers to the best advantage. The bent system developed from this innate sensibility through time and experience, driven to a great extent by need. The eternal question of the builder has been, "How best to use these timbers?" The common pattern that resulted in timber framing was one of bents and bays. By spacing the bents at the greatest practical distance the early builders realized they could create comfortable, human scale living spaces in the most efficient manner.

The New England Cape, as an example, humble in its stance, is the result of hundreds of years of subtle yet determined evolution and experience, and provides at least one answer to the question, "How best to use these timbers?" The result is a timeless design that sits as comfortably on the landscape today as it did in the 15th century.

The most common traditional timber houses were made up of four bents and three bays. The bents were commonly spaced between 8 to 16 feet. In a common house frame the two outer bays were larger, 14 to 16 feet, and the

The traditional four bent high post cape is a timeless design. The 28′ x 40′ frame to the right can easily accommodate 3 or 4 bedrooms and bath upstairs as well as comfortable open living areas on the first floor. Kitchen/dining area in the east bay, living room/study in the west bay. Bathrooms can be stacked easily in the north side of the chimney bay. The stairway in the chimney bay provides central access to bedrooms and also acts as a visual barrier between living area and kitchen/dining areas, reducing the need for interior partitions.

central bay narrower, from 8 to 12 feet. The central bay was called the chimney bay. This is the area where the chimney, stairway, closets, and hallways were placed. It is essentially the mechanical and transitional area of the house. The two outer bays, being larger, were used for the kitchen, dining, living room and parlor on the first floor. On the second floor the stairway led to a small hall. The bedrooms were above the two outer bays. This was a practical and efficient design, resulting in little wasted space.

To provide for our modern needs, the chimney bay can be used for the bathrooms, first and second floors, keeping the plumbing all in a central location. The chimney, mechanical and HVAC systems are still appropriate to place in the chimney bay without hindering the open living areas.

When designing living spaces in a timber frame house there are many creative avenues to pursue and discover by working within the modular dimensions and parameters within the timber framework. These concepts and their design implications will be discussed fully later in this book.

Traditional four bent frame with chimney bay. The frame is enclosed with stress skin panels.

Enclosure Methods

In recent years, stress skin panels have become the most common timber frame enclosure method. The speed of application, energy-efficiency and ability to keep all timbers exposed are definite credits to the system. However, there are several issues concerning foam core panels that can create heated discussions between both advocates and opponents of the system. These range from cost to environmental concerns and longevity.

While stress skin panels remain one of the most convenient options for enclosing a frame, there are a number of innovative natural alternatives based on traditional systems that are worth considering.

The traditional method of enclosing a timber frame throughout Europe and Asia for the past millennia has been wattle and daub. This is a dense clay and straw mixture (daub) that is worked by hand into a wickerwork of split hardwood saplings (wattles) held in place by hardwood staves. Of all the clay systems with which I have worked, this is most enjoyable as it progresses rapidly; uses abundant and easily worked material, few tools, and it looks beautiful in every step of the process. However, due to its density it has a low insulation value, making it impractical for enclosures in northern climates. It does, however, remain practical for interior partitions. For northern climates, clay based systems require greater wall thickness and a greater ratio of fiber to clay than wattle and daub provides.

Frame during stress skin enclosure process. Gypsum blue board was first applied to the frame followed by the chip/chip panels.

Wattle & daub wall panel on the Dining Hall at the school site in Maine.

Finished interior of a wood chip clay infill house. The infill was undertaken in a one week workshop in Corbett, Oregon. Clay plaster was used on both the interior and exterior.

A typical caged wall system for wood chip clay infill. The cavity is 12 inches thick. Spaced lathing is stapled to both interior and exterior. The light framing inside and out allows for an uninterrupted thermal shell. Two by two studs can be used for straight wall sections and 2x4s for door and window openings.

Laying hardwood floor over radiant heat tubing in the office at Fox Maple School. Compressed straw panels were used for the enclosure. The frame was cut in the spring 1996 workshop.

In the mid 1970s a revolution of traditional clay building techniques erupted in Germany. It was prompted by the government in part to revive a traditional craft intrinsic to their building heritage, but also on a more practical note, to repair the many half-timbered houses which were damaged during the war.

Immediately following the war great numbers of centuries-old timber frames were repaired with portland cement-based infill material in place of the original clay-based wattle and daub. By the late 1960s it became apparent that problems with these initial repairs were beginning to occur on a widespread basis. Rot was a primary problem due to the nature of cement to wick moisture. This prompted a revival in the trade of the clay builder.

Spurred along with government support, an initiative was undertaken to restore these buildings to their original state using the traditional clay systems that had proven effective for so many centuries prior to the war. Once initiated, this led the newly revived Guild of clay builders to begin research and development of new innovations of traditional clay based systems appropriate for new construction that would meet the stringent German building codes for energy efficiency, fire codes, etc. This resulted in a variety of innovative natural light clay systems to be developed that combined mixtures of clay with cellulose fibers: straw, wood chips, hemp, peanut shells, reeds (virtually any cellulose fiber can be used), to construct practical, energy efficient enclosures.

The two most efficient systems to come out of this, I believe, were straw-light clay and wood chip light clay. The term light implies a greater ratio of fiber to clay, therefore a lighter mix, increasing insulation values. Each of these systems require a wall thickness of 10-12 inches and provide a tested R-value of 2 per inch of material. While there is little space to cover these systems in detail in this book, as the subject here is the system of timber framing, I highly suggest further investigation to anyone wishing to use a natural enclosure system. I have been working with these systems for nearly 15 years, and am a stronger proponent today than ever.

Another viable natural enclosure alternative is compressed wheat straw panels. By compressing wheat straw under heat the glutens produce a natural glue which structurally binds the straw. Compressed straw is the natural alternative to foam core panels. The office and workshop at our school site are both enclosed with compressed straw panels made by Stramit. While Stramit has been producing these panels in England for over 50 years, the industry is only recently emerging in the U.S. I would highly suggest further investigation of compressed straw panels to anyone interested in natural enclosure materials in a panel system.

Chapter 2
Tools

Carving pegs on raising day 1976. This is how we did it in the old days. We'd usually arrive at the building site and first thing scout out a suitable red oak, or locust tree if there happened to be any, and chop it down into bolts. The crew would take turns riving pegs with a broad hatchet from the time we arrived until the last peg was driven. Family and friends were always welcome to join in on raising day. It was not about efficiency, as we had better ways to make pegs in the shop, but more about connecting with the owner and the land. There is something special, and perhaps even magical about pegging your frame with the wood that grew where the frame stands. It is one of those little things in life that just makes you smile and feel good. Perfection and grace... puts a smile on your face.

Smoothing pegs in the Head-of-Jeddore Workshop, Nova Scotia, Canada, 1995.

The Timber Framer's Tool Box

One of the first questions I'm asked by workshop students is invariably, "What tools do I need to build a timber frame?" My retort is usually quick, "a chisel and a mallet." This may not be the whole truth, but I've always felt that tools should be purchased only after they've proven to be absolutely essential to the work being done. With a chisel and mallet, a brace and bit, and a hand saw, an experienced carpenter could build anything—given the time. When learning a new trade, it's best to start out with only the minimum of essential tools of that trade. The first priority is to learn how to use these few tools really well; to execute your work accurately and efficiently, and to understand the nature of the work—inside and out—before you go out and spend a bundle on a cache of tools that may spend most of their time in the tool box. Tools will not necessarily make a person a better craftsman, but a craftsman can expand the capabilities of just about any tool he touches. This comes from experience, and from spending a lot of time working with a short tool box. The more you have to stretch the limitations of your tools, and imagination, the better a craftsman you'll become, and the better equipped you'll be to tackle any project that comes along.

In what may actually be a blessing in disguise, most carpenters and builders are limited by economic realities and cannot purchase every tool on their dream list in just one outing. After all, half the fun of having a dream list is dreaming about it; just as the greater reward we get from building may be in the act of building, or in the process of completing, and not necessarily in the completion itself. If this is the case—and I believe most craftsmen would agree that it is—then the tools we use, or choose not to use, become an all important aspect of our work. It's not necessarily how the tool is designed to work, it's how the tool works in *our* hands. They need to *fit* our hands, literally and figuratively. They need to *feel* right. They need to have balance so that they can naturally act as an extension of our hands. Tools may be designed to cut, plough, rip or gouge, but it's our hands that must guide them to make them perform to our will, and it is through our own eyes that we make cuts true. The eye develops aside from the tools, but a good tool that feels comfortable in your hands can reduce fatigue and help to maintain a sharp eye throughout the day. I tend to judge the worthiness of a tool in the way it feels, and in the way that I feel after using it all day. If I feel good at day's end, then perhaps my work has maintained a sharp edge, and perhaps I will look forward to work the next day. The insight that I give to my students about tools is based to a large degree on this approach.

The photo above shows the hand tools used to carry out most of the hand work of cutting joinery: 1-1/2 & 2 "chisels, mallet and hand plane for chopping, paring and smoothing; and tape measure, framing square, combination square, and scoring knife, for marking and gauging. Once the tools are in hand, the challenge is to learn how to use them to create fine joinery. That's where the camera comes in—to take a picture of your fine work when it is done.

A combination square is perfect for checking mortise and tenon joinery for accuracy.

Timber framing is demanding work, both on the tools and on the body using them. Perhaps more than any other type of house building, timber framing demands a level of intimacy and dedication that tends to make people extend the limits of their abilities. When people extend their limits, then surely the tools will be asked to do the same. For this reason, cheaply made, misaligned tools have no place in the shop. We have a ritual at the beginning of every workshop in which we check all of the tools before we start. The framing squares are checked for square, the tape measures checked for accuracy, the chisels are checked for trueness. Inevitably, we throw more tools in the cull tool pile than those that pass the test. On this first day, the answer to the question first posed by the student begins to unfold, as well as an appreciation for the meticulous and careful approach to selecting the essential tools which make up the timber framer's tool box.

The Timber Framer's Tool Box

Anyone engaged in a trade or craft quickly learns what tools are indispensable, and soon begins to develop a list of additional tools that may increase productivity and efficiency, but are not essential to performing the work. So it is with timber framing. A basic set of tools should include all the essential tools to cut joints, pare clean lines, and assemble the frame. In the tradition of trade guilds, the young apprentice started out with only a handful of tools—only those that would fit into a small knapsack—but by the time the journey was completed, the apprentice was expected to own a complete set of the tools essential to his trade.

These consisted primarily of hand tools, and today, small hand operated power tools should be included as well. The larger, stationary tools would be provided by his employer. We find this naturally to be the case today, and

Paring a tenon face with a 2 inch framing chisel.

even more so in timber framing because of the many costly and specialized tools that are available. With this in mind, the tools of the trade can be broken down into two basic categories: 1) *Personal Tools*—those that a joiner would be expected to own and maintain, and 2) *Shop Tools*—larger specialized power tools shared by everyone working in the shop. Regardless of whether you are working in a commercial shop, starting your own small two to three man shop, or planning to build your own house, these categories apply equally as well.

Personal Tools

A fully equipped timber framer's personal tool box actually contains a rather small number of tools, considering the nature of the work. Many are the same tools that any general carpenter or builder might use, although the way in which they are used, the design, and quality criteria may be quite different. It should include a selection of both hand and power tools, and if the set is complete, there may be no limit to the quality and complexity of timber frames that could be built. To be sure, additional tools could be purchased which may help to increase productivity, but depending on the scale of the work you plan to do, they may not be necessary until you've first gained a little experience with hand tools. The cost of the basic collection of tools is actually quite reasonable. If purchased wisely, the out-of-pocket cost for the essential hand tools purchased new may fall in the $400 to $600 range. To set up your own small shop to cut your own frame, you may get by for as little as $1,500. For a carpenter planning to cross over, you may be able to round out your tool box for as little as $300 to $500. Aside from the basic tools that no carpenter should be without (cords, tape measure, hammer, etc.) a list of the essential tools is as follows:

Flushing up a peg with a hand saw.

Paring to the shoulder score line with a chisel and mallet.

Hand Tools

Framing chisels, 1-1/2" & 2" - If any tool is synonymous with timber framing, it's the framing chisel. Framing chisels come in two basic types; tang chisels and socket chisels. For timber work, the socket version is much preferred because it can take considerably more abuse, and there is less shock and vibration transferred to the hand from repeated mallet blows. Broken handles can also be replaced quickly with just about any piece of hardwood lying around. A tang chisel, on the other hand, will transfer more vibration to your hand, which creates more fatigue. Replacing handles also proves to be a little more difficult—and their handles are always breaking.

A chisel should be judged by the quality of its steel, its weight, balance, and most importantly, it's *feel*. The *feel* of a chisel may seem a somewhat nebulous term, but it can be quickly understood by chopping a few joints with one that has it, and then chopping a few joints with one that does not. Most mortises are either 1-1/2 or 2 inches wide, therefore, one chisel of each size is essential.

Good chisels can be hard to find unless you know where to look, and know what you're looking for. It may take a little experience working with both good and bad chisels before you begin to understand and appreciate the qualities of a good one, and precisely what a good chisel means to a timber framer. A chisel, after all, is the defining tool of the timber framer.

Used chisels can be found in antique stores and yard sales, but the chances of finding a good one are hit or miss at best. Chisels with a thin cross section and a silky smooth feel are a sign that they were made of a finer grade of steel, and most often worth buying. These were made after Henry Bessemer altered the nature of steel making in the 1860's.

Student paring the tenon face on a rafter foot. Waldoboro, Maine Workshop, Fall 1994.

The Bessemer process, which was patented in 1855, revolutionized the steel making industry and allowed the Industrial Revolution to move into high gear. Before this invention, high carbon steel was made in small batches, essentially by alchemist craftsmen, and cast into ingots to cool. It was through this process that they controlled the carbon content. The rate of cooling, the size and thickness of the ingot, and even the location and time of year all affected the quality and hardness of the steel. Chisels stamped *cast steel* are a sign that they were made prior to 1870, and are the work of a craftsman who made his own steel in small batches according to their own secret recipes and alchemical magic. The result was high carbon steel that was hard and brittle, and incapable of being struck with hammers and mallets directly, so it was hammer forged, or laminated, to softer steel that would absorb the stress. Because of this, these *cast steel* chisels usually have a very heavy cross section.

For many hundreds of years the highest quality steel came from Sheffield, England. Ashley Iles, the renowned Sheffield edge tool maker, once told me that many attributed its superior quality to the unique mineral content of the water in the river Don, which was used to quench the steel.

The selection of new chisels now on the market is limited as well. The best chisels I've found, by far, are made by Barr Quarton, of Barr Specialty Tools, in McCall, Idaho. Barr, who is an apprenticed Japanese sword maker, hand-forges a line of socket timber framing and log building tools that really have no equal in any mass produced line. I'd recommend Barr tools as a first choice to any serious timber framer or woodworker. Henry Taylor (a corporation), of Sheffield, England, also makes a line of socket framing chisels which can be purchased through many tool catalogs in the U.S. These look great, but in my experience they can be difficult to sharpen and maintain a good edge. Unfortunately, this is about all that is available on the market for new socket chisels.

For tang chisels, Sorby, also of Sheffield, makes a great line of quality tools, including a set of tang framing chisels. While the tang is not preferred, the quality of the steel in the Sorby chisels is superb. Coupled with the feel that they've managed to capture, they are a great alternative if a quality socket chisel cannot be found.

Framing Mallet, 32 to 48 ounce - My preference in a framing mallet is a one piece, turned mallet, 16 to 18 inches long, with a head about 3 to 3-1/2 inches in diameter. These, of course, you have to turn yourself. In New England, the best wood is American Hop Hornbeam. It is best to use hornbeam grown on rocky mountainsides as opposed to sandy soil. Sugar maple (also called rock maple), beech, Osage orange and locust, also make good mallets. If you don't have the wood, or the lathe, you'll have to find someone who does, as this design of mallet cannot commonly be purchased on the street. Dead blow hammers can also be used, however, they create more fatigue, produce more heat through friction, and have less *feel* than a solid wooden mallet. Carpal tunnel and or tendonitis may also result by using these hammers over a period of time.

When using a mallet, the handle wants to be grasped loosely in your hand so the shock does not drive into your hand, wrist and forearm. For this, you want the handle to be large enough so that you can just touch your finger tips when grasped. Skinny handles make you want to grip to tightly, creating much more stress, increasing the possibility of injury. The mallet is designed to do the work, so let it absorb the shock, and don't try to drive the mallet through the wood, let the chisel do its job. When pounding a chisel with a mallet, you should be able to feel the edge of the chisel cutting the wood. I find that anything other than a turned wooden mallet (with the pounding face parallel to the grain of the wood) creates too much shock and vibration, and this *feel* is lost.

Framing Mallets, chisels, drills and bits suitable for timber framing. The mallets are turned hornbeam and sugar maple, and the style I prefer. Beech, Osage orange and locust are also suitable. Hickory & white oak, however, are too dense to use for a mallet as they do not absorb the shock. A mallet should fit loosely in the hand with a fairly fat handle—let the mallet do the work. Gripping a small handle all day will cause greater fatigue and possible injury.

Student finishes off an interesting joint with a chisel, mallet and a combination square—the essential timber framing tools.

Squaring up timbers is one of the most important uses of a square in timber framing. For this it is imperative that the square is square. Above, a student squares up a timber using the new Chappell Universal square.

Protractor squares, below, are handy for checking and gauging angles.

Framing Square - A framing square is without a doubt one of the most essential tools to the timber framer. Developed by and for timber framers back in the middle ages, the steel framing square today still is one of the most useful layout tools available to not only the timber framer, but also to the general carpenter and builder as well. To the timber framer, the framing square is essential to check the squareness of timbers so that accurate layout can be made across and around all sides of the timber. The first step in joinery layout is to square the timber. To do this accurately it is essential that the framing square itself is square and true. This may seem obvious, but the truth is over 30% of all squares on the rack are out-of-square from the factory. Therefore, it is important to check for squareness before purchasing.

Aside from using the square to square up timbers and to make straight lines at 90 degree angles to the side faces of timbers, it is also an ideal template for laying out 1-1/2 and 2 inch mortises, and for stepping off mortises and tenons consistently to the same distance from the side face, or center line, along the length of a timber. While these are the most fundamental and practical benefits of a ruled, rigid square, the full appreciation of a framing square becomes evident when using it to lay out roof systems.

As with many tools, the best framing squares are the most expensive, and as mentioned, it is absolutely imperative that the square is *square*. Check for square by measuring the diagonal from 12" to 16". This should read *exactly* 20".

After years of watching the quality of framing squares decline, coupled with the desire to update the rafter tables on the square to more fully accommodate the needs of the modern builder, I finally sat down and developed a framing square to meet and exceed the modern builders needs. The result is the new, and patented, *Chappell Universal Square.*

With the introduction of this new framing square, I really cannot recommend any other. For one, I designed the square because I could not find a decent framing square on the market. Secondly, it is designed specifically to meet the needs and requirements of timber framing, especially when laying out compound joinery, as it includes information that allows one to project tenons from compound cuts. My goal in designing the square was to provide not only timber framers, but all carpenters and builders, with a modern square that was made of stainless steel and guaranteed to be square. The result is a square with expanded rafter tables that will allow anyone in the field to determine rotational angles and length ratios for virtually every rotation in both equal-pitched and unequal pitched compound roof systems—including backing angles and fascia miter angles. It also has rafter tables for hexagons and octagons that include the full array of angular and length ratios.

The square is ruled using a metric inch, with minor divisions in 1/20. These fall on the 1/4, 1/2 & 3/4 inch marks of the imperial inch, so one can easily transition from the imperial to the decimal inch. The practicality of the decimal inch is that there is no need to convert decimal results on the calculator to imperial fractions to apply them to the square. Decimals can be applied directly to the ruling on the Universal square. The square is also truly *Universal*, as the name implies, in that it fluently works cross-platform between metric and imperial units of measure without any conversions necessary.

The tables on the Chappell square are all based on the decimal units of 1 and 10, allowing rapid mental calculations and application. The tables on the standard framing square were developed in 1901, and include only 4 basic pieces of information—so it is about time for an update to the carpenters framing square. There is also a line of smaller center squares and flexible stainless steel center rules, all ruled in the decimal inch, to go along with the framing squares. These are all designed to make the layout process a breeze.

Combination & Bevel Squares - Combo squares are used for marking and gauging, and usually not for layout, so even the lower end models will do. The most important requirement is a tight locking nut to prevent the rule from slipping. Bevel squares are handy because they can be set to any angle and set up for repetitive layout and for gauging angle cuts of joinery. They are a cheap alternative to a protractor square, but do not take their place.

Protractor or Compass Square - Compass squares are a handy tool for determining and checking preliminary layout when cutting compound angles, and for gauging the angle and depth of angled mortises. They're a great addition to your tool box, and will certainly become a tool that gets quite a bit of use. Woodcraft Supply and Lee Valley sell a number of makes, ranging in price from $50 to over $100. Starrett is the top of the line and will last a lifetime. Brown & Sharp made a line of fine machinists tools, and may be the best brand available, but these are no longer manufactured, so check out the flea markets or ebay. The type with the double shoe is best as you can use the set from either direction.

Block Plane, low angle and standard - Aside from your chisel, block planes are one of the most frequently used tools of the timber framer for flattening tenon faces, cheeks and shoulders. Low angle block planes are great for planing end grain, and a standard plane is great for all around work. Stanley still makes good planes, but you have to buy the professional models, or find an older used one. These cost new about $35 to $75, and should be available at most hardware stores. In the past few years a number of high quality planes have become available. Lee Valley's Veritas brand, and Lie-Nielsen's extensive line of professional planes are each top-of-the-line, and though they are expensive, once you use them you will see, and feel, the value immediately.

Rabbet Plane - For cleaning the tenon faces up to the shoulder (90°), rabbet planes are the fastest and cleanest tool to use. In timber framing, rabbet planes are the kind of tool that once you start using, you'll wonder how you ever got by without it. Both Veritas and Lie-Nielsen make a couple of models of rabbet planes of superb quality. The English Stanley #78 may be the best reasonably priced rabbet plane available and can be fitted with after market Hock, Veritas or Japanese plane irons available from many tool suppliers.

The hand tools used to cut this rafter foot to post joint comprise only of the basics.

Clamping the framing square into a square jig set to the roof pitch allows for accurate repetitive layout for rafters and angled joinery. The jig can easily be made with plywood or solid wood strips, ripped and joined to 1-1/2 inches, and secured with screws.

Black & Decker drill on the left is capable for hogging out 2-inch and larger holes for mortises. The Makita drill on the right is ideal for pegging and drilling with bits 1-1/2 inches and under. It can bog down in oak. The short bits are made by Greenlee, #45 Short Unispur, but are no longer available new. Look for these in yard sales and antique stores, or call Greenlee and order one. If enough people call, they may start producing them again. The 18"long 1-inch pegging bit is style you want, but no longer available. Wood Owl makes a good line of pegging bits in 8" and 18" lengths.

Hand saw, rip and cross cut - Since the development of the circular saw, rip saws have all but disappeared from the modern carpenter's tool box. To the timber framer, it's an essential tool for completing the side cuts of tenons where the circular saw can't reach. Sandvik and Disston both make a fine saw (buy the professional model only). The Japanese Ryoba saw is also an ideal saw for timber framing in that it has both rip and crosscutting edges. They're great for finesse cuts, and the flexible blade makes it the best saw for cutting off pegs. The Stanley Shark saw (available in just about any hardware store) is also an excellent all-around saw for both ripping and crosscutting large timbers. The Japanese style teeth (though they cut on the push stroke) have a large set which prevents them from binding, so fast clean cuts can be made.

Power Tools

Circular saws - If you already own a circular saw, the odds are that it will work fine if it is a professional model. A 7-1/4 or 8-1/4 inch saw is required for general work. Both sidewinders and worm drives have their place, and if at all possible, owning both is ideal. Angle cuts on large timbers can often be approached from only one direction, therefore, the flexibility of being able to set the worm drive and sidewinder angles in opposite positions can be a time-saving advantage. I find worm drives to be much better at making long rips, while sidewinders offer a little more two-hand control for cutting to scored shoulder lines across the grain. Although you're working with large timbers, the work is closer to building cabinets than pole barns, so a saw with a solid heft and no vibration is essential. Makita makes a great all-around 7-1/4 inch saw. It's solid, has little or no vibration, and like most Makita tools, has a powerful motor. The newer professional lines of American saws—DeWalt, Porter Cable, and Black & Decker—are also a good choice. Above all, choose a saw that feels comfortable in your hands.

1/2 inch Drill - If you don't own a mortising machine, you'll find a good 1/2" drill to be one of the most used tools in your tool box, so make sure you choose a drill that's capable of handling the job, but also one with the most versatility. Makita and DeWalt both make a similar model, 6 amp, 550 rpm, medium to heavy duty 1/2" drill which is great for all-around use. They're both light enough for one-hand drilling, but also deliver enough torque to handle a 2" bit for roughing out mortises in softwoods. Both have a forward/reverse toggle trigger switch, which can save time when drilling a number of repetitive holes. If you'll be working primarily in pine, these drills will do just about everything you'll need, but for hogging out 2" mortises in oak, you'll have to step up to a more rugged drill. Milwaukee, Black & Decker and DeWalt all make a model of rugged 450 rpm heavy duty drills capable of drilling up to 2-1/2" holes in oak. These are quite a lot heavier than the drills previously mentioned, so you'll want to do all your drilling at, or below, waist level. The slower rpm is necessary to prevent the lead screw from stripping out, especially when drilling oak. With the exception of Makita, avoid the Japanese brands if you plan to do heavy work. Ryobi and Hitachi seem to make drills which are too lightweight to handle their own rpm, torque and load ratings.

Hand mortiser and an electric drill—both can do the job. Advanced Workshop, Fall 1991.

Drill Bits - Along with a good drill, you'll also need a set of drill bits. You'll need bits to serve two essential functions: 1) drilling peg holes, and 2) hogging out mortises.

The availability and supply of drill bits in recent years has changed dramatically. The stalwart manufacturers have nearly all gone by, and you can no longer expect a drill bit to last more than a couple of frames. Irwin, however, still makes one of the better pegging bits available—and they can actually be purchased for about $15 off the rack of any neighborhood hardware store. These come in sizes up to 1-1/8", with an 6" twist and 8 inches overall. Pegs can vary slightly in size from batch to batch (whether you make them yourself or purchase them) and most often need to be calibrated with the bit. These bits are cheap enough to be field dressed without loosing sleep. The most common peg sizes are 3/4" and 1", so to accommodate all peg dimensions and variations, you'll need an 11/16, 3/4, 7/8, 15/16 and a 1 inch bit as a starter set.

In the past few years a new bit of excellent quality, marketed under the trade name of Wood Owl, has come onto the market that is great for drilling peg holes. This three spur ships auger comes in lengths of 8 inches and 18 inches and diameters from 3/8 to 1-1/2 inches. They cut very clean, straight holes. These can be purchased by Timberwolf Tools, and you can easily find local distributors by doing a google search.

Using a framing square to lay out tenon on a rafter foot for an English tying joint.

Student handles a 16" saw at the Summer 1996 Workshop in West Falmouth, Mass.

For pegging in general, you'll want a single or double spur bit. A good source for drill bits are electrical or plumbing supply houses. They generally have the catalogs of all manufacturers and can order from any of them. Avoid spurless bits, such as the Nail Eater® or electricians bits. They cut ragged holes and tear-out on both the entry and exit.

Mortising Bits

Unfortunately, in the last several years most manufacturers have stopped making bits larger than 1-1/2 inches in diameter. The best bits made for the drilling mortises were the Greenlee #45 Short Unispur bits. Greenlee dropped the line in the mid 80s, but if you ever run into any, snatch them up. Wood Owl makes a 1-1/2" bit, but it tends to clog up a lot, in part because it 3 spurs. For hogging out mortises, single twist, unispur bits work the best. Double spur, double twist bits tend to clog up quickly, especially in oak timbers and in knots. Milwaukee makes (or at least markets) a great single spur bit which cuts quickly and cleanly in both hardwoods and softwoods, but unfortunately, they don't make anything larger than 1-1/2 inch. I suggest buying a 1-1/4 and a 1-1/2 inch Milwaukee, then go to your local electrical or plumbing supplier and seek out the larger 2" and 2-1/2" bits, hopefully from a German manufacturer.

Stay away from forstner bits, spade bits and multi spur bits. They tend to wander, are difficult to pull out of deep mortises, and can be dangerous if they run into a hidden knot.

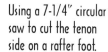

Using a 7-1/4" circular saw to cut the tenon side on a rafter foot.

Shop Tools

If your intentions are to make timber framing a business, sooner or later you'll find the need to bring in some larger, more powerful, and more specialized equipment. The two most time-consuming aspects of timber framing are cutting through large timbers, and making mortises. If efficiency is to be gained and production time saved, purchasing machinery to perform these tasks will prove to be the most helpful.

To cut through large timbers, a chain saw can be used, however, it takes quite a bit of experience to master the art if fine cuts are to be made. For more controlled cuts, a 16" saw may be preferred. For mortises, a chain or chisel mortising machine is the answer. The following are a few of the tools that will be the most helpful.

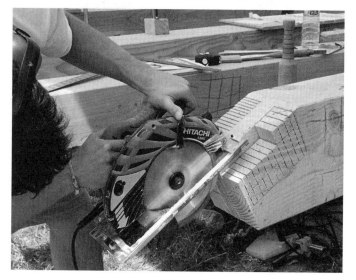

Circular Saws - For making the shoulder cuts of tenons and off-cutting larger timbers, a step up from a 7-1/4" circular saw will cut production time dramatically. If the budget allows, three sizes should be purchased; a 10", 13" and a 16". The 10" saw will cut a full 3-1/2 inches and is ideal for cutting tenon shoulders. The 13" saw will cut a full 5 inches, and is only slightly larger and heavier than the 10", making it an extremely practical and efficient saw. At the moment, these are only available from Makita, and even at that, you might have to search for one. If only one size is affordable, my choice would be to go with the 16 inch.

Makita and Hitachi both make a 16" saw, and the German manufacturer, Mafell, makes a 14" saw (as well as a two-man 25" saw). Of the two Japanese models, the Makita is the most rugged, has less vibration, and seems to have the best feel. As with the smaller Ryobi's and Hitachi's, the larger saws seem to be lightly made, and the torque seems to exceed the tool's limitations. These saws all cost in the neighborhood of $750 to $950 (prices are unstable, so you might find the prices even greater). All in all, the differences are slight, and with the scarcity and escalating prices, if you can find a good buy, any one of these tools will do the job. The Mafell is a little more pricey, but it is designed with that German *feel*, and smooth clean cuts are the result. The Mafell, however, requires a little more respect and finesse when operating and handling. It's not the kind of tool that gets thrown in the back of the pick-up and left in the rain.

Saws, drills and planers are the essential tools if you want to produce a frame efficiently, but do not plan to go into high production.

The Makita 16" saw (pictured) is a great saw and can take quite a bit of abuse, however, finesse is required to make accurate cuts on a consistent basis. Mafell makes a line of large saws that are better engineered, take less know-how to use, but the cost (double the Makita) makes them practical to only the professional timber framer. Smaller saws, 7-1/4" & 8-1/4" are more readily available, but stay with the top-of-the line models. Planers worth purchasing are limited to Mafell and Makita. Again, Mafell has the quality, but Makita makes a tool worthy of a professional at half the cost.

Mortising Machines - Mortisers come in two varieties: chain mortisers and chisel mortisers. Makita and Hitachi make both types. Mafell and ProTool, both European manufacturers, make only a chain mortiser. The best chain mortisers of all are the European style mortisers like those made by Mafell, ProTool and others.

Unlike the Japanese models, the design of the European models do not require that they have to be clamped to the timber while mortising. The flat base is simply set on the face of the timber and a side plate butts to the side face, and away you go. Setup time is reduced to near zero as there are no clamping bases or knobs to adjust. These are also generally lighter and not as unwieldy. The reason for this is that the chain in the European designs cut across the grain (which is the easiest cut in wood). Therefore, as it plunges the chain pulls the side plate tighter to the timber. Because the chain is cutting across the grain, there is also no kickback to worry about.

The Japanese models, however, all cut with, or parallel, to the grain. This requires that the mortiser be tightly clamped to the timber, and even at that, when plunging oak, or cutting through knots, care must be taken to control the plunge to avoid jumping and kicking. The one catch is that the European models costs around $3,000 to $4,500 and the Japanese models all cost in the $1,250 to $1,750 range. To justify the additional expense, you need to be serious about producing frames.

The Japanese chain mortisers cut with the grain, so it is necessary to clamp them to the timber. The Makita, to the right, has a rotating head that allows three plunge positions with each locked setting. Chain mortisers can hog out plenty of wood in a day, but afterwards you know you have worked, and you will still need to clean up the mortise with a chisel.

In saying this, the Japanese models are workhorses and extremely rugged. The Toyota definitely gets you where you are going, but it sure is nice to dream about the Mercedes.

Comparing the two Japanese models, their basic operation is on a fairly equal par. The one advantage to the Makita is that the standard base can clamp to a 12 inch timber, while the Hitachi can only clamp to an 8 inch. Base extensions can be purchased for about $300, but most people I know have the extensions made up at a machine shop for about $100.

Chisel Mortisers - While chisel mortisers make sharp clean cuts with flat bottoms (doing away with the cleanup that is often necessary with chain mortisers) they cut a little slower, and are limited to cutting softwood and shallow, narrow mortises such as brace pockets. Again, the two Japanese models are on a fairly even par, and the decision of which one to purchase may justifiably be based on the best price and availability. Chisel mortisers cost about the same as the chain version. If only one mortiser is going to purchased, I'd choose the chain version, which cuts quicker and is generally more versatile.

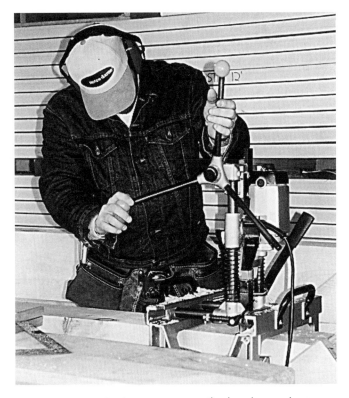

Chisel mortisers make nice and clean flat bottom mortises, but are a bit slower and work best when mortising soft wood timbers such as white pine and doug fir.

The European design chain mortisers to the left are lighter and more flexible as they do not need to be clamped to the timber. However, the price tag makes them a little out of reach to the casual timber framer. Here we have a Scottish and an English bloke trying to figure out how to turn it on at the Asturias, Spain 2008 workshop.

Student chopping the slot dovetail shoulder on a tie beam for an English tying joint with a vintage cast steel chisel.

Checking the tapes measures before getting to work. All tapes will vary slightly. When laying out timber joinery it is important that all crew members are using calibrated tapes.

Squaring timbers before layout is the first priority to making fine joinery.

Sawing the angled shoulders of a dovetail pocket with the saw set to 20.5°, which is the ratio of 3/4" to 2", the common dovetail angle.

Chapter 3
Structural Design Considerations

Clear span roof framing offers one of the most difficult challenges to a timber framer. Coupled with compound hip and valley framing, it requires a thorough understanding of all aspects of joinery and structural design. Indianapolis, Indiana, 1992.

Arch braced roof lower strut to post and tie beam.

Structural Design Considerations

Not everyone can expect to become fluent in engineering formula and theory just by building one, or even a dozen, timber frames. Engineering is a very complex science, and in most cases, it's better to not even begin confusing the mind with such concepts as **moment of inertia** or **modulus of elasticity**, etc., unless you plan to become a professional timber frame designer. You do not have to be an engineer to design and build your own timber frame home, but there are some basic principles one should understand that will help in the process.

Traditional timber frame designs of Colonial America were the results of hundreds of years of evolution in Europe. Reviewing the evidence of early Greek and Egyptian architecture leads us to believe that structural engineering was quite advanced early on in history. As the use of timbers to build dwellings began to emerge in Europe in the Middle Ages, the chore at hand was to devise methods of securing these timbers in accordance with their already considerable knowledge of structural design. Thus was born the mortise and tenon joint, the basic joinery of timber framing.

In light of this historical evolution, I believe one should follow their lead by first gaining an understanding of the basic concept of structural design, followed by an understanding of joinery. The rich history of timber framing left to us by colonial and European housewrights, coupled with the ever growing body of knowledge available from modern timber framers, opens the doorway to all who wish to build a timber frame.

The key to this doorway is to gain a thorough understanding of the elements which set timber framing apart from what we consider "conventional building." Primarily this would be joinery, but it also includes a basic understanding of the general principles of structure, i.e., imposed loads and their impact on each structural member.

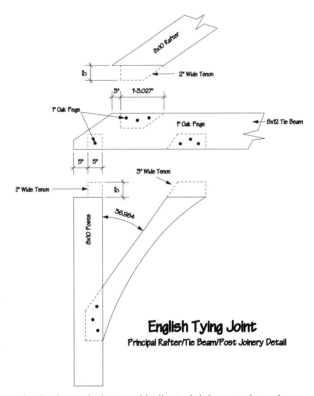

English Tying Joint
Principal Rafter/Tie Beam/Post Joinery Detail

The development of joinery like the English tying joint, simple yet eloquent, allowed sophisticated structures to be built and ushered in a renaissance of building across Europe by the end of the first millennia AD.

Structural Design Considerations

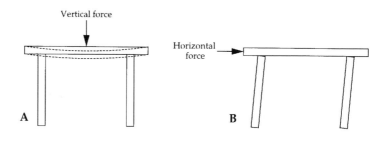

Post and Lintel Framework

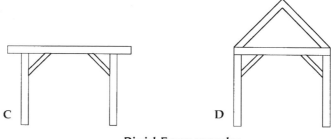

Rigid Frameworks

Structural Frameworks

The frame below uses a simple post & lintel rigid framework relying on the intrinsic beam strength to resist both the dead and live loads (externally applied forces). The internal struts from the posts to longitudinal beam are not designed to transfer loads, but rather to add rigidity and to beef up the support girder.

The nature of structural design is to assure that the resistive forces—in a beam or a structural framework—are greater than the externally applied forces. The goal is to transfer the combined forces through the framework to the foundation. In its most fundamental application, this would be to place **posts** (vertical members) to support a **beam** (horizontal member). As reviewed earlier, this is known as post and lintel construction. In the diagram above we see the evolution of a structural framework. Diagram A and B, are simple post and lintel frameworks. The lintel (beam) is subjected to vertical loading and must sufficiently resist motion due to its intrinsic strength properties. Resistance to horizontal forces are minimal due to lack of bracing. By adding braces (Dia. C) a rigid framework is created. A rigid framework is a basic structural form which is commonly used in many building applications. By introducing rafters (Dia. D) we have created a simple bent. In this form, the bent is not a truss, but a simple, rigid framework. As with the post and lintel framework, its ability to resist external forces is directly related to the strength of the beams. The addition of the braces only act to stiffen the frame. The next evolution would be to create a truss. A truss, by definition, is *a rigid framework which has four joints and five members all lying in one plane.* They do not rely on beam strength, but on a system of joints which replicate the dynamics of a single beam. Truss dynamics will be discussed more fully in Chapter 6.

Load Distribution

While conventional stick-framed buildings are designed to distribute loads through many pieces, subsequently lessening the demand of each individual member, a timber frame tends to concentrate loads on a few members. This allows for larger open spaces, and greater flexibility in design, but offers less margin for error.

To understand just how this translates, we can compare the load that is imposed on each rafter of a conventionally framed house to that of a timber frame. Assuming the house is a 28' x 36' cape with a 12/12 pitch, the total roof load, based on a common safe load of 50 pounds per square foot (lbs psf), would be 25,200 pounds for each side of the roof or roughly 1,400 pounds distributed load on each conventional rafter at 2 feet on center. In a timber frame, with bents spaced at 12 feet on center, the rafter would be expected to carry a load of up to 8,400 lbs. The requirement of the timber frame is to effectively transfer this load through purlins to rafters to posts and, ultimately, to the foundation.

The two post & lintel frameworks in this frame run the length of the building and utilize opposing struts to increase the net beam depth of the upper girder. This system relies essentially on pure post & lintel structural dynamics, without any trussing action.

To gain an understanding of how this may be accomplished, it may be easier to break the frame down to its three basic elements, which are: 1) **Timber strength**; 2) **Structural design**; and 3) **Joinery**.

Timber Strength — This deals with the raw science of wood, i.e., the physical and mechanical properties of a particular timber of a particular species. To determine the safe working load for a given beam, three considerations are necessary: *design for bending*, *horizontal shear*, and *deflection*. The formulas and criteria for determining these aspects of beam design will be covered in Chapters 5 & 11. Once the appropriate sized timber to carry a given external load has been determined, the internal forces imposed on the joinery must be analyzed. This is really the more difficult process because each aspect of the joint must be analyzed—tenon, pegs, mortise sides, etc. Joints under tension must be scrutinized more thoroughly than those in compression. By first determining the requirements of the joints, then sizing the timbers to meet the requirements of the tenon/mortise/peg interfaces and bearing surfaces, the timbers will often exceed the required design loads.

Structural Design — Structural design has to do with the placement and arrangement of timbers within a framework. The required dimension of a timber may be substantially increased or decreased in accordance with its placement and relationship to each adjoining member. Proper design aims to increase strength while at the same time decreasing timber size. Understanding the basic mechanical concepts of structure will allow builders more

Longitudinal plate with buttress arches.

creativity and confidence in expanding their design talents. Through proper design we can save time in the cutting and raising, reduce costs, increase usable living area, and create more aesthetically pleasing and functional homes.

One of the unique aspects of timber framing is that most often it is the builder who is also the designer of the frame. This was especially true back in the early days of the revival when there were no other options. In great part, this was the original impetus to write this book—so that my students could become composers as well.

Structural Design Considerations

The aisled barn frame above is made up of the basic elements of traditional bent framing—principal posts, rafters and tie beam; and secondary members—interior posts, queen posts and collar ties. The tie beam joins to the post using a wedged half-dovetailed through tenon. The rafters join directly to the posts with a reverse teasel tenon birds mouth. The queen posts join to the collar tie in direct line with the aisle posts. The posts join directly to timber sills. The bents are not trusses, but rigid frameworks that effectively redirect outward thrust of the roof load to vertical loads on the posts. This was the frame project for the Stow, MA Workshop, 1995.

I have always equated timber framing to a musical expression, and have forever called it the jazz of building. It shares a similarity to jazz, in that there is a certain amount of improvisation involved in composing a system of joinery that is *right* for each frame. No two frames are ever the same, and while there may be similarities in the joinery employed, there are always slight variations, or improvisational twists, required. When the frame is completed the joinery stands out as if they were the individual notes in the scales of structure—nothing is masked or hidden.

I liken the early days of the timber frame revival to the early days of rock 'n' roll, when the Beatles and Bob Dylan ushered in the era of the singer songwriter. Their art did not fit in the box, and the only way they could really express it was to compose it and *perform* it themselves. Before the Beatles and Dylan it was the rare musician who performed their own compositions, though today it has become the norm.

So it was with timber framing. The only way to express your art back in the early 1970's was if you were able to compose it and perform it as well. To this day there remains a broad window open to the timber framer who chooses to become the designer builder. But first, one needs to understand the basic elements of structural design. And just as the aspiring musician must first study and methodically practice the musical scales until they know them by rote before they can unleash their creativity to improvise hot, musical licks, so must the aspiring timber framer study the modes and scales of structural design if they wish to be truly creative in this craft. A large part of this book deals with structural design concepts, as I am confident that if one wants to play, they first have to know the scales.

Joinery —Timber framing is essentially a delicate marriage between structural design and appropriate joinery. Joinery may be considered the scales within the modes of structural design, in that they are both necessary to create a structurally harmonic balance. And just as structural design can increase strength by distributing loads, so can properly designed joinery by maximizing the beams potential. The execution of joinery is equally important. Gaining a solid working knowledge and understanding of the vocabulary of joinery is one of the most important aspects of timber framing, and will result in the greatest creativity and design flexibility.

Joinery design is not merely a static science, but rather, a rhythmic vocabulary that must shift and change to best define the conditions at hand. It has regional accents and unique colloquial expressions. These revolve around fundamental structural laws, but they also allow for flexibility and creativity.

To understand what forces are at play, let's take a look at a typical bent, identifying its members and the forces acting upon them.

Effects of Loading

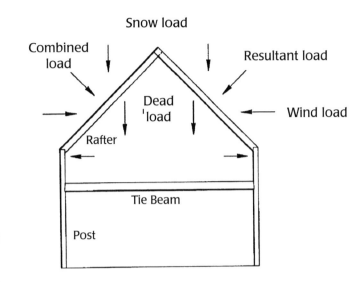

A) This simple framework is made up of posts, rafters and a tie beam. The external forces are acting on the framework which will produce internal reactionary forces. The combination of live loads (snow, wind) and dead loads (weight of the structure itself) results in a combined roof load that must be resisted. This bent relies on timber strength and joint strength to prevent failure. To prevent the lateral racking forces braces would be necessary, however these are left out to illustrate the fundamental force loads acting on the frame. The reaction to force loads are shown below.

B) The combined roof load imposes bending stresses on the rafters (1), horizontal bending stresses on the top of the posts (2), and places the tie beam in tension (3). The posts and rafters must be of sufficient strength to resist bending, and the tie beam to post joint must be sufficiently strong to resist horizontal thrust. Under severe loading, failure could occur at all three locations but would likely occur where the greatest force is imposed at the tie beam to post joint (3). This is a very unstable structural framework.

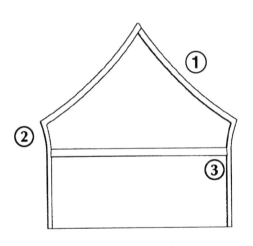

C) The horizontal load transferred to the posts places the tie beam in tension. This places bending stresses on the post and shearing stresses on the pegs, tenon and mortise sides. The joint must resist the combination of all forces. Failure will most likely result due to horizontal shear in the pegs or tenon. Failure always occurs at the weakest link. In the design process the weak link must be identified. Proper bent design relies on the uniform distribution of all forces throughout the framework.

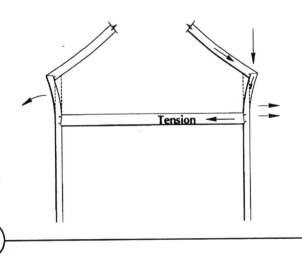

The frame above is another example of a bent that is made up of the basic elements of traditional bent framing—principal posts, rafters and tie beam; and secondary members—king post, queen posts, collar tie and struts. The rafter, tie beam and posts join using English tying joints. The lower struts transfer the loads to a vertical load at lower 3rd points of the post, allowing a clear-span first level, and represent the first design evolution in making a hammerbeam bent. Lithia, Florida, 2005.

Bent Framing

The high post cape is perhaps the most vulnerable design to failure due to the extended, or cantilevered post above the tie beam. For this reason it provides a great example to study the nature of structure.

The tie beam in this design is doing just what the name implies—tying the two posts together, therefore preventing collapse due to the outward thrusts of the rafters. If the tie beam was joined directly to the top of the post (as in the English tying joint in the photo at left), there would be no lateral forces transferred to the post and the requirements of the post, and the tie beam to post joinery, would change dramatically.

If you look around at some of the old high-posted capes built during and shortly after the Civil War (when common rafter roof systems started to become dominant), you'll see many with bowing walls at the eaves. This is due to the horizontal force of the rafters pushing out the top plate, and is affected more dramatically over long-term loading. This is what we want to avoid. For this reason, the high post design is a good example in which to illustrate the forces acting within a timber bent, from which we can determine proper design approaches.

Principal Frame Members

The Principal Frame Members are those timbers which make up the basic design (or form) of the bent structure. In the example depicted in Diagram A (pg. 39), the Principal (or primary) Members are the **Posts**, **Rafters**, and **Tie beams**.

The bent shown in Diagram A, has five principal members: two posts, two rafters and one tie beam. It is possible that this bent could stand alone, with no added members if the timbers were large enough. This may be practical in a very small frame with a 12 to 16 foot tie beam, however, in a larger frame the timbers would have to be of such great dimension that it would be wasteful and inappropriate. By analyzing the force loads acting on this bent we can begin to understand what may be done to resist these forces. The primary forces affecting a frame will be:

1) **Dead Load** - Being the force of gravity acting on the weight of the structure itself.

2) **Live Load** - Being the forces acting on the frame as a result of its intended use, such as occupants and furnishings.

3) **Snow Load** - Based on the maximum accumulation of snow that can be expected to fall on the roof (the snow load is also considered a live load).

4) **Wind Load** - The horizontal force exerted on walls and roof by wind.

5) **Resultant Load** - The combined effect and resulting direction of all loads acting on the roof structure; wind, snow and dead loads. Also called the **combined load**.

Diagram A, illustrates the forces affecting a bent. The sum of all forces are considered to be the **combined load**.

In Diagrams B and C we see the exaggerated effect that these forces will produce in the framework. The rafters are subjected to a **uniformly distributed load**. The immediate reaction of the rafters under this load is to spread or flatten out, transferring the vertical load to a horizontal thrust at the rafter feet. This load force places two distinct stresses on the posts: the vertical roof load, which places the posts in **compression**; and **bending stress** imposed by the horizontal force of the rafter's tendency to spread or flatten. If the resistance of the post is sufficient to prevent lateral movement or deflection, the rafters will then be subjected to a secondary bending force as depicted by (1) of Diagram B.

The horizontal force pushing on the post places the tie beam in tension resulting in a strain on the post/tie beam joint. Both the tie beam tenon and the pegs securing the joint must be of sufficient strength to resist the shearing stress imposed by the load. This is not the optimum condition. I tend not to rely on pegs alone for strength, but only as a binding agent, just as a stone mason relies on stone upon stone for strength—not the mortar. It is entirely possible to design a frame that does not require pegs as a structural element. This can be accomplished by adding additional members to redirect the loads so as to alleviate or reduce tension on joints completely. The photo below shows an example in which all of the joints are in compression. More on the concepts and design of tension joints will be covered in detail in Chapter 5. For now, let's see how we can reduce the amount of thrust on the post by using proper structural design.

One can see the same structural design elements in the hammerbeam bent above as in the queen post truss in the photo on the opposite page.

In this gambrel frame, the interior posts transfer the roof load to the foundation directly. Sag Harbor, NY 1984.

The queen post bent above directs roof loads to upper tie beam and directly to foundation via secondary interior posts. Center trusses are clear-span, and the queen posts are in tension. The gable truss is in compression.

The bent framing in the frame above and below addresses horizontal thrust directly by joining the rafter directly into the one piece tie beam by using the English tying joint. In this design, the collar tie resists the load on the rafters to prevent deflection. All joinery is in compression.

Secondary Frame Members Within a Bent

To make this bent a structurally sound framework we must find a way to substantially reduce or redirect the roof load to relieve the thrust placed on the posts and subsequently the tie beam joint. By relieving the horizontal thrust, we will simultaneously relieve the bending stress placed on the posts.

We have reviewed the primary frame members, now let's take a look at the secondary frame members to see how they affect the structure.

The primary reaction of the rafters under loading is to bow inward at mid-span (assuming that the posts are fixed and immovable). To resist bowing, or deflection, we could calculate the load and use a timber large enough to resist the load, but this may not be the best approach. If we were in need of an 18 foot rafter and the bents were spaced at 12 feet, the rafter dimension would need to be 7" x 20" in softwood, 7" x 15" in oak (assuming mortises were cut on the top edge for purlins). Obviously, this is excessive. The most practical approach would be to place a **collar tie** between the rafters. By placing the collar tie within the middle third of the rafters we would effectively reduce the required depth of the rafters in half, to 10 inches. This, however, has not completely compensated for all the forces acting on the frame.

As shown in Diagram D, the placement of the collar tie counteracts the bending force on the rafters, but we still must deal with the total roof load and the subsequent horizontal thrust on the posts. (In this example we are assuming that the rafter feet are not fixed because the posts may deflect under loading. If the rafter feet were fixed and immovable, the placement of the collar tie may be all that is necessary). Our concern now is the portion of the rafter below the collar tie which is still being subjected to bending stresses. Again, we could attempt to size the rafter to resist this bending stress, but the most practical approach would be to further divert the load by placing additional members within the frame. It must be remembered that a collar tie is actually designed to be a compression member. If the rafters actually do bend below the collar tie, then the collar tie becomes a tension member. Though we may design a collar tie to resist tension, it is not optimal as our goal is to avoid tension members—and hence, tension joinery—through proper structural design, thereby relieving the stress on both joinery and member sections in the frame.

Transferring Loads with Secondary Members

Diagram D

1) Placement of collar tie resists bending stresses on rafters. The collar tie is in compression. The arrows denote the resistive forces.

2) The roof load is concentrated at the rafter section from collar tie to rafter foot.

3) The roof load still imposes outward thrust on top of posts; possible failure.

Diagram E

4) Placement of secondary queen posts to support the roof load relieves the bending stresses imposed on the principal posts and rafters, tension on the tie beam, and shearing stresses on tenon and pegs.

5) The tie beam must now carry a portion of the roof load. The tie beam is no longer in severe tension.

6) At least one post must be placed under the tie beam to support the transferred roof load. The addition of 4 timbers and 2 braces transformed the unstable framework into a structurally sound bent.

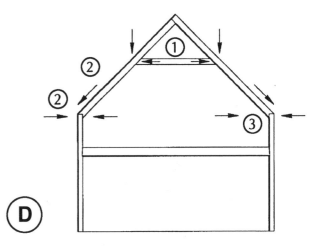

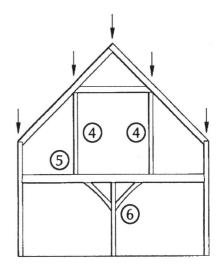

The high post bent to the left uses queen posts to redirect roof load to the 24' tie beam, which is supported by a centered post. Spring 2004 class project.

Hammerbeam trusses can transfer roof loads effectively so long as the proportional ratios are followed. It is important to understand that the post is a part of the truss, as is the lower chord, or floor system. Spring 2004 class project at Fox Maple.

Finally, we have two forces exerting severe stress on two member sections: the post/tie beam joint and the rafter section below the collar tie. Since the structure is only as strong as its weakest point, if one member section fails, complete failure is likely. Likewise, if deflection or slippage occurs on one, a proportionate increase in strain will be placed on the other.

To review, the requirements for this situation are: 1) *to prevent horizontal deflection of the post* (thereby reducing shearing stresses on the tie beam tenon and pegs); and 2) *to prevent any deflection whatsoever of the rafter section from collar tie to rafter foot.* This may be accomplished by: *1) adding additional members to relieve the load and subsequent stress placed on the post/tie beam joint;* or *2) beefing up the post to a size that could resist the total horizontal roof load.* Of these two options, the first is the most viable, and the path that we will examine. And remember, we want the collar tie to remain a compression member.

The easiest way to relieve the stress placed on the post/tie beam joint is by placing a queen post to support the collar tie close to where it joins the rafter (see Diagram D). The queen post could also join directly to the rafter as depicted in the top left photo. Though it is a hammer post, it is serving the same structural purpose as the queen post. This will reduce the outward thrust by transferring the major portion of the roof load directly to the tie beam. This is a simple and direct way to relieve the stress on the post to tie beam joint, while at the same time alleviating any concentrated forces on the rafters below the collar tie. The collar tie remains a compression member.

This does bring up some new considerations. Up to this point we have considered the tie beam as the primary member under tension only. By placing the post from collar tie to tie beam we are effectively transferring a

This arch-braced truss effectively transfers the force loads imposed on the post due to horizontal thrust to a vertical load at the post/tie beam intersection by making the post a part of the truss. Strong, Maine , 1990.

portion of the roof load to the tie beam. This is effective for reducing the tensile stress on the tie beam joint, and bending stress on the posts, but now we have to consider what new forces are in play on the tie beam.

With the roof load being partially supported by the tie beam, we have to ensure that the tie beam will support this load. For practical purposes, spans of 16 feet are the limit for unsupported beams. I have a rule for this, which I call the *Sixteen foot rule*. This essentially states that *no simple beam can span more than 16 feet.* In other words, a 20 foot beam would require a secondary post to support so it so that no section exceeded 16 feet. In our example we have a 24 foot tie beam, so we could choose to put one post to divide the beam into an 8 foot and a 16 foot span and meet the rule. However, in this case the tie is not a simple beam because it has two point loads at the third points. If the bay spacing were 12 feet, this point load would amount to approximately 4,800 pounds on each post. By placing one post at the mid span with two braces (which are essentially struts in this case), we can safely transfer the roof load further to the foundation.

If the bent is 24' wide or less (as in our example), a single post at the midpoint will sufficiently stiffen the tie beam to support the floor load and that portion of the roof load transferred by the secondary queen posts. If the span increases beyond 24 feet, then you would need two posts to address the point loads. In this case the posts would be placed directly below the queen posts.

Braces extending on both sides of the post to the tie beam are necessary structural elements in this situation. This is one instance where braces can be used effectively to transfer a load from a beam to a post because they are directly opposing each other. In most cases, knee braces are relied upon only to prevent racking, not transferring loads. No doubt, some portion of the load is always being transferred through knee braces, thereby stiffening the horizontal members but one should not rely upon this, nor try to measure their effect, but rather be reassured that you have exceeded the structural requirements at hand by designing conservatively.

Keep in mind that this is a simple overview of the basic elements of a timber frame structure. For every example there is usually an exception, and for every exception a new example. While there are many different designs which have not been discussed, most of the basic rules of structure hold true and are apparent in almost every building, whether a timber frame or not. This will become increasingly evident through experience and observation.

I believe that most people have an innate ability to understand and acknowledge proper design when they see it—something given by nature—much like the skills birds have in building nests or beavers have in building dams. All we have to do is realize it.

In this yellow pine frame both queen posts and king post secondary members were used as truss elements. The queen posts were designed as tension members to stiffen the tie beam and to reduce thrust. This frame also had a king post bridge truss that spanned two valley frame sections. Lithia, Florida, 2005.

Though it may be difficult to see in this photo, the frame to the right uses a scissor truss as a design element in the upper portion of a hammerbeam truss to make a cathedral second floor. Scissor trusses are a very efficient and attractive truss system. Sag Harbor, NY 1989.

This scissor truss was used to make an 8' wide dormer. This same design would be capable of making a clear span of up to 16' with no additional elements. Indianappolis, IN 1991.

Chapter 4
Bent Framing & Joinery Design

The structural bent framing design is the essential canvas upon which the designer/builder is allowed the freedom to create and define living spaces—spaces that reflect the building's use or occupant's needs. The joinery employed can be seen as the individual patterns or tones that add detail and harmony as if they were musical notes. Understanding the underlying structural principles of bent design, coupled with a broad vocabulary of joinery systems and designs, should be the goal of all aspiring timber framers. Hunt Valley, Maryland, 1998.

This 32′ clear-span, king post truss frame was the Spring 2004 class project at Fox Maple. The 4 bent frame has a purlin roof system, with bay spacings of 16 feet. The frame design represents the most efficient and practical use of timbers to provide the greatest enclosed space following the ground-rules as described in this book. The rafters are 20′ long, posts 12′ with the ties and king post being 16′. Spring 2004 workshop project.

Joists & Purlins

Floor Framing & Connecting Member Joinery

Dovetail joinery is most commonly used to join the connecting members in a frame, i.e., floor joists, summer beams and purlins. The requirements of these connecting members are twofold. The first, and most rudimentary, is to create the framing to which the exterior sheathing and flooring may be nailed. This may be boards, stress skin, or any other suitable enclosure or flooring material. The second requirement—which has a greater importance to the structural integrity of the frame—is to tie the primary bent framing firmly and securely together. The nature of the dovetail as a tension joint, with its ability to draw the joining members into each other once wedged, makes it a great joint for floor joists and purlins.

Shouldered Dovetail

The types of dovetails used in these connecting members may be broken down into three basic types: 1) **Simple wedged dovetail**; 2) **Housed dovetail**; and 3) **Shouldered dovetail**. A particular joint may incorporate one or more of these elements. That is, one might choose to use a housed/shouldered dovetail or a simple/shouldered dovetail, etc. Let's take a look at the individual properties of each of these joints and find out where and why we would use them.

Simple dovetail pocket in rafter. The depth of the mortise should be no more than 5/8 the depth of the beam.

Simple Wedged Dovetail

The simple, wedged dovetail is probably the most common type of dovetail in use today. Structurally, it has all of the properties one looks for in good timber joinery, and it has a romantic allure that seems to pervade the collective woodworking consciousness. When wedged, it is a self-locking tension joint. It must be clear that the wedge is an integral part of the joint, without which it will not effectively do its job.

Dovetails are best suited for joining floor joists to connecting girts, tie beams or summer beams, and purlins to rafters. In most cases the simple wedged dovetail is used where the dimensions of the connecting member (the joist or purlin itself) are 7"x7" or less. This is partially dictated by the size of the timber the joist or purlin is to be joined. The suitable tenon length for most simple dovetails range from 2" to 2-1/2", however, the general rule-of-thumb of 1/3 the beam depth should be loosely followed. For the greatest strength, the angle of the dovetail should be about 20°, or a ratio of about 3 to 1. This is usually mapped using the ratio of a 3/4" side cut to the length of the tenon. Most common dovetails have a 2" to 3" tenon.

The actual width of the tenon should be slightly narrower than the mortise, so that the wedges may be easily started. The wedges driven on both sides of the tenon will pull the members tightly together, making a clean, tight fit and will strengthen both the mortised and tenoned members. The shoulder cuts on the tenon should be scored with a sharp knife, cut shy of the line and pared with a chisel. This will create a tight, even joint where the timbers meet. It is also very important to square the surface of the connecting beam. These steps should be carried throughout the joining process to assure a clean and accurate job.

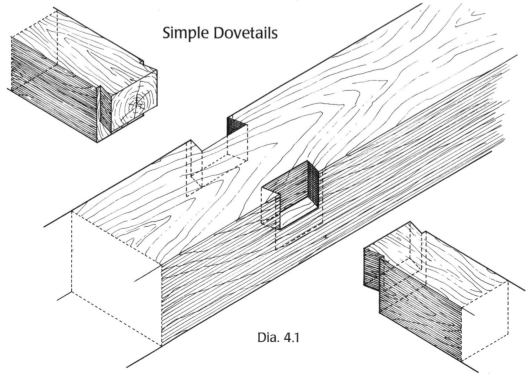

Simple Dovetails

Dia. 4.1

Housed Dovetail

A housed dovetail is a simple dovetail in which the whole timber is let in, or recessed into the joining member. All of the proportions remain the same on the tenon. The housing is usually from 1/2" to 3/4" deep. Housing the dovetail is primarily done for visual reasons, however there are some instances when they may be used for structural support. In these cases, the housing should be a minimum of 1 inch deep.

When relying on a housing as a bearing surface, greater care must be taken in the lay out and execution. The bottom shoulder of the housing should be considered the bottom of the tenon, and therefore subject to the 3/4 rule. The critical aspect lies in the fact that both horizontal surfaces must be precisely cut so that they make contact simultaneously (bottom of timber/ bottom of tenon). If the bottom of the timber makes contact with the housing surface first, you run the risk of the subsequent load crushing the surface resulting in an unsightly, and to all appearances, failing joint. On the other hand, if the bottom of the tenon makes contact first there will always remain a gap on the bottom surface, which will only become larger with time. The optimum condition is to pare the tenon so that the bottom of the timber makes contact with the housing slightly before the bottom of tenon. In pine this should be a scant 1/32 of an inch, for oak it should be a scant 1/64 inch. This allows good clean contact with the housing. The small amount of crushing is not enough to damage the shoulder but will help to ensure a tight fit after aging and shrinkage occurs.

It is extremely important to perfectly square the surfaces of the beam that is entering the housing. This should be done in relation to the bottom surface (square the sides to the bottom). After the squaring is completed, exact measurements of the timber should then be taken and transferred accurately to the mortise housing. The housing mortise should be slightly smaller than the dimension of the beam being housed (about 1/32 of an inch or so). The housing layout should be carefully scored with a knife and pared to the line with a chisel. Housings also need to be flared slightly at the top to allow entry.

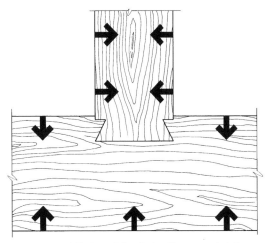

Dia. 4.2) Housed dovetail in the original state indicating the direction of shrinkage.

Dia. 4.3) Housed dovetail showing exaggerated effects of shrinkage. A housed dovetail may produce gaps on the side faces, but with proper wedging will not create gaps on the side face of adjoining member.

Simple dovetails before wedging. Note spacing on sides to fit wedges and on the end to allow joint to tighten. Also note the beveled corners of the pockets to allow entry of the joist without crushing.

Shouldered summer beam joining to tie beam.

Setting dovetailed purlins to rafters in a red oak frame. Purlins are usually spaced at 4´ o.c., with the top purlins offset toward the peak to compensate for the thickness of panels if they are used.

Careful direction is necessary when assembling. Slight compression of the fiber is preferred. If, however, crushing or tearing occurs, the timber must be gently removed and carefully planed or pared in place just enough to stop the tear. It is best to start with a slightly undersized housing and carefully adjust the timbers entering to size on an individual basis. This takes more time but the end result is worth it if perfection and grace is the goal. The goal when housing dovetails is to make the timbers look like they grew there. If you can't do that, then why bother housing at all?

Housing requires considerable extra work, and in many cases the timber shrinking in the housing will leave unsightly and uneven gaps—even if executed perfectly. Aged, dry timbers should be used for the housed members to reduce shrinking. After years of housing joists, I have concluded that the simple wedged dovetail ages better than the housed version, so I rarely use this type unless the housing serves a structural purpose.

As with all dovetails, housed dovetails require wedging.

Shouldered Dovetail

Shouldered dovetails are used when the members being joined are subjected to a secondary or concentrated load, such as a summer beam connecting to a tie beam. The shoulder allows for a distribution of forces on two bearing surfaces. This distribution allows for maximum resistance to horizontal shearing stress on the tenoned member, while retaining the maximum amount of meat, and therefore, strength, in the mortised member. The dovetailed upper tenon allows the members to be drawn tight with wedges. It is very important that both horizontal surfaces make simultaneous contact.

The shoulder length should be from 1 to 1-1/2", and the dovetail portion another 2" to 3" long, making a total tenon length of 3 to 4-1/2 inches. I usually make the dovetail section 3" thick, and the shoulder should be laid out no more than 2" from the bottom of the timber. This proportion should be in general accordance with the 3/4 inch rule. When sizing beams and the proportions of the mortise and tenon the following rule-of-thumb guidelines can be used. This rule simply states that: *The depth of the tenon should be no less than 3/4 the depth of the tenoned member, and the depth of the mortise should be no greater than 5/8 the depth of the mortised member.*

I call this the 3/4 & 5/8 rule, and we can use it not only to design joinery, but also to divine comfortable, human scale proportions throughout the frame. Let's see how the 3/4 & 5/8 rule applies to sizing a common floor system.

Shouldered dovetail
summer beam tenon
with a 1 inch shoulder.

Dia. 4.4

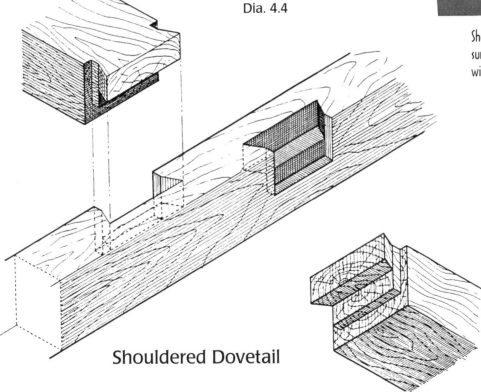

Shouldered Dovetail

The shouldered dovetail is used primarily where concentrated loads are present, such as a summer beam that carries the loads of additional floor joists. Its ability to distribute stress to two bearing surfaces, while allowing a minimum of meat to be taken away from both tenon and mortise, makes it effective for joining summer beams to tie beams or connecting girts. This joint has strict tolerances that must be maintained.

Dia. 4.5

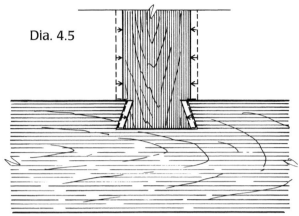

Shrinkage of joist with simple dovetail. Even with shrinkage the 3/4 inch shouldered dovetail is sufficient to conceal mortise.

Dia. 4.6

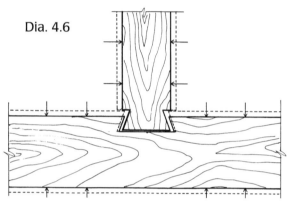

Simple dovetail showing original and exaggerated effects of shrinkage in both tenoned and mortised members.

Dia. 4.7

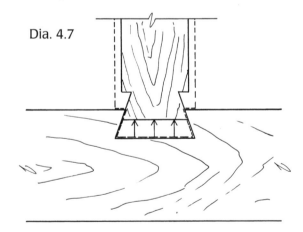

As the dovetail shrinks in width the result is that the shoulder of the joist may open. Wedging is used to prevent this pull out. A properly wedged dovetail will maintain compressive force on the tenon even after drying, reducing pull out to a negligible amount. Perhaps more importantly, the wedged tenon maintains the compressive strength of the extreme fibers in the mortised member by filling the mortise with an amount of force equal to, or even exceeding, that of a solid beam.

3/4 & 5/8 Rule — Let's say we have a frame with bents spanning 24 feet and a net bay spacing of 15 feet, and have determined that a 12 inch deep tie beam is required. We also plan to span the bay with 2 summer beams, which will divide the bay into three, 8 x 15 foot sections. By using the 5/8 rule to find the maximum depth of the mortise on the side face of the tie beam we can then use the 3/4 rule to determine the maximum depth of the summer beam.

To find the maximum depth of the mortise on the side face of the tie beam multiply the depth of the tie beam by 5/8: 12 x 5/8 = 7.5 inches.

If we now divide this maximum mortise depth by 3/4 we can find the maximum depth of the summer beam: 7.5 ÷ (3/4) = 10. This tells us the maximum depth of the summer is 10 inches, but we still have the option to use a shallower timber, say 9 inches, in order to retain a little extra meat in the tie beam. In many cases summer beams are 12 inches wide, so let's first see if a 12 x 9 white pine is suitable for this situation.

We can now find the minimum depth for the tenon for the 9 inch deep beam by multiplying the beam depth by 3/4: 9 x 3/4 = 6.75. This can be rounded to 7 inches, which gives a little more strength to the tenon and also remains above the maximum depth of 7.5 inches for the mortise. This also allows the lower shoulder to be 2" from the bottom face of the beam. The next step is to determine the size of the floor joists and joinery proportions using the same process.

The maximum mortise depth on the side faces of the summer beam would be: 9 x 5/8 = 5.625. I would round this down to 5 or 5-1/2" to allow more meat in the mortise. Using 5" as the tenon depth we can find the maximum joist depth by dividing this by 3/4: 5 ÷ (3/4) = 6.6. This could be rounded up to 7 inches if need be as we have already diminished the max from 5.625 to 5 inches. My first tendency would be to round down to see if a 6" beam is adequate for the joist in deflection.

By using these ratios we have determined the appropriate beam dimensions for the summer beams to be 9 to 10 inches deep, and the joists 6 to 7 inches deep—based on a 12" deep tie beam. This allows for all the timbers to diminish by 2 to 3 inches as they step from the tie beam to floor joists. This proportional change is extremely important to the visual aesthetics of the floor system. I would always opt to use the shallower depth of both summer and joist unless it proved not to meet the other design specs.

The next step is to determine if these sizes are adequate to carry the loads. We will cover this process more fully in Chapter 11, but just for curiosity the beam design for shear, bending and deflection are as follows:

Summer beam, 12 x 9: H = 55.1 psi*, D = .5, D_{allow} = .75

Floor joist, 6 x 6: H = 24 psi*, D = .085, D_{allow} = .4

Where: H = horizontal shear stress, psi, D = deflection, D_{allow} = allowable deflection.

These are all well within the safe range, so it looks like we will be in fine shape.

*Includes reduction factor for square tenons notched at the bottoms.

Soffit and Tusk Tenons

To complete the options of joinery commonly used to join connecting members to the primary bent framing, we must also include the soffit and tusk tenon. The terms *soffit* and *tusk* are often used interchangeably to describe a horizontal tenon which extends from the bottom, or near the bottom, of the member. Literally, a soffit tenon is a tenon which extends from the bottom surface (no bottom shoulder cut), as depicted in dia. 4.8. A tusk tenon extends from some point up from the bottom surface (two shoulder cuts, top and bottom, as in the photo to the right). In both types, the upper shoulders are often cut at an angle to increase shearing area.

Soffit tenons are commonly used for joining smaller dimension timbers, such as floor joists and purlins into principal members. Tusk tenons are used more often for larger timbers, such as summer beams to tie beams. In this case the shouldered tusk tenon (as in the photo to the right) would be used. Both types create a stronger joint for two reasons: 1) *the full, or nearly full, cross section of the tenoned member is utilized because there is no notch (or a minimal notch) at the bottom*; 2) *the closed mortise on the side of the carrying timber maintains continuous beam fibers on its top surface, therefore the timber will resist deflection greater than timbers with open mortises cut on the top edge.* Because of this, the reduction factor to compensate for the removal of wood in the mortised area is not necessary when analyzing the beam design.

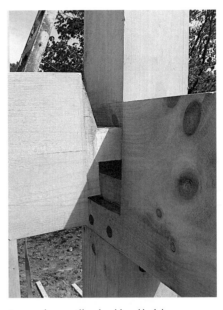

Summer beam with a shouldered tusk tenon joining to tie beam. In this detail the lower shoulder is 1-1/4 inches and is cut lower than 5/8 of the tie beam depth because it is supported directly by a post.

The drawback to this type of joint is the difficult assembly procedure. Where dovetail joints allow the members to be dropped in after the bents are raised and secured, tusk tenoned members all have to be placed in the frame—all at one time—as the bents are being raised. This requires many hands, and can be a little more dangerous.

There are a two situations in particular where soffit or tusk tenons are very appropriate. One is when joining floor joists to summer beams when the other ends are either drop-in dovetails, or are resting on top of the wall plates (such as the eavesdroppers on pg. 86). Possibly its most appropriate use is in place of the shouldered dovetail for joining summer beams to tie beams, as shown in the photo above.

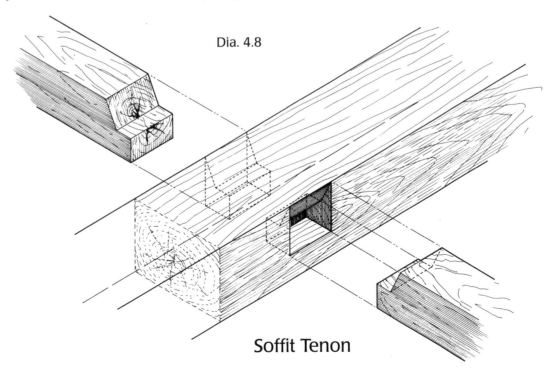

Dia. 4.8

Soffit Tenon

Paring dovetail tenons to the score line. The depth of the tenon should be no less than 3/4 the depth of the beam.

Depth of Dovetail Mortises on Supporting Members

As a general rule, mortises cut on the side faces of timbers, such as dovetails in summer beams, tie beams and rafters, should be kept above the neutral plane. From the diagrams on pages 62 and 63, we see that horizontal shearing stresses are at zero on the top and bottom surfaces of the loaded beam, and reach a maximum at the neutral plane (also called the neutral axis). The neutral plane *theoretically* lies along the horizontal center of the beam. Being that this is the location of maximum horizontal shearing stress, failure is most likely to occur along this plane. Horizontal shear is generally the first, and most common cause of beam failure. Due of the beam's tendency to fail along this plane, mortises cut on the side faces below the neutral plane will impose additional vertical stresses (shear perpendicular to the grain) at an already highly stressed point, and may proportionally increase the likelihood of failure.

In small dimension members (1" x 1" test pieces) the theoretical horizontal stresses and the actual horizontal stresses are more accurately aligned along the center of the member. In larger timbers however, experimentation has indicated that the actual location of the neutral plane shifts downward toward the tension side, with the maximum shearing stresses resulting in the lower third portion of the beam.

Design criteria for large beams rely on a combination of factors that include analysis of small dimension testing, coupled with actual case studies in the field, empirical evidence, and to a lesser degree, direct laboratory experimentation on large timbers.

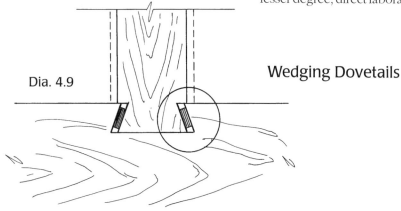

Dia. 4.9

Wedging Dovetails

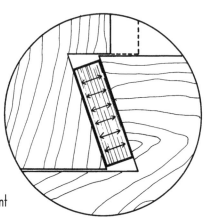

Driving wedges into the sides of the dovetail to the point where compression becomes evident will dramatically reduce the amount of pull-out possible as the timbers dry. Wedging also increases the stiffness and strength of the beams by placing the tenoned member in tension. In this case, the tenoned member is designed as if it were fixed at both ends as opposed to a simply supported beam. The mortised member is strengthened because the compressive force of the wedges replicate the continuous grain fiber on the compression side of the beam.

From this analysis, assumptions must then be made based on the average reactions to the conditions at hand. These may include: beam width to depth ratio, types of supports, loading conditions, physical qualities of the beam (species, grain pattern, defects, moisture content) and joint connections to name a few. From this research it has been shown that large timbers react differently to loading conditions than smaller beams of similar species and grades. The following phenomenon is very helpful in determining the placement of mortises in main carrying timbers.

In beams from 8 to 14 inches deep (but no greater than 16 inches deep) that have a width to depth ratio between 1:2 and 3:4, experiments have shown that the maximum extreme fiber strain is not proportional to the distance from the neutral plane, but moves increasingly downward under loading from the compression side to a maximum at approximately 1/3 the beam depth. This results in a corresponding shift of the neutral plane toward the bottom, or tension side, of the beam.[1] Considering this, we can assume that the maximum fiber strain in compression in an 8 inch wide by 12 inch deep beam would fall at four inches from the top surface (12 ÷ 3 = 4). This would move the neutral plane down from the midpoint (6 inches) to the lower third of the beam, or 8 inches from the top surface. Using this phenomenon we can substantiate the following rule-of-thumb guideline: *The bottom of a mortise cut into the side face of beam should be no greater than 5/8 the depth of the beam from the top (or compression) surface.* This results in a mortise above the actual neutral plane.

It should be noted that beams over 12 inches deep are subject to a phenomenon where the value for the modulus of rupture decreases as the depth increases. This requires a *depth factor* in the flexural formula to account for the decrease. While the decrease begins to show up in beams 12 inches and greater, it is insignificant until beam depths reach 16 to 18 inches, and is therefore accounted for mostly in glue-lam beams.

In the process covered previously we used this rule to determine the mortise and tenon depths for a sample floor framing situation. We also used it to determine the required beam dimensions. In that example the maximum depths were backed off to allow extra strength in both the mortised and tenoned members. While this is not a hard and fast law, it will result in beam dimensions that will meet the design requirements for most common situations and also result in human scale beam proportions that look and feel attractive, as if they were meant to be.

1. Kenneth R. Lauer, *Structural Engineering for Architects* (New York: McGraw-Hill, 1981), p. 321-322.

Drive oak wedges evenly on both sides of the dovetail to draw the joint tight. Wedging dovetails puts the tenoned timber in tension, making it stiffer as if it were fixed at the ends. The mortised member is strengthened because the wedged tenon replicates the continuous beam fiber.

Chopping the side shoulder of a dovetail to the scored line.

Rules of Deflection

1) It is directly proportional to the cube of the length of span for beams of the same width and depth.
Tripling the span gives 27 times the deflection.

2) It is inversely proportional to the width for beams of the same span and depth. If the width is tripled, the deflection is one third as great.

3) It is inversely proportional to the cube of the depth for beams of the same span and width. If a depth is tripled, the deflection is 1/27 as great

Sizing Joists, Purlin & Dovetail Tenons using the 3/4 Rule

As we have seen in our previous example, the maximum mortise depth in the main carrying timber should be no greater than 5/8 the beam depth. We have also discussed the 3/4 rule used for determining the beam dimension and vertical tenon depth for a shouldered dovetail. To understand this fully, let's take this one step further by considering another example.

Structurally, as well as visually, it is preferable to keep common floor joists as near to eight feet in length as possible. If you are faced with a span much over 8 feet (12' would be the max length of a common floor joist), the wisest choice is to divide the span with a larger carrying timber and join shorter and smaller dimension floor joists in between. It is important to note that the size of beams subjected to a distributed load, such as a floor joist and purlins, are often dictated more by the allowable deflection than by other more dramatic failure modes (it's safe to assume that if a beam is not allowed to deflect under loading beyond its allowable limits, then in most likelihood it will not fail due to shear or bending). Excessive deflection creates bouncy floors, which we want to avoid—even if the deflection is within allowable limits.

With this in mind, it must be understood that the *deflection of a beam is directly proportional to the cube of the length of the span for beams of the same width and depth*. It is also *inversely proportional to the cube of the depth for beams of the same span and width*.[2] In other words, if we increase the span of a given beam from 8 feet to 12 feet (1.5 times its length) it would deflect 3.375 times greater (1.5^3). Inversely, by increasing the depth by 50% (1.5), the deflection would be only 1/3.375 as great. We could therefore maintain the same deflection by making the beam 1.5 times deeper.

To get a bearing on this, a 6 x 6 white pine joist spaced at 30 inches on center and spanning 8 feet has a calculated deflection of .0853", or slightly over 1/16" (at 40 psf floor load). The same beam spanning 12 feet would deflect .432", nearly 7/16". While this may be marginally acceptable structurally, visually it is not, and would surely raise comments from everyone entering the room. To find an acceptable deflection we would need to use a 6 x 8, which has a calculated deflection of .182", or just under 3/16. Design standards use an allowable deflection for first floors of 1/360 of the span, and for second floors 1/240 of the span. To determine the allowable deflection, simply divide the span in inches by the appropriate factor. A 12 foot joist in a second floor would be: 144/240 = .6 inches; for a first floor: 144/360 = .04 inches.

To understand this further, let's see how a 12 foot joist would affect our sample floor system. In our earlier example we determined that a side mortise in a 9" deep summer beam should be no more than 5-1/2" deep. By using the 3/4 depth of tenon rule, we can determine the maximum joist depth by dividing the mortise depth by 3/4: 5.5 ÷ (3/4) = 7.33". This would normally be rounded down to the next full inch, giving a maximum joist depth of 7", but we have determined that we need a 6 x 8 to span 12 feet. We must now go back to our original 10 inch deep summer to see if it will work by using the formula: 10 x 5/8 = 6.25. Rounding down to 6 inches and using the 3/4 rule we can determine the maximum joist depth: 6 ÷ (3/4) = 8. This works perfectly.

By increasing the span we have also increased the load. We now have a floor area of 12' x 15' equals 180 sq. ft., at 40 psf, totals 7200 pounds. Using the formula for horizontal shear (for a notched beam), design in bending and deflection we find the following:

H = 80 psi; D = .54 inches; D_{allow} = .75 inches.

These are within our safe margins, so we should be fine. However, this is approaching the limits I want to see. I am not so happy at having a summer beam deflect more than a half inch, even if it is allowable. This will always be the case when you try to extend the floor joists over the rational limit of 8 feet. Deflection becomes enemy number one. Can you do it? Perhaps. But do you want to?

2. Frederick F. Wangaard, *The Mechanical Properties of Wood* (New York: John Wiley & Sons, 1950), p. 68.

Green Timbers & Long Term Loading

Deflection values are derived from formulas based on dry timbers. Green timbers will deflect approximately 50% more than dry timbers if allowed to dry under a load, and therefore will show increased deflection under long-term loading.[3] Partially dried timbers will sag more or less in proportion to their moisture content. It is therefore best to allow a minimum of 12-16 weeks for timbers to cure in proper conditions prior to loading. To compensate for green timbers it is common to design for initial deflection based on values reduced by half of the allowable long-term deflection, and proportionally less for semi-dry timbers. This effect is greater for larger timbers with longer spans, such as summer beams. This is one reason why I developed the *16 foot rule* for timber spans. Cubing the increased margin over 16' rapidly becomes unwieldy.

As an example, an 8 x 12 white pine timber cured for 12-16 weeks may require a reduction factor of 25%, while a 6 x 6 timber similarly cured would likely require no reduction at all. However, reducing the allowable deflection by 25% across the board is not a bad idea, and will only result in better aging over long-term loading.

Beams Notched at the Bottom

The basic law concerning beams notched at the bottom is that the horizontal shear stress of the beam is proportional to the square of the depth of the tenon (d) divided by the depth of the timber (h): $H_z = (d/h)^2$ = proportional horizontal shear stress.

In other words, a beam with a tenon 1/2 its depth has only 25% the shear strength, and a tenon 3/4 its depth has only 56% the shear strength of the solid beam: $(3/6)^2 = .25$, and $(4.5/6)^2 = .5626$. The example of a notch 1/2 the depth of the beam is used only to illustrate the rapid reduction of strength in a notched beam, and should never be used. The absolute minimum tenon ratio is 3/4 the full beam depth.

In the case of horizontal shearing stress you can use the formula above to determine the stress ratio of a notched beam and reduce it from the horizontal stress as calculated for the full beam cross section as illustrated in diagram 4.12, page 63. The full equation to determine horizontal stress directly for a notched beam is also illustrated in diagram 4.12. The 3/4 rule is derived from the fact that you never want the d/h ratio to ever be less than 3/4, or 75% of the full beam depth.

The formula to determine the vertical shearing stress on the tenon is illustrated in diagram 4.13. This formula gives the load that will result in failure of the tenon due to *direct* vertical shear. An allowable load can be determined by dividing the results by 8. It is unlikely however, that vertical shear of the tenon would ever occur before horizontal shear failure, but it is always good to know the potential of all failure modes.

You might ask if it is necessary to have the extra depth to the timber at all. I believe it is for two reasons. The first is purely structural, and the second has to do with proportion and aesthetics.

The stiffness of a beam is directly related to its width, depth, span and mechanical properties, and not necessarily in relation to the tenon to beam depth ratio. More depth generally means greater resistance to deflection. If a beam is designed to meet or exceed the imposed vertical and horizontal shearing forces with a tenon notched on the bottom, then the extra material, breadth and depth, is an asset and increases the beam stiffness, and therefore resistance to deflection.

The second factor is proportion, which I believe plays a large role in the beauty of a finely crafted timber frame. Scant, deep members covering long spans tend to conjure up notions of condominiums in Colorado, not colonial or

3. Forest Products Laboratory, *Wood Handbook: Wood as an Engineering Material*. Agric Handb. *72* (Washington, DC: U.S Dept. of Agriculture, rev. 1987), p. 8-4.

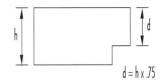

Horizontal Shear Stress for Notched Tenons

$$d = h \times .75$$

$$H_z = (d/h)^2$$

H_z = percentage of shearing stress
d = depth of tenon,
h = depth of beam

The horizontal shearing strength of a beam with a tenon notched on the bottom is reduced from that of an unnotched beam by the square of the ratio of the effective tenon depth (d) to the actual beam depth (h), as in the formula above. The ratio of tenon depth (d) to beam depth (h) should never be less than 75% of the full beam depth.

Dovetailed joints should follow the 5/8 and 3/4 rule as described on these pages. Spacing of floor joists should be 30 inches on center nominally, with spans no greater than 8 feet to achieve both a comfortable visual balance and structural integrity. Purlins are commonly spaced at 48 inches on center.

medieval timber frame dwellings. Just as natural, harmonic proportions in nature effect us in a positive way, so does this natural proportion effect us in our built environment. The ratios and proportions we have covered here tend to give the frame a human feel and sense of scale, and even if we do not understand overtly when we enter the space, we can not help but feel comfort. As the designer or builder, this is what you want to impart to all those who may ever enter the space.

By following the *16 foot rule, 8 foot joist rule*, and the *3/4 and 5/8 rules* throughout the frame design process you will find that your beam design will always end up in a safe range.

This second floor system follows the rule-of-thumb guidelines for both sizing and spacing joists, and determining joinery specifications. By following these rules a structurally sound floor system will result, but perhaps as equally important, an aesthetically pleasing and comfortable 'human scale' living space will result as well.

Spacing Floor Joists & Purlins

The fact that timber framing is a nonstandard building form allows for some nonstandard standards. By this I mean that maintaining centers on standards of sixteen or twenty four inches is not always warranted or desired. I have found that floor joists spaced at approximately 30" on center, or about 24" inside to inside, is ideal, both visually, as well as structurally. The approach we use in our shop is to divide the space equally into divisions as close to 30" o.c. as possible. This will usually result in spacing from 29 to 31 inches on center. Closer spacing results in a cluttered look, and further spacing begins to stretch the limits of the flooring material and will even begin to negatively effect the deflection of the joist.

Purlins are usually spaced at four feet on center. This is primarily to accommodate stress skin panels, but also, people do not usually dance on roofs, so we are not concerned with vibration or flexing in the roof under foot—only the pure structural elements to resist the *maximum deflection, extreme fiber stress in bending*, and *horizontal shear* due to the maximum assumed loading conditions at hand.

Rule-of-Thumb Guidelines

1) *The sixteen foot rule states that no simple beam can span more than 16 feet without additional supports.* As we have discussed to some extent, there are several factors that will effect beam strength. One of the most significant is the fact that deflection increases by the cube of the length of the span. Combining this with the reduction factors for defects, notched tenons, green and mortised timbers, it becomes clear with just a few calculations that the practical clear-span limit of any simple load bearing beam is sixteen feet.

A simple beam is one that is supported at each end and loaded with a distributed load. This rule states that if the span of a beam exceeds 16 feet then a secondary support must be placed so that no portion or segment of the timber exceeds 16 feet. This goes for rafters, tie beams, and all horizontal load bearing beams. A rafter that is longer than 16 feet needs a collar tie or a queen post so that no segment exceeds 16 feet. A 32 foot tie beam would need one support post at mid span. A 24 foot tie beam requires one post, at mid point or at a third point. A 48 foot tie beam would need two posts. In each of these situations, the beam dimension would not necessarily need to be increased.

2) *The length of a tenon should be no less that 1/3 the depth of the timber.*

There is a very delicate balance between the length of a tenon and the depth of a mortise on the side face of a timber. If the tenon is too long, then the mortised member is weakened. On the other hand, if the mortise is too short, then it has reduced compressive and vertical shear resistance to the load. The general rule-of-thumb is to make the tenon length 1/3 the depth of the beam. This would be rounded to the nearest 1/4 to 1/2 inch.

3) Mortises cut on the side faces of a timber should be no deeper than 5/8 of the depth of the timber from the top face, or compression side of beam.

As explained previously, the rule of 5/8 of the timber depth proves to be a comfortable margin for the vertical depth of mortises in members subjected to uniformly distributed loads. This effectively places the mortise above the actual neutral plane. When a beam is subjected to concentrated loads, additional considerations should be made. More on this will be covered later in the book. Before applying this rule, it should first be determined that the principal carrying beam (usually the tie beam) is sufficient to safely carry the intended load. This should follow the standard design procedures for determining design in: *bending*, *horizontal shear*, and *deflection*.

4) Tenon depths should be no less than 3/4 the depth of the timber. When tenons are notched on the bottom of a beam the neutral plane moves up proportionately toward the top of the timber (compression side). This has two implications on the strength of the beam; 1) *the vertical shear strength of the tenon*, and 2) *the horizontal shearing strength of the beam*. Though direct vertical shear failure is extremely rare in a solid beam, the likelihood increases significantly in beams with tenons that are notched on the bottoms. The vertical shear formula (diagram 4.13, page 63) can be used to determine the vertical shear strength that includes the tenon to beam depth ratio. The results should exceed the imposed vertical shear stress as determined using the equation, $V = P/2$. As an example, a 6 x 6 with a tenon 1/2 its depth can resist a maximum vertical shear stress of 510 pounds, while a tenon 3/4 the depth could safely resist a load of 1,147.5 lbs. This is nearly twice the strength of the first example and becomes important when we consider there may be defects in the timber that may reduce its strength.

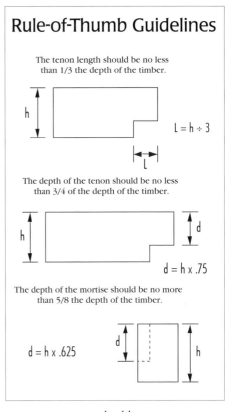

Rule-of-Thumb Guidelines

The tenon length should be no less than 1/3 the depth of the timber.

h

$L = h \div 3$

L

The depth of the tenon should be no less than 3/4 of the depth of the timber.

h

d

$d = h \times .75$

The depth of the mortise should be no more than 5/8 the depth of the timber.

$d = h \times .625$

d

h

The second aspect regards the horizontal shearing strength. Horizontal shearing stresses on a notched beam are proportional to the square of the depth of the tenon to the total beam depth, $H_z = (d/h)^2$. The amount of stress can be determined directly by using the equation for the proportional horizontal shear in diagram 4.13, pg. 63. Using either the vertical or the horizontal shear formulas, it becomes clear that the proportional change in the shearing strength diminishes rapidly to unsafe levels when the ratio exceeds 3:4. Hence, the 3/4 rule.

General Considerations

It must be pointed out that all of the safe load tables for beams and the specifications for mechanical properties of wood are based on solid clear timbers without mortises. Allowances for timbers with knots and defects should be made and poor workmanship should be compensated for, even if not anticipated. Mortises need not reduce the strength of beams if the tenon of the timber filling the mortise creates the same or greater compressive resistance as that of an unmortised timber (this is why wedges are important for all dovetails). Engineers, as a rule however, will consider beams with mortises cut on the top edges to be the size of the remaining solid cross section only. In other words, if an 8" x 12" beam had two opposing mortises on the side faces that were notched 2" deep into the top 8 inch surface—in one or more locations along the beam—the net cross section of solid wood remaining at that point would be 4" x 12". Most engineers would use this net remaining section to make their calculations. This is done justifiably because they have no control over the quality of workmanship in the field, and timbers are not always stress graded, which means that worst-case scenarios must be assumed.

The rule-of-thumb design approach described here will produce timber proportions that are tasteful and aesthetically pleasing in a timber frame. One should not rely solely upon these rules to design beams, but by using them to develop a general plan and then checking using the scientific approach, you will find that you will often end up exceeding the requirements. If not, you will be very close to where you want to be and can adjust accordingly.

The timbered ceiling in a small house helps define space without framed partitions. This frame was the Spring 2003 workshop project at Fox Maple.

Stresses Acting on a Beam

By examining a typical floor timber in a frame we find that three distinct stresses are produced as a result of the imposed force load. These being: *compression*, *tension*, and *shear*. Let's use a summer beam as an example because it is the most critical and difficult beam to design because they must carry the sum of the floor load.

As the beam begins to bend under the force of the load—which is being applied at a right angle to the beam—the fibers on the top half of the beam are placed in compression, due to the forces tending to shorten or compress the fibers. The fibers on the bottom side of the beam however, are said to be in tension as they are simultaneously being pulled or stretched. The plane established at the neutral point, that is, the plane along the horizontal mid section of the beam affected by neither compression nor tension is known as the *neutral plane*, and is said to be in *horizontal shear*. In effect, the fibers in compression on the top of the beam are being forced to slide along the fibers on the lower section of the beam. Under a severe load, the timber would tend to fail by shearing horizontally along this neutral plane.

Whereas the extreme fibers (those at the top and bottom surfaces) are subjected to the greatest forces of compression and tension, the neutral plane is subjected to the greatest shearing stresses. The primary cause of beam failure is due to horizontal shearing stress. A more thorough explanation of horizontal shearing stresses will be discussed later in this manual, however, a basic understanding of the forces at play will be helpful in understanding the beam design procedures and rule-of-thumb guidelines discussed in the preceding chapter. By determining the amount of horizontal shearing stress acting on a beam we can then determine the appropriate beam dimension.

Let's say we are building a 28' x 36' four bent frame giving us three equal bays 12' x 28'. If we were to then divide each bay into three smaller bays of equal size by adding two summer beams connecting the two tie beams, we would be left with three equal openings of 9'4" x 12'. Based on the standard requirement of 40 psf floor load for second floors in residential houses, each summer beam in this case would be expected to carry a distributed load of roughly 4,500 pounds.

Summer beams are often sized with the visual impact in mind in near equal measure as with the structural considerations. This seems to have been true for many centuries, as it is most common to see summer beams in colonial American and European frames rotated so that the horizontal width is greater than the vertical depth. This is really one of the rare cases in all of timber framing when this is done. In following this tradition, let's make this example a 12 x 8 inch white pine. Now let's

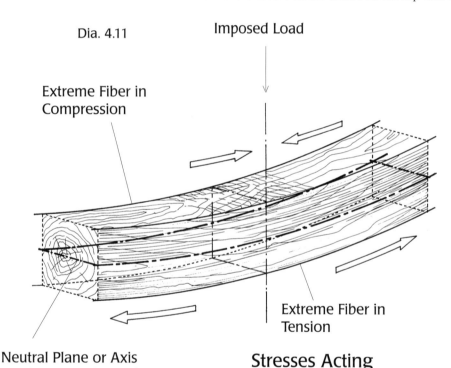

Dia. 4.11

Imposed Load

Extreme Fiber in Compression

Extreme Fiber in Tension

Neutral Plane or Axis
Maximum Horizontal Shear

**Stresses Acting
on a Beam**

see how we would determine if it is adequate to resist horizontal shear.

By cutting mortises into the side faces of the timber we are in effect reducing the size of the timber. From a conservative engineering standpoint we should consider the amount of solid wood left after mortising to be the effective beam size (even though we are filling the mortises with wedged tenons that will actually exceed the compressive strength of the solid beam). If the joist mortises were cut 2" deep into each side face of the summer beam (perpendicular to the side faces), we would conservatively be left with a remaining cross section equivalent to an 8 x 8 inch timber. This is conservative, but let's see where it takes us.

The equation to determine horizontal shearing stress for a simple beam is: **3V/2bd**. In our example the total load, represented by the letter **P**, is 4,500 pounds.

V = P / 2 = 4,500 / 2 = 2,250;

V = 2,250

3V = 3 x 2,250 = 6,750 lbs

2bd = 2 x 8 x 8 = 128

6,750/128 = 52.734 psi.

The safe shearing stress for white pine is 120 psi. If we use the horizontal shear equation to include the tenon the horizontal shear stress increases to 68.878 psi. To determine the proportional increase in stress due to the tenon we can reverse the H_z equation to: $H_z = (h/d)^2 = (8/7)^2 = 1.306$. The horizontal shear stress is increased by 130%. So, 52.734 x 1.306 = 68.87. The results are the same. Even with the reductions we are within the safe zone. Additional calculations must be made for final approval, but because most failures occur in horizontal shear, it is likely that no changes will be necessary.

It should be noted that the H_z equation can be $(d/h)^2$ or $(h/d)^2$. Using $(d/h)^2$ results in .765, which reflects the percentage of decrease in strength. To find the amount of shear stress simply divide: 52.734 ÷ .765 = 68.87.

4.12) Shearing Stresses within a Simple Beam

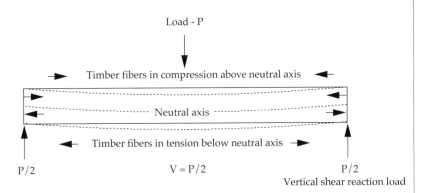

Equation to determine horizontal shearing stress for rectangular beams:

$$H = \frac{3V}{2bd}$$

H = Horizontal shearing stress, psi
V = vertical shear, pounds
  (end reaction, P/2)
b = width of beam, inches
d = depth of beam, inches

Vertical load transferred to horizontal shearing forces in timber.

Neutral axis

The failure of a beam will occur first in horizontal shear along neutral axis. Once this occurs, complete failure is likely.

4.13) Formula to Determine Tenon Shear

To determine the proportional horizontal shearing stress of a beam with a tenon notched square at the bottom use the following equation:

$$H_z = \frac{3V}{2bd_e}\left(\frac{h}{d_e}\right)$$

H_z = Horizontal shearing stress, proportional, psi
V = Vertical shearing stress, lbs
b = width of beam, inches
h = depth of beam, inches
d_e = depth of tenon, inches

The horizontal shear strength of a beam is reduced proportional to the square of the tenon depth (d) to the total depth of the timber (h). The neutral axis moves up from the center of timber to a line parallel to the center of the tenon: $H_z = (d/h)^2$

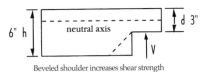

Beveled shoulder increases shear strength

Equation to find maximum vertical shear stress of tenon:

$$V = \frac{2Hbd(d/h)}{3}$$

V = load resulting in failure of tenon, lbs
b = width of beam
d = depth of tenon
h = depth of beam
H = Shear parallel to grain, maximum shearing strength.

A beam with a tenon 1/2 the depth of the timber has only 1/4 the shearing strength (vertical or horizontal) of an un-notched beam. If the shoulder is cut at a bevel, not square-cornered, the shearing strength increases to the net depth of the tenon, d, therefore, the d/h factor does not apply in the equation.

Calculation for a 6x6 white pine beam:

$$V = \frac{2 \times 680 \times 6 \times 3 \times (3/6)}{3} = 4,080 \text{ lbs}$$

To find the safe load, use the following equation

$$\text{Safe load} = \frac{V}{8} = 4,080 / 8 = 510 \text{ lbs}$$

For green Northern red oak, H = 1,200 psi. For green Eastern white pine, H = 680 psi.
For a list of other common wood species see Table 7: Mechanical Properties of Wood, page 236-7.
By replacing the value for the maximum shearing strength (H) in the above formula with the value for the Basic, or Safe Shearing Stress from Table 8, page 238, the result will be the safe horizontal shearing stress directly, with no need to divide by the factor of safety.

Struts and braces come in many forms. Top: King post with struts in barn frame, 1986. Bottom left: Natural curved and sawn knee braces were used in this scribe-rule frame cut by students in Monteverde, Costa Rica, 2005. Bottom right: Upper strut joining to post and tie beam, 1995.

Braces & Bracing

Natural curved sills and tension braces were used in this 17th century
German Barn, at the Kommern open air museum near Koln, Germany.

Braces & Bracing

Quite often joined timber frames are referred to by architects and engineers as *braced frames,* and appropriately so. A joined frame is really nothing more than a structural skeleton made up of an arrangement of vertical and horizontal members that rely on diagonal braces to keep it both rigid and square. The term suggests that the frame is a complete structural system—one that needs no further elements, such as enclosure membranes or shear walls to provide for its rigidity. This is true, and the fact that the structure happens to become a thing of beauty is merely an added benefit. This may be one of the reasons why braced timber frames have survived well over 1000 years as a viable structural system.

As in all structural frameworks, a timber frame is designed to be a body at rest, and we want to keep it that way. This is made possible in large part through bracing. While the primary frame members are designed to resist vertical motion, braces are designed to resist the horizontal racking motion created by external loadings such as wind and seismic action, or combinations thereof. The traditional timber frame designs we are familiar with today are the result of hundreds of years of design experience. Many frames, no doubt, fell down throughout the ages to become compost for another generation of trees and new timber frames. Those that remain are the successful examples to study and to replicate.

The ability to withstand vertical forces is directly related to the size of the structural members, the type of material, and their number and placement in the frame. Whether it be pine or oak timbers in a joined frame or a modern steel skyscraper, the same basic principles of engineering are applied.

This, however, is only one aspect of the design process. The designer must also take a close look at the entire structural framework to see how it works as a unit—in relation to all of the forces that will be acting upon it. Whereas the live and dead loads impose vertical load forces, the combined, or resultant effects of the snow load, wind load, and seismic loads are basically forces acting on the structure as a horizontal, or lateral force. This horizontal force is what bracing is intended to resist or counteract. While sizing a simple beam to support a given load is fairly straightforward, understanding the complete interrelation of all forces acting on all members can become quite complex, requiring some very thorough technical savvy in engineering.

Fortunately, we have a rich history of timber framing to study that gives us a wealth of empirical knowledge concerning braces and bracing in a braced frame. Because of this we are spared some of the rigorous calculations that may normally be necessary, and can also devise some rule-of-thumb guidelines that will assure a sufficiently braced frame.

Conventional frame construction relies on an external membrane, *sheathing,* as the bracing. It may either be plywood, diagonal boards or California braces

Tension braces are the primary bracing element of this English half-timbered frame. The principal corner brace joins to post and sill at a 45 degree angle. The brace to its right joins to the post and sill at a 30/60 degree angle.

(diagonal braces which are let into the outside of studding so as to be flush with the outside framing surface). In practice, the system of bracing conventional stud, or balloon framing, is pretty straightforward. I don't think that you'll find too many builders racking their brains trying to figure out an appropriate bracing scheme for their current building project. Likewise, it was probably just as rare to find an early carpenter in a fuss over where to put his braces. They followed a basic rule-of-thumb that simply states: *a brace is required at every location where a horizontal member joins to a vertical post.*

Upon considering this you will soon realize the redundancy of this practice—which is precisely the point. Bracing in a timber frame relies on the structural principal of *redundancy*, and may very well have been the first instance of its use in the history of building. In modern stick frame construction redundancy is the fundamental rule. The definition of *redundancy* as it relates to engineering is; *the inclusion of extra components that are not strictly necessary to functioning, in case of failure in other components.*

So, in the definition itself we find a bit of a loophole in that some of the braces are *not strictly necessary.* Of course, this is assuming the lowest common denominator. The next question is, how many braces are not necessary? This may be synonymous with the question as to how many studs can I remove from a stick frame before it will fall down? Standard stick frames use studs at spacings of 16", but it is not uncommon throughout the stick framing era to find frames that used spacings of 24". This is a 25% reduction of studs, and still the frame is considered structurally viable. Now, if one were to go around and randomly pull out a stud here, and a stud there from a stud wall with 16" spacings, they could pull out a considerable number (perhaps as many as 25%) without structurally affecting the frame—so long as they were randomly spread out about the frame. However, in a frame with 24" stud spacings, one would have to seriously consider which stud was safe to pull out as this would result in a 4 foot spacing which is beyond the structural limit of a stud frame. So here we may have found the practical limit of redundancy in a stick frame. If we go beyond that we quickly loose our redundant factor of safety.

This brings us to a second rule-of-thumb which states that; *assuming that at every intersection of a vertical and a horizontal member there is a brace, it may be assumed that in any given frame design 15% can be eliminated due to excessive redundancy.*

Now, this is only a general rule-of-thumb. One should not simply remove braces on a whim, but must carefully consider which braces are over redundant and which ones are critical. There must be a good and compelling reason to remove the brace, such as when it will interfere with a door or window

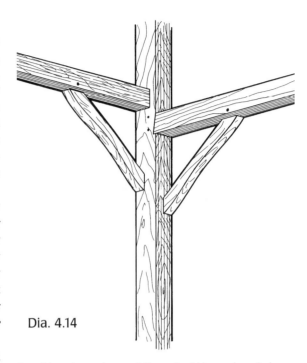

Dia. 4.14

Typical knee brace placement. Knees should be positioned at approximately the upper third of the post, extending at a 45 degree angle to the adjoining horizontal member.

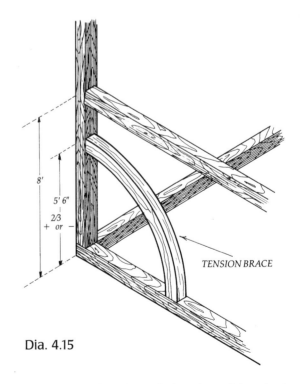

Dia. 4.15

Tension braces should extend from the lower horizontal member to the upper third point of the post or adjoining vertical member.

In this frame the natural curved knee is used to both resist racking, and as a strut to transfer a portion of the roof load from the upper plate to the opposing horizontal plate. Note also that the rear tie beam to the post has no braces. This is possible because it is connected to a fully braced frame, and is in essence being buttressed.

opening. By removing the brace there must still remain an adequate and equal number of braces working in opposing directions in the wall plane or bent. To understand this a little better, let's consider the following example.

Say we were to design a two bent, one bay cape frame that followed the rule of placing a knee brace at every post and beam intersection. If the bents were spaced at 16 feet and the tie beams were 24 feet long (requiring an intermediate post at 12 feet) we would have 2 braces from the posts to plates, front and back, and 4 braces on each gable bent, making a total of 12 braces in the frame. This frame would be considered to be braced sufficiently. Now, let's consider making another identical frame and placing it to one side of the first frame, say at a distance of 12 feet. Both frames are independent, and structurally complete. After a while, your wife starts complaining that the houses are too small, and she doesn't like walking in the rain to get from the living room to the bedroom, so you decide to connect the two frames by simply placing plates and purlins between the two frames. Your wife is very happy because you have increased the living space by 45% and it "only took you 2 weeks", whereas the two frames took many months, seeming more like years, which you fortunately just managed to finish moments before the divorce papers arrived thanks in large part to that long Thanksgiving weekend that put off the postman for four days. So, pleased with the new space, and you, your wife decides she wants to make a patio off the new middle bay and put a 12 foot sliding glass door in the space. Being the thorough student you are, you have already put braces from the post to the new plate in this bay, so you say, "Sorry honey, but I can't put the slider in because of the braces." To this she retorts, "Find a way." Divorce papers may be forthcoming, so what choice do you have but to finally resort to Chappell's book.

So, the question is, can you take your chain saw and cut these braces out to fit the 12 foot slider? The answer is yes! For one, the two frames were already deemed structurally complete on their own. The connecting ties only help to buttress the two frames to work as a single unit. So, when you are determining your brace plan, it is helpful to identify the complete frames within the overall frame—just as the two, 2 bent frames in our example were combined to become one 4 bent frame. This amounts to removing 14% of the braces considering the full 4 bent frame would have had 28 braces—12 in each frame plus the four in the new connecting bay— and you removed 4. Fits quite neatly into the rule-of-thumb.

Compression of framing members. Vertical post is subjected to compression along, or parallel, to the grain. The horizontal member is subjected to compression across, or perpendicular, to the grain.

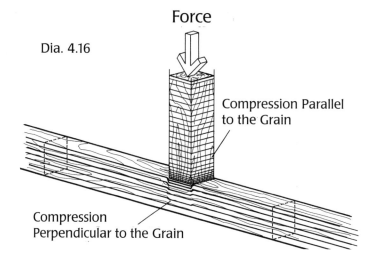

Force

Dia. 4.16

Compression Parallel to the Grain

Compression Perpendicular to the Grain

Types of Bracing

Knee Braces

The most common bracing method in use today, as well as in early Colonial and European frames, is to place the diagonal brace from the post to an upper horizontal member i.e., wall plates, tie beams, etc. This form of brace is commonly referred to as a knee brace. The common placement is to enter the post at its upper third point, and extend at a 45 degree angle to the adjoining horizontal member. For a nominal 8 foot post this would be at 32 inches and the brace hypotenuse would be 45.255 inches. Knee braces are most effective when in compression.

Tension Braces

When braces are placed joining from the posts to the sills, or a lower horizontal member, they are quite often referred to as tension braces. Tension braces are very common in barn framing in New England, and are found in a very large percentage of timber frames throughout Europe. In most cases, tension braces are used only on the corner posts and usually run from the top third of the post at a 45 degree angle, down to the sill plate or other adjoining member—making them a much larger member than the average knee brace. The name tension brace may be somewhat of a misnomer. While the larger size of tension braces, with its proportionately larger tenon, will withstand the forces of tension much greater than smaller knee braces, the fact is, tension braces also perform best under compression.

Sizing Braces

Braces are subjected only to the forces of tension and compression parallel to the grain. Because of this we are spared from much of the engineering considerations that are imperative to most of the other elements of the frame. Wood is greatest parallel to the grain. As an example, the compressive strength of northern red oak perpendicular to the grain is 500 pounds per square inch (psi), and 1,350 psi parallel to the grain. In tension, red oak's relative strength is 750 psi perpendicular to the grain, and 2,050 psi parallel to the grain (see table 1, pg. 98). This is illustrated in diagram 4.16, where the sill plate is subjected to compression perpendicular to the grain, and the post is subjected to compression parallel to the grain. While both members are subjected to the same force load, deformation will occur first on the sill plate.

Dia. 4.17

Horizontal Racking Force

Tension   Compression

When subjected to horizontal forces, braces are placed in compression or tension, according to the direction of force. Placing braces in equal numbers in opposing positions will resist these forces to the fullest degree.

This barn frame combines both tension braces and knee braces. Multiple opposing braces are necessary in barns due to the open interior space. As a horse barn, all the lower timbers are hemlock. Warrenton, Virginia, 1986

Bent Framing & Joinery Design

Brace with housed tenon. In the photo above the mortise is offset from the beam face so that the brace flushes to the outside face of the timber.

The brace above on an interior queen post to a collar tie has the brace mortise offset from the center line of the timbers so that the brace projects from the center of the post.

As may be evident from these figures, appropriate bracing may be achieved by using relatively scant members. The only real factor to consider is how the mortise, tenon and peg resist shearing when the brace is in tension. As we've already discussed, a brace is most effective when in compression. Therefore, when designing a frame the *braces should always be placed in equally opposing positions, so that for every brace subjected to tension in a given load situation there is an equal number of braces placed in compression.*

Aesthetics

As we've seen, braces are always subjected to end grain loading, or parallel to the grain. The amount of force on any one brace will be affected by the total number, location and overall arrangement of braces in the frame. The more braces, the less stress on each one. From a pure structural standpoint the size of the stock needs to be analyzed only in relation to its compressive and tensile strength parallel to the grain, however, there are some aesthetic and proportional considerations that should be understood. From an aesthetic point of view braces need to appear that they are of sufficient size to perform the job to the untrained eye, but they also don't want to appear to bulky, boxy or cumbersome. By slightly arching the braces, a nice balance can be achieved that preserves the sense of strength as the full dimension of the brace enters the post and beam, while adding an subtle, delicate and elegant touch.

On the small side, one should not use material less than 3 x 4 inches. This size allows for a 1-1/2 inch wide tenon—sufficient to resist tension if oak is used. In softwoods, I would make the tenon 2 inches wide. The four inch depth of the brace allows an adequate area for the peg to be driven. The length of the tenon for common knee braces should be 3 to 4 inches long, and tension braces should be a minimum of 5 inches. If the braces are to be straight, I would choose 3 by 5's for hardwood braces and 4 by 6's for softwood braces. These sizes will not look too bulky if left square. If they are to be curved, 3 by 8 or 4 by 8 inches allows for an appealing curve, leaving 5 to 6 inches at the narrowest point. *When sawing curves and arches, no more than 1/3 of the timber dimension should be removed at its narrowest point.*

Types of Wood

Oak is my first choice for braces, even in pine frames. I began using hardwoods—oak, maple and beech—in the early days because it has stronger properties in shear than pine, and also because the majority of early frames in our area of Maine used oak, beech, maple and chestnut braces, even in the pine and hemlock frames. If hardwood was not used, hemlock seemed to be the next wood of choice. Pine, however, is certainly adequate for most conditions, though I have never seen a pine brace in a New England frame built before 1980.

While I will admit there may be a few redeeming characteristics in good hemlock, I seem to have cultivated a significant distaste for the stuff, as did Socrates. Horses also seem to share this distaste, as it is one of the few woods they won't chew. For this reason most of the barns in New England were framed with hemlock, and this is still one of the few places I will use it. Other than horse barns, I seldom think of hemlock as a choice for anything. A fairly clear description of hemlock may be had by asking any experienced sawyer what they think about it. The comeback will usually be short and to the point, and most likely include a four letter word that surprisingly smells very much like the wood itself.

The problem with hemlock is due to the inconsistencies of the species (which, by the way, is actually a completely different type than what grew two hundred years ago in New England). Western hemlock is generally of much higher quality and more like that which was indigenous to the Northeast. Commercially, hemlock is of little value because an average load of logs may contain up to 30% or 40% unusable or low grade material. I've seen no appreciable increase in its price in the last 35 years, if this tells you anything. If you go to the cull pile at any sawmill, it will usually consist of about 95% hemlock. Hemlock is prone to any number of defects, few of which can be foreseen prior to milling or aging. In timbers, they may twist, shake, split, or maybe even stay absolutely straight and solid, looking like the best timber ever. The point is, you never know. One thing is certain, whatever it does, or doesn't do, it is at an extreme level. Enough on hemlock. Every once in a while I just have this incredible urge to complain about it. This should last for a while.

Roughed out brace tenons being pared to the score line. Note the beautiful curls.

Pre-fitting braces to assure tight fits prior to assembly. Note that the brace on the left above has the pocket offset so that the brace will be flush to the outside face of the post. The brace on the right has the pocket offset to one side of the center line of the timber so that when inserted the brace will extend from the center of the timber. This is done for all braces joining to interior posts. All braces will be made identical using this system regardless of where placed in the frame. Not also the spar tenon for a continuous top plate.

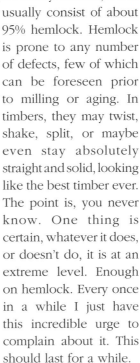

Housed Tenon Knee Braces.

Natural curved brace with centered tenons.

Paring brace shoulders to the scored line.

Assembling braces into frame.

Brace Joinery

Many of the joinery details used by modern timber framers are based on the tried and true methods that have historical evidence dating back hundreds of years with virtually no change in design. Then, of course, there are those joints that are used quite readily in modern timber framing which seem to have limited, or no historical precedence. When analyzed, it becomes evident that some of the newer techniques are applied because they are easier and faster to produce. This does not mean that all speedy joinery is less effective. The only point to be made here is: whatever joint one decides to use in a given situation, it should be used only if all of its implications and characteristics are understood.

When it comes to brace joinery, there are really only two joints used to any extent today that have any merit. One is a *housed tenon*, which is really the superior joint, and the other a *lap tenon*. Of course, as with almost any aspect of joinery, there are a number of variations to be found in both basic types. For instance, the housed tenon may also be shouldered (the whole brace being recessed into the joining timber). In the case of the lap tenon, it may be half dovetailed in an attempt to give more strength in tension. It will help to discuss each type.

Housed Tenon

The housed tenon is really a basic mortise and tenon joint. In a brace, it is cut at a 45 degree angle to the post or tie beam into which it enters. In most cases, the tenon will be 1-1/2" wide and extend into its mortise 3 to 4 inches. In any case, the mortise should be cut 1/4" deeper than the tenon length so that it will not bottom out as the timbers dry (this is a basic rule for all mortises). The tenon can be cut as a half lap, with the tenon to the inside face of the brace, in effect, housing the tenon face, thereby alleviating a shouldered edge which may open with aging.

Despite the fact that braces are one of the smaller members in the frame, they can be one of the most difficult members to join accurately, requiring the greatest amount of care in the accuracy of layout and in cutting. Accurate measurements are extremely important. A measurement off by only 1/32 of an inch on the mortise and brace length can the result in a gap of up to 1/8 inch.

Prior to the lay out of the brace mortises the timbers must be squared and prepped, making sure to check for any variations in dimension along their length—both at the point where the two members join, as well as the point where the brace is to enter (see diagram 4.18a). If any variations occur, compensation must be made in either the distance the mortise is laid out from the intersecting joints, or in the length of the brace. However, it is best to maintain a standard length for all braces and make any adjustments necessary on the post or horizontal member. Fewer mistakes will be made. If planed S4S (surfaced 4 sides) timbers are used, this step is usually not necessary, however, checking the timbers is always advisable.

The advantages to the housed tenon over the lap tenon are clearly visible. First of all, the tenon is locked into the mortise, resisting twisting action. The second factor is that the peg, being driven through two mortise faces, is considered to be in double shear. This means, theoretically, that it will take twice the force to rupture the joint. This joint will also resist the effects of aging better than a lap tenon because it does not, and cannot, pivot on one plane.

Lap Tenon

In the early days of the timber framing revival the lap tenon seemed to be used quite extensively for braces. It was, and still seems to be used to some extent in joining collar ties to rafters. To state it simply, lap joints are one of the more questionable joints to use in a joined timber frame. In New England, lap joints were reserved mostly for joining sill beams. In rare instances they were used to join top plates in barns, and in some cases they can be seen in collar ties in small house frames. For the most part however, these were frames built by farmers—not by carpenters. The period around the Civil War may have been the hay day of the lap joint revival here in northern New England. I always thought it curious that the frames built during the 1860's would use so many lap joints for all manner of joinery details until one day it dawned on me that all of the carpenters were off fighting and the building was left to the older farmers and young kids.

The lap tenon was popular throughout Europe for a number of centuries, but stopped being used in favor of the housed tenon by the 1500's. Some years back I was visiting an open air museum in the Black Forest near Frieburg, Germany. The director of the museum was giving a tour of the medieval structures and he pointed out an example of a lap tenon brace in a structure built in the early 1400's. He used it as an example, saying that, "You can judge the age of this building by the brace joinery. We learned long ago not to use this type of lap joint for braces due to it's inherent weakness. If you see this joint, then the structure was most definitely built prior to 1500." I pondered this for a minute, and considered that he was pointing out a structural defect in a frame that was over 500 years old. I just had to pose the question. "So, if this is such a bad joint, how is it that it has lasted these last 500 years, and in such fine shape?" He stood and looked blankly for a few moments and finally retorted, "They must have been damn good zimmermen back in those days, eh?" A German carpenter is called a zimmerman, which literally means *room builder*.

The truth is, the lap tenon does have an inherent weakness due to the fact that the peg, tenon, and mortise are all more or less pivoting on one shear plane. Under a load, especially in tension, the joint is likely to give considerably because there is nothing to stop the peg from pivoting, and therefore compressing, into its adjoining members. It would be much stronger to nail or bolt a lap joint than to peg it.

When used for braces, the lapped joint will not resist the brace's tendency to twist if it is so inclined. In effect, the brace will tend to pull away from its adjoining timber, causing an unsightly opening and a significant reduction in strength. The frame that employs lapped braces must rely more on the enclosure sheathing to prevent racking, and to hold the brace in place for the long term. Without these other materials present, the brace could literally fall out of the frame in ten years or so. Lap joints are certainly easier and faster to use, and in the initial placement, easier to fit accurately. They may even be placed after the frame is erected.

So, how do I explain the lap braces in the 700 year old building in the photo to the right? "Damn good carpenters back in those days, eh?

The oldest timber frame in the south of Germany was built in the town of Ependorf in 1317. As was common prior to 1500, the braces are all half lapped into the timbers using a slight half dovetail angle. This structure was built on top of a Roman wall that was built soon after Caesar's march to the Rhine in 56 BC, which marked the Roman conquest of Germany.

Dia. 4.18a

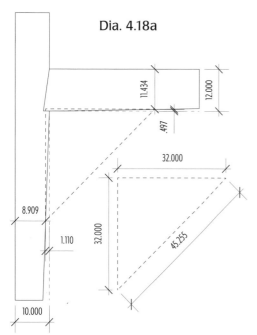

Mortise layout may need to be adjusted based on any variance in the timber dimension. The dotted triangle represents the two legs of the brace and the brace length. The dotted lines on the post and beam show a change in their dimension. The post in this diagram diminishes from 10" to 8.909" at the brace location, a difference of 1.11"; the tie beam diminishes by .497". The layout along the tie beam would therefore be marked at 30.89", and layout on the post would be marked at 31.503" from the inside corner of post and beam intersection. The brace length would remain unchanged, at 42.255".

4.18b) The Effects of Compression and Tension on Knee Braces

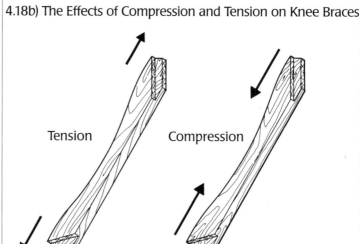

Tension   Compression

All braces are subjected to two distinct forces throughout the life of the building: compression and tension. Compression is the force which tends to compress the wood fiber. In the case of the brace, this would be the force pushing on the ends of the brace, tending to shorten the fibers. Tension, on the other hand, is the force which tends to pull or stretch the brace fibers.

Braces, as is the case with most members, are most effective when in compression. In this situation, the strength of the whole cross section of the brace is fully realized. The surfaces of the brace shoulders are in full contact with the adjoining members and not reliant solely upon the tenon or peg for strength. When a brace is in tension, it is relying not on the complete strength of the brace itself, but on the strength of the tenon and the peg securing it. This is why it is important to always plan and design your frame so that there are an equal amount of braces placed in opposing positions. In this way, there will always be braces in the wall or bent in compression, which will be opposing those in tension.

Brace pockets are cut with the nose angle of 90 degrees and the back side at 45 degrees. These angles need to be made accurately to assure perfection & grace is the end result. The brace tenon will normally be offset to project from the inside face of the brace, just like a lap tenon, but will be housed by offsetting the mortise to align with the inside face, as depicted in the photo to the left. Interior members will use the centerline of the of timber as one side of the brace mortise, always offsetting the mortise consistently to one side in the frame.

Tie Beam Joinery

The tie beam is the bottom chord of this 24′ clear-span scissor truss. English tying joints are used to join the tie beam to posts. This frame was the class project in the Head-of-Jedore, Nova Scotia workshop in the summer of 1995.

Tie Beam Joinery

Tie beams are the main connecting timber within the bent structure and performs two essential functions. As the name implies, its primary function is to tie the framework together so as to prevent spreading or possible collapse resulting from the outward force or **horizontal thrust** of the rafters. In this capacity, the tie beam is in tension, and is considered a **tension member**. Tension members perform best if they are one continuous piece, spanning the full width of the bent or framework with no intermediate joints. This will not only save layout and cutting time, but also produce the best long-term results because tension scarfs—no matter how well they are executed—have a tendency to spread slightly over time. To quote Ed Levin, "God makes the best scarf joints."

English Tying Joint cut by students in the Spring 1994 workshop at Fox Maple.

The design criteria for tension joinery is the strictest of any in timber framing. Therefore, if they can be avoided by using continuous members, it's wise to do so. Colonial housewrights understood this and would often use tie beams up to 45' or even 50' long. One might find fuel for a good argument that the design of colonial homes and barns were dictated more by the length of available timbers than by square footage requirements.

The secondary function of the tie beam is to act as the main floor carrying timber into which all of the other floor timbers are joined and supported—either directly or indirectly. In this situation the tie beam is subjected to **vertical loading** which imposes bending stresses along the length of the beam. The total vertical load is a combination of: 1) the **dead load** (the weight of the timber framework itself); and 2) the **live load** (the weight of the objects being placed on the framework in use). The combination of the live and dead load is known as the **combined floor load**. To determine the appropriate joinery specifications and beam dimensions for a given situation, the maximum vertical and horizontal loading conditions must first be determined.

Because so much of the structural integrity of a traditionally joined frame relies on properly designed (and executed) joinery, this is where the design process should begin. In many cases beam dimensions will be dictated more by the requirements of the joinery than by the loading conditions on the beam itself. Complete understanding of structural beam analysis is quite complex, however, the following basic guidelines can make the design process easier and less confusing for the novice.

The 16 Foot Rule

For practical purposes, 16 feet is the maximum safe span for a simple beam. This is partially due to the fact that as the span increases, the stiffness of the member decreases proportionally by the cube of its length. In other words, a timber spanning 20 feet will have nearly twice the deflection of a beam spanning 16 feet. This is only one aspect to consider when designing beams, but if we analyzed this further, we'd find that attempting to increase beam dimension in order to accommodate spans much over 16 feet is the wrong approach.

Understanding this, we can design more cost-effective frames by using the following rule-of-thumb guidelines:

1) *Maintain a standard tie beam dimension of 7 or 8 inches wide, by 10 or 12 inches deep—regardless of the overall tie beam length*;

2) *Place an intermediate post under all beams so that no single span/section exceeds 16 feet.*

Clear-spans in excess of 16 feet can be designed, however, these must rely on truss dynamics, rather than beam strength. For more on this see *Clear-Span Truss Designs.*

Tension Joinery

There are a variety of traditional joinery details to choose from to make an effective tie beam joint. The choice of which joint to use may be based on the conditions that best suit the frame design, aesthetics, or ease of execution, but most importantly, it must serve the purpose based on a sound structural basis. Some of the general considerations that must be taken into account from a structural standpoint will be discussed, followed by specific details and a description of each.

The tensile strength of wood parallel to the grain is its strongest mechanical property. It is highly unlikely that a beam in tension would ever fail across its full cross section due to tensile stress, however, the reduced cross section of tenons need to be analyzed carefully. A beam in tension does not necessarily imply that the forces imposed on the individual components of the joint—tenon, mortise, pegs—are subjected to tensile forces. Identifying the type of stresses acting on the components of the joint is the first order of business.

When we deal with the mechanical properties of wood, in regards to strength, we are essentially dealing with how the external forces affect the internal structure of the beam or beam section. If the wood fibers crush, break, or slip by each other, the beam is said to fail. Any deformation of more than 5% of a sectional area may be considered to have failed. Without going into the subject in excessive detail, a general overview of the types of basic stresses will be helpful in understanding the joinery discussed in this chapter.

Stress is essentially the internal resistive forces of a structural member or material to an externally applied force. In wood, the resistive strength is determined by the type of wood (species) and the direction of the force in relation to the grain (wood fiber). There are three basic types of stress: **tension**, **compression** and **shear**.

Peg Spacing for Joint in Tension

Dia. 4.19

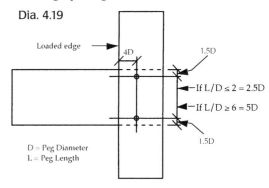

Determining Critical Length of Pegs

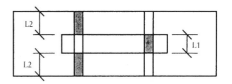

Critical length for Tenon = L1
Critical Length of Mortise = L2 + L2
If mortise sides (L2) are less than
1/2 tenon width (L1), critical length for
tenon becomes L2 + L2.
For a more complete review, see Chapter 5.

Half-dovetailed & wedged tension joint.

To assure maximum strength the half-dovetailed tenon surface must make complete surface contact with the angle on the bottom of the mortise. In this photo a student is checking that the bottom of the tenon is cut absolutely square.

Tensile forces tend to stretch or pull a structural member. The direction of the applied force in relation to the grain of the wood dictates the relative strength of the member, so tensile forces are further qualified as: **tension parallel to the grain** and **tension perpendicular to the grain**.

Wood is strongest in its resistance to tension parallel to the grain. Failure will always occur at the joint or joint section before failing across the full cross section of a beam.

Tension perpendicular to the grain is closely related to side hardness and cleavage. Mortise sides may fail due to tension perpendicular to the grain. However, there are no straightforward formulas to determine consistent results for pegged joinery because the area calculated as the resistive section is difficult to determine. Laboratory testing for bolted connections resulting in ratios of bolt diameter to edge spacing, and tenon width to mortise side widths are usually used to determine the strength of the complete joint and do not determine factors specifically for mortise sides. *(For more on this subject, see Chapter 5, Tension Joinery.)*

Compressive forces tend to shorten or compress a structural member. Compression is also qualified with regard to direction to the grain; **compression parallel to the grain** and **compression perpendicular to the grain**.

Compression parallel to the grain is the second strongest mechanical property of wood, and rarely becomes a significant concern in timber framing. Failure due to extreme end loading of posts and columns will usually result from horizontal shear—due to bending of the loaded member—before end grain crushing will take place.

Compression perpendicular to the grain may be a factor in some joints if the shoulder of one member does not make full surface contact with the joining timber, or if the contact surfaces are not of sufficient area for the species of wood and load. This will rarely result in catastrophic failure, but may appear only as unsightly crushing of the surface fiber. In both of these cases, if serious problems were to ever occur, it would only be after other, more serious failures were taking place in the frame. While compression may not be the direct cause of failure, compressive forces within a beam are often contributing factors under extreme conditions.

The equation to determine compressive stress per square inch (psi) is: $S_L = PA$, where S_L is the compressive stress, P is the load in pounds, and A is the sectional area. The compressive stress should not exceed the allowable stress given in Table 1.

Potential tensile failure perpendicular to the grain (cleavage) of mortise sides due to outward thrust of the rafters

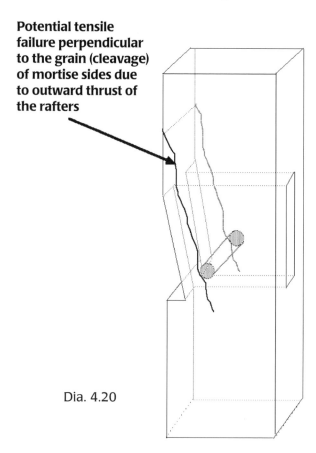

Dia. 4.20

Shearing Forces in Tension Joint

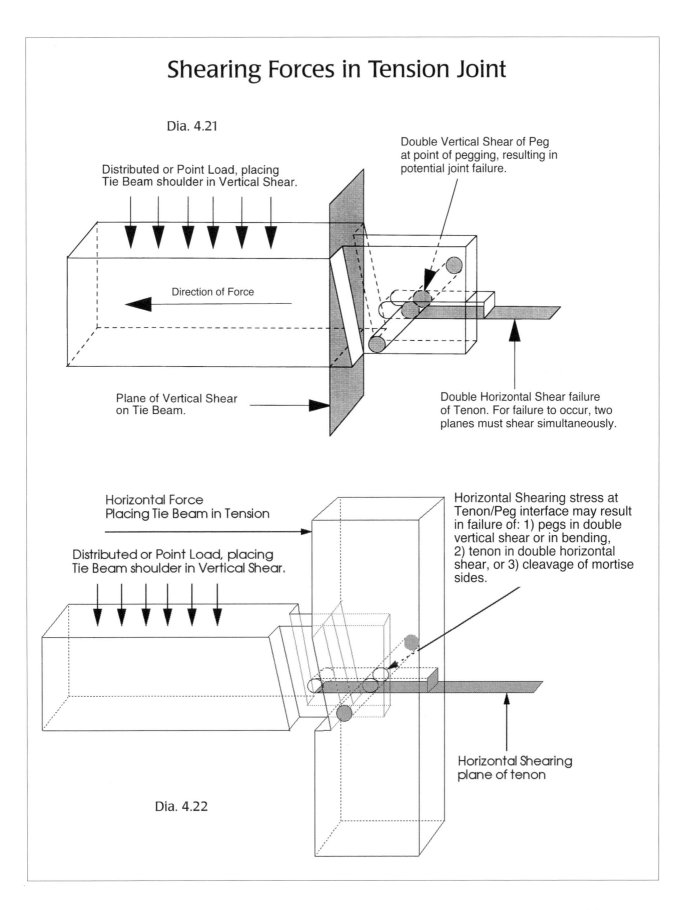

Dia. 4.21

Distributed or Point Load, placing
Tie Beam shoulder in Vertical Shear.

Double Vertical Shear of Peg
at point of pegging, resulting in
potential joint failure.

Direction of Force

Plane of Vertical Shear
on Tie Beam.

Double Horizontal Shear failure
of Tenon. For failure to occur, two
planes must shear simultaneously.

Horizontal Force
Placing Tie Beam in Tension

Horizontal Shearing stress at
Tenon/Peg interface may result
in failure of: 1) pegs in double
vertical shear or in bending,
2) tenon in double horizontal
shear, or 3) cleavage of mortise
sides.

Distributed or Point Load, placing
Tie Beam shoulder in Vertical Shear.

Horizontal Shearing
plane of tenon

Dia. 4.22

One final check of the depth of dovetail cut in mortise and tenon prior to assembly.

Shearing forces tend to make the parts of a structural member slip, or slide past each other. Shear is also qualified with regard to its direction to the grain: **horizontal shear** (parallel to the grain) and **vertical shear** (perpendicular to the grain).

By far, the most common cause of beam and joinery failure is due to horizontal shearing stresses. When a simple beam is loaded, the fibers on the top of the beam are in compression and the fibers on the bottom are in tension, resulting in horizontal shearing stress along the neutral axis (the longitudinal center of the beam). When a beam is loaded beyond its limits, actual slippage occurs, hence, failure. This is usually the first failure in a beam. Once this occurs complete beam failure is likely, which may appear as direct vertical shear, or a snapping of the wood fiber. Horizontal shear is also one of the primary causes of failure for tenons and even pegs in joinery. However, in the case of a tenon, it will be due to direct shearing stress and not a result of bending. Pegs, though they are subjected to vertical shearing forces, will likely fail first in horizontal shear due to bending because the tenon and mortise sides will compress under loading. When designing tension joinery it's imperative to determine the maximum load (thrust) so that sufficient shearing surfaces (relish) can be allowed to remain on the tenon behind the pegs. This is also necessary to determine adequate peg size and number. More on this will be covered in Chapter 5.

While vertical shearing forces can cause direct failure of a beam—such as tenons which are supporting connecting beams—it is extremely rare unless the builder has no common sense about building. The term vertical shear is commonly used to denote the amount of shearing stress that is acting on the cross section of a beam at any point along its length as a result of vertical loading. The value is then used to determine the horizontal shearing stresses.

The half-dovetail on the tie beam tenon must be mapped to the actual cut on the bottom angle cut in the mortised post to assure a full surface contact.

Horizontal Shear of Simple Beams

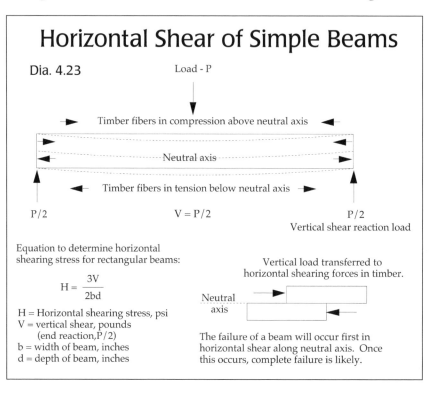

Dia. 4.23

Load - P

Timber fibers in compression above neutral axis

Neutral axis

Timber fibers in tension below neutral axis

P/2   V = P/2   P/2

Vertical shear reaction load

Equation to determine horizontal shearing stress for rectangular beams:

$$H = \frac{3V}{2bd}$$

H = Horizontal shearing stress, psi
V = vertical shear, pounds
    (end reaction, P/2)
b = width of beam, inches
d = depth of beam, inches

Vertical load transferred to horizontal shearing forces in timber.

Neutral axis

The failure of a beam will occur first in horizontal shear along neutral axis. Once this occurs, complete failure is likely.

The equation to find vertical shear force in a simple beam of rectangular cross section is: $V=P/2$. In which: V = vertical shearing force, and P = total load in pounds. By using the following equation we can find the horizontal shearing stress (H) in pounds per square inch: $3V/2bd$.

Designing joinery requires a basic understanding of how forces are transferred within a framework and the mechanical properties of the wood being used. The correct evaluation of all of the forces acting on the individual members is essential if a proper joint is to be designed. However, by following a few common sense guidelines and the examples of fine joinery left to us by our predecessors, the mysteries will soon seem to fade.

This may all seem somewhat confusing, however it really is straightforward, and may be easier to understand when analyzed in relationship to the actual joinery details that have traditionally been used for tie beam joinery.

Traditional Tie Beam Joinery Details

Tie beam joinery can be broken down into two types as follows:

Tie beam to post joinery—*when the tie beam enters directly into the post below the top plate level.*

Tie beam to plate joinery—*when the tie beam rests directly on top of the post or plate.*

Tie beam to post joinery

Simple Mortise and tenon
Shouldered Mortise and tenon
Wedged Half Dovetail mortise and tenon

Tie beam to plate joinery

English tying joint
Modified English tying joint

The overall design of the frame, the planned raising sequence (dictated to some extent by the equipment available at the time of raising) and the structural loading conditions will all play a part in what type tie beam joinery will best fit the situation at hand. Let's take a look at these, one by one, and discuss the appropriate uses of each.

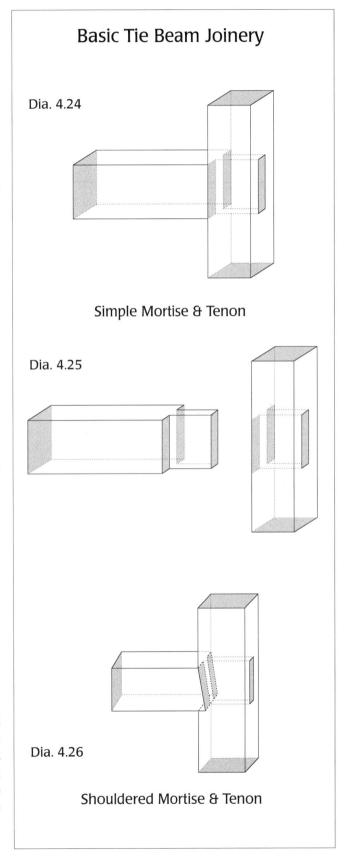

Basic Tie Beam Joinery

Dia. 4.24

Simple Mortise & Tenon

Dia. 4.25

Dia. 4.26

Shouldered Mortise & Tenon

Paring the shoulders and flattening the tenon on a shouldered through tenon.

Simple Mortise and Tenon

The simple mortise and tenon is one of the most common joinery details used throughout the centuries, and is really the basis of all timber joinery. New England house and barn frames built in the early 1700's used the simple mortise and tenon joint extensively for plate to post joinery, and increasingly for tie beam to post joinery, especially in barns. During this period, in part due to the economy of a rapidly expanding frontier, timber frames were beginning to be seen more as a purely functional structural system, and the joinery was evolving to reflect this new economy. By the late 18th century many of the beautifully embellished and classic joinery details brought from Europe began to be modified into a more practical and efficient American style of joinery, which placed more emphasis on efficiency and function over form. It may be no coincidence that this took place about the time that the colonies won their independence from England. In most 19th century house frames the timbers and the joinery were usually covered completely by plaster. This, however, does not diminish the elegance and style of the 19th century American timber frame. It is actually this period that personifies the craft at its zenith—and a truly American vernacular form—prior to the industrial revolution.

The non shouldered tenon must rely completely on the size of the tenon for its strength to resist both horizontal and vertical shearing forces. If the tenon is too narrow, and the span and load forces on the beam are too great, this is one case where the tenon could potentially shear off directly due to vertical shearing forces. The vertical shearing stress in this situation is greatly affected by the placement (or lack of placement) of interior posts under the beam and their proximity to the exterior post. This joint is most appropriate for connecting plates up to 16', or tie beams of short span (16' and under) that are subjected to little or no horizontal thrust, as in the first floor tie beams in a two story colonial.

If the maximum 16 foot span rule is followed, vertical shear failure of the tenon is of little concern. For pine timbers, the tenon should be a minimum of 2 inches wide, and if the span is 16 feet or under, an unsupported 7 x 12 can be used. In this case, the tenons would have 24 square inches of shearing surface resisting vertical shear. This would allow a safe vertical load of 6,960 lbs on the tenon*—within the safe margin if we maintain the 16 foot rule throughout the frame. If oak were used, the tenon could be reduced to 1-1/2 inches, and a 7 x 10 could be used, however I would tend to stick with a 2 inch tenon to help prevent twisting of the timber (the tenon width has a direct relationship to resistance of twisting). It might be said as a general rule-of-thumb that the *tenon width should be between 1/3 to 1/4 the beam width.* Using timbers less than 10 inches deep may result in problems joining floor timbers, so I would attempt to maintain this as a minimum standard for all tie beams that will be carrying additional floor timbers.

Tie beam to post assembly using half-dovetailed through tenon tension joint. Wedges are at the right in photo.

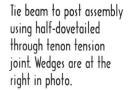

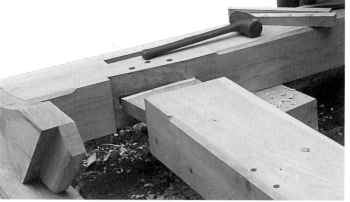

The amount of tensile stress on this type of joint is determined by the point at which the rafter foot is joined to the post, and its distance from the joint. In the case of a tie beam in a full two story frame, the first floor ties are not subjected to tensile forces because the thrust is being placed on the uppermost tie, at or directly below the rafter feet. The simple mortise and tenon is appropriate for the lower tie in this situation as long as the tenon is designed to adequately carry the floor load. However, for tie beams one should always consider the shouldered mortise and tenon.

*Using the value in Table 7) Mechanical Properties of Wood, for green Eastern white pine, Side Hardness—load perpendicular to the grain, pg. 236.

Pegging

If the tying joint is not in tension, two 1 inch pegs are sufficient, and the pegs should be spaced 2 times their diameter from the loaded edge. When the tenon is in tension, the pegs should be 4 times the peg diameter from the loaded edge. In either case, the pegs should be a minimum of 1.5 times the peg diameter from the top and bottom tenon surfaces (parallel to the grain).

The center-to-center spacing between pegs on the side face should be 4 times the peg diameter. If three or more pegs are used, the pegs in line parallel to the grain of the mortised member should be alternately offset at least 1.5 times the peg diameter from the center line of the pegs nearest the loaded edge (see dia. 4.19 pg. 77).

For tension joints, the pegs should be at least 7 times their diameter from the end of the tenon in softwoods, and 4 times for hardwoods. For joints in compression, or neutrally loaded, the end distance should be 4 times the peg diameter.

It may be wise to point out the difference between a tie beam (connecting post to post) and a collar tie (connecting rafter to rafter). A collar tie within a pair of rafters is not really a tie in its truest sense, because it is subjected to the inward compression of the rafter load rather than pulling or spreading tension. Therefore, it is not tying, but bracing. There are conditions, such as when the collar tie is joined within the lower third section of the rafters, when it is actually working as a tie, and therefore in considerable tension. In this case, it should be analyzed as a tension member. For more on this, refer to *Structural Design Considerations*.

Shouldered and wedged half dovetailed tie beam to post tension joint, above and below.

Shouldered Mortise and Tenon

When a tie beam will be subjected to an excessive vertical floor load, or when there is a point load in close proximity to the joint, the shouldered mortise and tenon is the appropriate joint to use. A shouldered tenon will dramatically increase the resistance to vertical shear and compression of the tenon, as well as reduce twisting.

There are two distinct advantages to the shouldered variety over the non shouldered type. One, just mentioned, concerns the properties of vertical shear of the member. The non shouldered tenon must rely solely on the strength of the tenon to support the vertical load and resist vertical shear failure. In cross section, a two inch wide by ten inch deep tenon has a shear plane of 20 square inches. The shouldered joint, cut on a 7"x 10" timber, has a shear plane of 70 square inches, making it three and a half times stronger than its non shouldered counterpart. Since the tenon of the shouldered type is not called upon to carry the total vertical load imposed on the tie beam, and if it is not subjected to a significant amount of tension, the tenon may be cut to a narrower size, allowing more meat to be left on the sides of the post mortise. This is particularly important in a case where wall plates or other members are entering the post at the same level as the tying member.

The second advantage is that the greater the area of contact between the tie beam and post, the greater the resistance to twisting. If one were to look at some of the old barn or house frames scattered about that did not employ shouldered joints (and there are plenty of them around) you will notice that many of the tie beams have twisted quite severely.

Pegging: The criteria for pegging this joint is the same as that of the simple mortise and tenon.

Assembling half-dovetailed
tie beam to post.

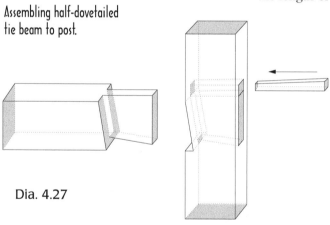

Dia. 4.27

Wedged Half Dovetailed/Shouldered Mortise & Tenon

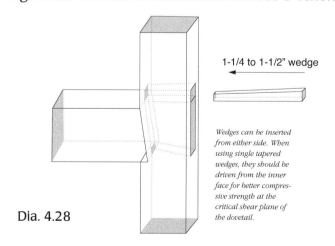

1-1/4 to 1-1/2" wedge

*Wedges can be inserted
from either side. When
using single tapered
wedges, they should be
driven from the inner
face for better compres-
sive strength at the
critical shear plane of
the dovetail.*

Dia. 4.28

Wedged Half Dovetailed Mortise and Tenon

Tension on the tie beam and tie beam joinery is most acute in a high posted design where the post is cantilevered or extended above the tie beam, but stopping short of another full story. The outward thrust of the rafters in this situation places a much greater amount of tension on the tie beam and its tenon, and a great bending force on the extended portion of the post. This condition calls for more than the simple mortise and tenon. The high posted design is an ideal situation to utilize the wedged half dovetail mortise and tenon.

Due to its ability to stand up to the forces of tension, this tie beam joint cannot be beat. Whereas the simple mortise and tenon must rely solely on the pegs for strength in tension, the half dovetail joint incorporates the strength of the dovetail tenon itself to complement the peg's holding action. The pegs themselves actually become a secondary element in this joint. As the diagram illustrates, the bottom of the tenon (and corresponding mortise) is cut with a 1-1/4 to a 1-1/2 inch half dovetail, depending on the length of tenon.

The top of the mortise must be enlarged the same amount to allow the tenon to be inserted and then dropped onto the corresponding angle on the bottom of the mortise. The space left at the top is then wedged snugly with an oak wedge, locking the tenon and mortise securely. The addition of two or three pegs, depending on the loading conditions, make this one of the strongest mortise and tenon tension joints to be found in traditional Euro/American timber frame joinery.

The spacing of pegs should follow the same pattern as mentioned previously.

For this joint to work effectively, it is imperative that the two dovetailed planes (post mortise & tenon) are in full surface contact, so that when the wedge is driven, there is no slop. This requires careful layout and extremely accurate execution. The shearing surface of the half dovetail will add an additional 18 square inches of total shearing surface to the joint if the post depth is 10 inches (1" of tenon length is lost to the shoulder angle). In pine, this adds 2,160 pounds of additional resistive shearing strength to the joint; in oak, 3,330 pounds (based on the safe working stress for pine in horizontal shear of 120 psi; oak, 185 psi).

English Tying Joint

One of the most common European style post/tie/rafter joinery details used throughout the centuries is what many call the English tying joint. There is very good reason for its widespread use. The English tying joint is a true compression joint and does just about everything you could ask the perfect joint to do. The rafter foot, being joined directly into the tie beam, alleviates all of the bending forces which may act on the post if the rafter foot were joined directly to its top. The tenon of the rafter foot, housed into the tie beam, is virtually flawless in its ability to resist the shear of both the tenon and the mortise (which is in double horizontal shear).

The post has a tenon extending through the top plate, which I call a *spar tenon*,

and a sleeved face wrapping around the inside face of the plate. From this inside sleeve a tenon, known as a *teasel tenon*, extends into the tie beam. As well, the bottom of the tie beam is cut with a 2" deep dovetail (occasionally deeper) which fits into a corresponding dovetail slot on top of the top plate. When joined and assembled (either pinned or not pinned), it is like a Chinese puzzle, and there is no natural force than can pull this joint apart. Its only enemy throughout the ages has been leaking roofs, causing the members to rot, and a failing foundation (if the joints were not pinned). I have seen and repaired many old barn frames where this joint had never been pinned, though most often the peg holes were drilled. I believe I have probably left a few unpegged myself.

This joint will not allow a full-bent raising because the top plate is continuous from post to post, however it creates the greatest strength in tying the bents together.

When using a true English tying joint, special consideration should be given to how the floor joists join to the top plate. The top of the tie beam (the floor level) is usually a full 7" to 9" above the top of the top plate. Using joists the full depth of the drop—from top of tie to top of plate—can visually affect the natural balance of the rest of the floor system if the joists are made the full depth. In many cases, this would require a joist deeper than the summer beam to which it was joining. There is a tasteful and aesthetically pleasing solution. I call them *eaves droppers*.

The ideal situation is to run the joist from the summer beam to the top plate. This keeps all of the floor joists in the same pattern, but requires a deeper joist running to the eaves.

Modified English tying joints were used on this barn frame in Warrenton, VA, circa 1986.

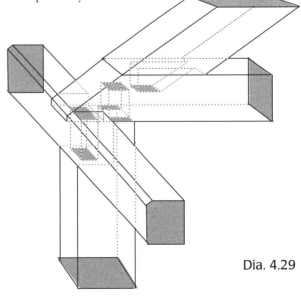

Dia. 4.29

English Tying Joint

The eaves dropper requires a joist that is the full depth of the drop—from the top of plate to the top of tie—(say it is 8 inches) plus one inch for a slot dovetail. The joist is ripped to match the depth of the regular joist depth to within 18 to 24 inches from the end that will rest on the top plate. The point where the rip stops is then gracefully curved between the two levels with a chisel. This detail looks great and appears to be something more than it is. In a small cape, where both sides of the house are visible without partitions or visual obstruction, it adds an interesting and distinguished feel to the space.

The southern yellow pine frame above (and below) used modified English tying joints with eaves dropper floor joists. Traditional English tying joints require a two-phase raising because the top plate runs continuously through the length of the eaves wall. The Modified English tying joint can be raised either as full bents or in two phases.

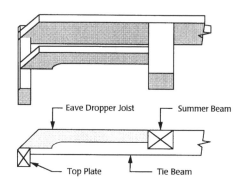

4.30) Eaves Dropper Joist

Dia. 4.31

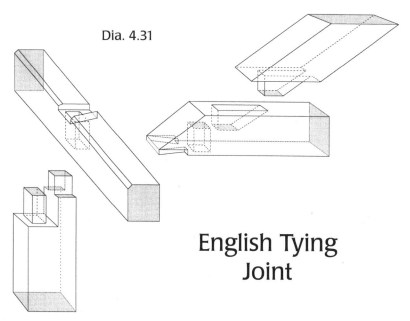

English Tying Joint

Modified English Tying Joint

The modified English tying joint is favored by many modern timber framers because it is the only way this joint can be used if the frame is to be erected as full bents. Full bent raising's require that all connecting members must be joined so they can be placed after the raising of the bents. The advent of stress skin panels has allowed the option of having no horizontal member at the eaves level (top plate). This is becoming a very common practice, but I personally avoid using it. The interface of wall to roof plane is extremely important in any frame, conventional or timbered, for fastening exterior sheathing and creating a solid tie between bents along the eaves. Relying on stress skin to maintain a tight, sealed fit seems to be asking too much, therefore I do not recommend this method.

Virtually all of the elements of the standard English tying joint are present in this modified version, with the exception of the continuous top plate. The post has a teasel tenon extending into the bottom of the tie beam, and the rafter is joined in the same way into the top of the tie. Instead of a continuous top plate, intermediate plates are joined from bent to bent. Top plate mortises of 1-1/2 to 2 inches wide and 3 inches deep are cut from the top shoulder of the post (open-ended) so that they can be dropped in before the tie beam is placed, or after, depending on the specific raising sequence. The top plate shoulders extend up into the tie beam 2 inches, though occasionally 1-1/2 inches, and are cut with a 3/4 inch angle to accept the dovetail notch on the sides of the tie beam. This helps to prevent rolling or twisting of the top plate.

The beauty of this joint is that all joining members are in compression. Pegs are necessary, however no additional strength in the bent is immediately achieved from their use. As the loading increases, the joint tends to get tighter. Many times I have waited to peg this joint until the final stages of completion to allow any shrinkage and settling that may occur during the process to be absorbed by the load. I have inspected many barn frames that did not peg this joint at all. The only problems that I've seen have been a result of the stone foundations caving in, allowing the teasel tenon on the post to drop out of the mortise. This is a good enough reason to peg the joint, but I would never feel at risk in a frame that utilized English tying joints, pegged or unpegged.

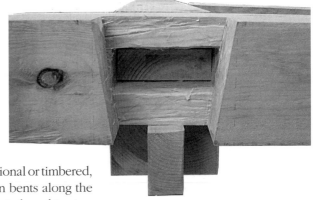

English tying joint with a continuous top plate. In this design the slot dovetail pocket receives the tie beam. The spar tenon passes through the plate and the teasel tenon locks the post directly to the tie beam.

Modified English Tying Joint

Dia. 4.32

Post & plate joinery for a modified English tying joint with dovetail notches in the intermediate connecting top plates.

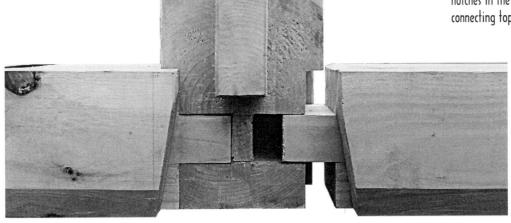

The post above, and top right, is designed to accept a continuous top plate in an English tying joint. In this design the plate is scarfed over the middle post with offset cheek tenons. This conceals the vertical butt cuts behind the sleeved post face, and to all appearances, the top plate looks as one continuous timber after assembled. The dovetail slot in the top plate and tie beam form an interlocking connection that prevents outward rolling of the plate, helping to secure the complete connection.

Top: Teasel tenons secure the tie beam to the post in an English tying joint, which is locked to the plate by the sleeved post face and the spar tenon that projects through the plate. This is an iron-clad joint that resists all forces in beautiful compressive harmonic balance—even without pegs. In the above photo a student checks the square of a teasel tenon. The spars have yet to be haunched as in the photos top and bottom left.

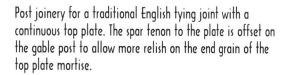

Post joinery for a traditional English tying joint with a continuous top plate. The spar tenon to the plate is offset on the gable post to allow more relish on the end grain of the top plate mortise.

Post joinery for a modified English tying joint. The housed side mortises in this post accept an intermediate top plate. A workshop student is paring the teasel tenon to fit into a recessed mortise. This conceals the mortise/tenon interface, making for a tighter, cleaner looking joint.

The Modified English tying joint, can be raised as full bents, or in two phases as in the frame above. Either way, the English tying joint—traditional or modified—is one of the most effective tie beam joints in timber framing because it absolutely resists thrust in a pure compression joint. 1995 FM course project.

The frame above used the English tying joint in a 32' clear-span King Post truss. This is the most efficient truss design for creating clear spans and one of the most elegant due to its simplicity. The frame below uses the English tying joint in a queen post truss. To accommodate a clear span, lower struts were used.

Half-dovetailed through tenon tie beam to post joinery is used in the Queen Post frame above (the bent raising is below). In this design the queen posts redirect the outward thrust to the tie beam, which must be supported by secondary posts as this is not a true truss. The hammerbeam gable dormer in the frame is being assembled and pegged to the right. The 4 bent frame and 4 valley dormer system were the Spring 2003 Intro & Advanced TF course projects at FM.

Chapter 5
Tension Joinery

Half dovetailed and wedged tension joinery is used to join tie beams to king post in the Library at Fox Maple School. The frame was cut in the spring 1996 workshop and enclosed with straw bales, finished with clay plaster and a thatched roof in follow up workshops.

When designing timber frames, or any structural framework, it's imperative that the designer recognize what forces are at play if a structurally sound framework is to be the result. If we assume that the net result of all externally applied forces are attempting to collapse a structure, then we must also assume that the nature of a structure is to resist these forces so that it will resist collapse. The law of force and motion states that: *for every action there is an equal and opposite reaction, and that, if a body is in motion, it will remain in motion unless an opposing force modifies or tends to modify its course.* In building, the goal is to prevent or resist motion. In timber framing, we rely on the balance of three distinct elements of the frame to accomplish this: 1) *the timbers themselves*; 2) *the overall design of the structural framework*; 3) *and the joinery employed.* Before we can determine the size of the timbers, or design the joinery details, we must first determine the forces acting on the structure.

Post to tie beam assembly using the wedged half-dovetail through tenon. This is a beautiful tension joinery detail, but it must be executed to strict criteria to achieve maximum strength. Note the oak wedges on the post that will be driven to lock the dovetails.

Analyzing Applied Forces

When a force is applied to a movable object, it moves. When we want it to move easily, we can put it on wheels. If we want to stop it once it's in motion, we can install brakes. For the brakes to be effective, they must be able to create a reactionary force equal to, or greater than: 1) *the combined force which set it in motion*, and 2) *the momentum generated due to the weight of the wheeled object.* In this example, the externally applied force which moved the vehicle is the action; the movement of the vehicle is reactionary. In applying the brakes, we set up a secondary internal reactionary force. When enough pressure is applied to the brakes to stop the vehicle—with the external force still being applied—we've reached the point of *static equilibrium*, or that point where the reactionary force is equal to the externally applied force and the body becomes at rest. Maintaining a state of static equilibrium is the goal of all structural design.

32' clear-span king post truss with queen posts, king struts and half-dovetailed tension joints to king post. The king post truss is an extremely efficient design, and actually fits the classic definition of a simple truss.

Whether we're dealing with moving vehicles, or timbers and joinery, the same principles apply. The only variables that we must include in the equation are: 1) *the amount of force* (magnitude); 2) *the direction of the force*; and 3) *the physical and mechanical characteristics of the materials resisting the force*. Applying this example to timbers we can see that the same variables are in action:

If we were to support a horizontal beam at both ends and apply a load at its center, we replicate the same force dynamics as that of the moving vehicle. In this case, the beam is the vehicle, the load at its center is the applied external force (the applied load plus the weight of the timber equal the combined momentum), and the physical and mechanical characteristics of the grain fibers in the wood act as the brakes. If the load is great enough to bend the beam, then the beam is set into motion. A reaction force (vertical shear) equal to one half the total load will be imposed on each end of the timber in an upward direction (or the opposite direction of the load). When this happens, a secondary internal reactionary force (horizontal shear) is imposed within the beam fibers. If the internal resistance force is not equal to or greater than the combined force generated by the weight of the timber and the applied load (momentum), the timber will break—the brakes will fail.

Referring to the diagram 4.23 on page 80 shows the distribution of forces on a simply supported beam. Diagram 1, below, shows how the forces in a simple framework are distributed.

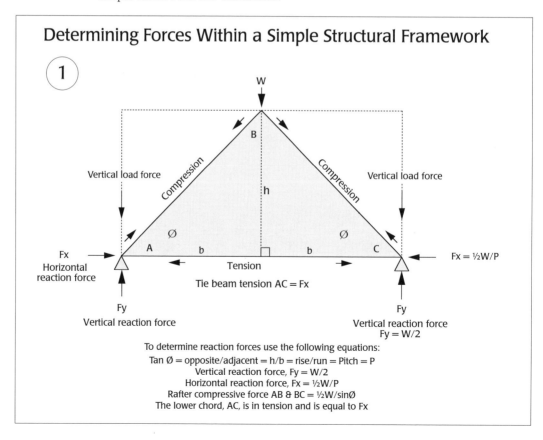

Determining Forces Within a Simple Structural Framework

(1)

W

B

Vertical load force

Compression

Compression

Vertical load force

h

Ø

Ø

Fx
Horizontal
reaction force

A

b

Tension

b

C

Fx = ½W/P

Tie beam tension AC = Fx

Fy
Vertical reaction force

Fy
Vertical reaction force
Fy = W/2

To determine reaction forces use the following equations:
Tan Ø = opposite/adjacent = h/b = rise/run = Pitch = P
Vertical reaction force, Fy = W/2
Horizontal reaction force, Fx = ½W/P
Rafter compressive force AB & BC = ½W/sinØ
The lower chord, AC, is in tension and is equal to Fx

Forces Acting on a Structural Framework

Just as the forces in the example of the vehicle are replicated in the simply supported beam, so are the same forces acting in a structural framework. When designing joinery to secure the structural framework, we must therefore identify: 1) *the amount of force* (magnitude), 2) *the direction of the force*, and 3) *determine the mechanical characteristics of the materials used.* Once we have done this, we can then determine the structural requirements of a given joint.

To understand how the forces are transferred within a framework, we can use the example of a ladder leaned up against a wall (see dia. 2). Let's first assume that the feet of the ladder are resting on a smooth surface, and the wall is also smooth, therefore offering little resistance due to friction. If we put the ladder nearly vertical, we can climb up the ladder and it will

2) Determining Force Loads
Transferred from Vertical to Horizontal

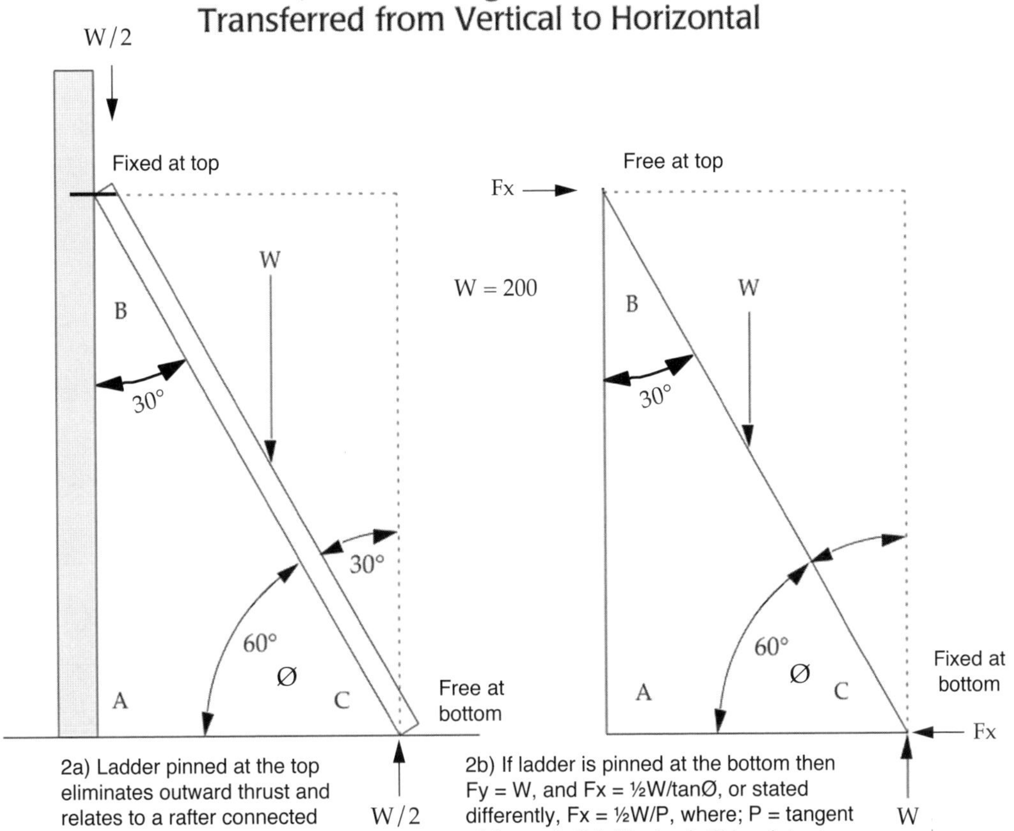

W/2

Fixed at top

W

B

30°

30°

60°

Ø

A   C

Free at bottom

W/2

Free at top

Fx →

W = 200

W

B

30°

30°

60°

Ø

A   C

Fixed at bottom

← Fx

W

2a) Ladder pinned at the top eliminates outward thrust and relates to a rafter connected to a ridge beam. In this case Fy = W/2. If fixed at top and bottom Fx = zero.

2b) If ladder is pinned at the bottom then Fy = W, and Fx = ½W/tanØ, or stated differently, Fx = ½W/P, where; P = tangent of the roof pitch (rise/run). This relates to a rafter fixed at the foot with no ridge beam. In our example: Fx = (200/2) / 1.732 = 57.73lbs

The example of a ladder leaning against a wall clearly illustrates the forces acting upon a roof system. If the weight of the applied load, W, and the angle of inclination are known, then all other force loads can be determined. In the above drawings we show a ladder fixed at the top (2a) and the bottom (2b), with the appropriate equations to determine both Fx and Fy forces. If the ladder were merely leaning, unfixed, and load W = 200 lbs, then Fy = W and the horizontal force, Fx, can be found by using the equation:
Fx = ½W/tanØ = 100 / 1.732 = 57.73 lbs

24' wide high post bent uses queen posts and collar tie to transfer outward thrust on post to tie beam. This frame also had a central post to support tie beam as this design is not a truss.

remain upright. If we move the feet out, there will become a point when it will want to slide out from under us and collapse. Like the vehicle with no brakes, i.e. no resistance, the ladder is set into motion. In this case the force of the vertical load is transferred to a horizontal force or thrust, increasing in magnitude as the angle becomes more acute.

If we were to securely fasten the top of the ladder to the wall so that it could not slide vertically, outward thrust would be eliminated, so long as the method of fastening (joinery) and the foundation supporting the wall were strong enough to support our weight and prevent motion. If we were to fasten the feet of the ladder so that they could not move horizontally, but allowed the top to remain free to slide, the vertical load would be transferred to an outward horizontal force at the foot of the ladder. The ability to resist movement, again, is directly related to the strength of the connection or joint. Which is why we must first determine the amount of force if we are to design appropriate joinery.

Translating this to a real building, we not only have to consider the joint, but also the strength of the member itself. To do this, we need to determine the internal reaction forces within the beam.

③ Transfer of Roof Loads on a High Posted Cape

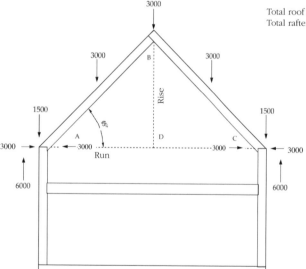

Total roof load = 12000lbs
Total rafter load = 6000lbs

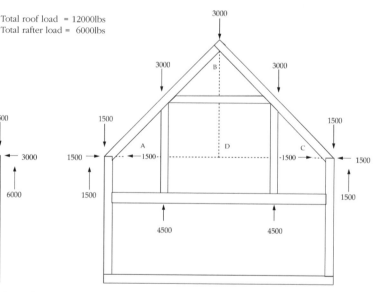

An extremely simplified version of a high posted cape without interior framing. Tie beam joints are in tension. Thrust at eaves is determined by using the equation: Fx = ½W/P, where Fx = horizontal thrust, W = rafter load (1/2 total load), and P = pitch (run/rise). In this example, a 12 on 12 pitch, P = 1, the total rafter load, W = 6000lbs: Fx = 1/2W/P = 1/2 x 6000/(12/12) = 3000lbs. The force load at the tie beam joint will be greater as it is subject to the lever rule. See page 97 for these formulas.

Addition of queen posts and collar tie diverts primary roof load vertically to tie beam. Horizontal thrust is reduced dramatically. Thrust depicted is theoretical only. If the tie beam was supported so that it could not sag, horizontal thrust would be reduced to zero, so long as collar tie and queen post joinery were properly joined.

Compression, Tension and Shearing Stresses

When a simply supported beam is subjected to an externally applied load *vertical shearing stresses* are produced. Vertical shearing stress is never the direct cause of beam failure, but is merely the measure of the reactionary forces acting on the cross-section of a beam (perpendicular to the grain) under a load. Vertical shear, in turn, produces internal stresses. There are three types of internal stresses: *tensile*, *compressive*, and *shearing*. Using a simply supported beam as an example (illustrated on page 80), we can see that as it begins to bend under loading the wood fibers above the neutral axis (theoretically the horizontal center of the beam) are compressed together, in effect making the fibers shorter—*compression parallel to the grain*. The wood fibers below the neutral axis, however, are being stretched apart, tending to make the fibers longer—*tension parallel to the grain*. This produces two opposing horizontal forces, or a sliding action, within the beam along the neutral axis. If the force is too great, the fibers will physically slip by each other. These internal reactionary forces produce *horizontal shearing stress* (shear parallel to the grain). When the fibers actually do slide, the result is horizontal shear failure. Horizontal shear failure is usually the first failure to occur in a beam under loading. Once this happens, complete beam failure is likely.

According to Gere and Timoshenko in the 3rd edition of *Mechanics and Materials*, "The intensity of force (that is, the force per unit area) is called the stress..." So, we can define stress as the average force acting per unit area inside a member. The amount of stress, being the measure of the intensity of an applied force acting on a beam, is measured in pounds of force per unit area (in the U.S. the norm is pounds per square inch, or psi). The amount of stress can be determined by using the equation: $S = P/A$

In which: S = unit stress; P = the magnitude of the force (load) in pounds, and A = the cross-sectional area, inches^2.

Vertical shear force at any point along a simple beam can be determined by the equation $V = P/2$ (see dia. 4.23 pg. 80).

If a beam is subjected to multiple loading conditions, determining the ultimate strength may require numerous complex calculations. For beams subjected to uniformly distributed loads, such as floor joists, purlins and common rafters, appropriate beam design requires three calculations to determine; *horizontal shear*, *deflection* and *design in bending*. Because horizontal shear failure is usually the first failure to occur, this is the place to begin. It is also a rather simple and straight-forward equation to carry out. If the horizontal stress is less than 50% of that allowable, it will likely pass the other design factors, i.e., design in bending and deflection.

The equation to determine the horizontal shearing stress (H) in a simply supported beam of rectangular cross-section can be found on page 80. This is a simplified version of the equation, and is applicable to beams of rectangular cross-section *only*. The equation (3V/2bd) results in a value of shear force per square inch of section area. As an example, say we have a 6 x 8 white pine beam spanning 12 feet, subjected to a 1500 pound (P) distributed load. We find:

$V = P/2 = 1500/2 = 750$ lbs.

$3V = 3 \times 750 = 2250$ lbs; $2bd = 2 \times 6 \times 8 = 96$ in^2;

$H = 2250/96 = 23.4375$ psi.

The safe working stresses in horizontal shear for white pine is 120psi. (see Table 1, page 98). In this case the beam is well within safe loading limits for horizontal shear. This is only one factor used in beam design. One should also check for design in bending and deflection. These formulas can be found on pages 230-232.

Dutch tenons make great tension joints and offer an attractive way to strengthen a joint to resist shearing forces in tension. The strength comes from increasing the area resisting the force by the elongated tenon. This tenon was carved by a student in the Spring 2000 workshop.

The frame below addresses tension forces in a high post bent design by joining what is essentially a hammer beam with an English tying joint to a queen post that is acting as a hammer post, only that it joins directly to the lower tie as if it were a queen. Oskaloosa, Kansas 2004.

Tension Joinery

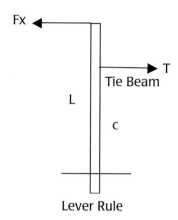

Fx
T
Tie Beam
L
c

Lever Rule

The lever rule can be used to determine load forces at the base of a lever arm, which is the condition faced in the example of the high posted cape. In our example: Fx = 3,000lbs, L = 12', c = 8' or 3000 x (12/8) = 4500 lbs.

Compression and Tension Members

As illustrated in diagram 1 (page 92), we can see that a simple framework consists of both compression and tension members. Ideally, we want to design frames so that all of the members are working in compression because the whole cross section of the timber is resisting the force—not just the joinery. Members in tension rely on a reduced section of wood—the area remaining in the tenon or mortise—to resist the force. While we may be able to design a frame that consists totally of compression members and compression joinery, there are times when tension joinery cannot be avoided, or is even desired, in order to create a particular bent design.

To illustrate the forces of pure tension on a member we can use the example of a High Posted Cape (Dia. 3, page 94). As we will soon find out, there are certain flaws in this design. For this reason, however, it proves to be a good example in order to gain a better understanding of how to determine force loads and subsequently, the design of tension joinery.

In our example, the tie beam is the only thing that prevents the building from spreading and ultimately collapsing. If the roof pitch is a 45° angle, and there are no other members transferring the loads within the framework (collar ties, king post or queen posts) then half of the rafter load, or 1/4 of the total roof load, will be transferred to horizontal thrust on the joints at the foot of the rafter. (To determine horizontal thrust for roof pitches other than 12 on 12, use; Fx = ½W/P)

The force on the tie beam joint, however, will be greater because the cantilevered post is acting as a *lever arm*, and is subject to the *lever rule*, which is a measure of length times force. The formulae in this application would be: $T = Fx(L/c)$, where; T = tensile force on tie beam joint, Fx = horizontal thrust at top of post, L = total length of post, and c = length of post from foot to tie beam. In our example Fx = 3,000lbs, L = 12', c = 8'. Resulting in 4500lbs

Depending on the total roof load, we may find that additional members are required to alleviate thrust, or we may be able to adjust the proportions of the mortise and tenon, add more pegs, etc. Before we build the building, it is necessary to analyze the forces and the components of the joints.

The frame to the right uses appropriate structural design to redirect all force loads in a 2 story clear-span structure into a bent design consisting primarily of compression members and compression joinery. This is essentially a double hammerbeam truss, with the lower hammer post supporting the upper hammer beam directly, as if it were an aisle post. Appleton, WI, 1991.

Tension Joints

Our sample bent has a total roof load of 12000 pounds, or 6000 pounds downward force on each rafter. As a result, the outward thrust at the foot of each rafter is 3,000 pounds; $Fx = \frac{1}{2}W/P$. Due to the lever rule as described above, the tie beam to post joint is subjected to a total of 4,500 pounds of tensile force. Assuming that the tie beam is a 7 x 12 white pine timber, let's see what is necessary to resist this load.

Diagram 4 shows a mortise and tenon joint which may typically be used to join a tie beam to a post. The tie beam is a 7 x 12 white pine and has a tenon two inches wide and ten inches long, which extends through a 7 x 10 white pine post. Two, 1 inch oak pegs and a wedged half dovetail secure the joint. To determine the safe working load we have three elements of the joint to analyze: 1) *the bearing strength of the tenon resisting the pegs in double horizontal shear, and the wedged half dovetail in single shear;* 2) *the strength of the two oak pegs in double vertical shear;* and 3) *the bearing strength of the sides of the mortise in tension perpendicular to the grain resulting from the stress imposed by the pegs.*

All trusses have both compression and tension members, and tension and compression joints. While the king post is a tension member, the top joint—joining rafters to king post—is a compression joint. The lower tie is a tension member and the joint as shown above—joining ties to king post—is a tension joint. In the truss above (and on page 92), which is a 32′ clear-span, strong backs are used to provide lateral support while the truss is being lifted.

This frame has a combination of compression and tension members. The main king post bents span 22 feet.. The tie beam and king post are tension members and are joined with wedged half dovetail tenons. The hammerbeam bent primarily consists of compression members and compression joints. The half octagon is essentially all tension members; struts, king post & plates are all in tension. Porter, Maine 2010.

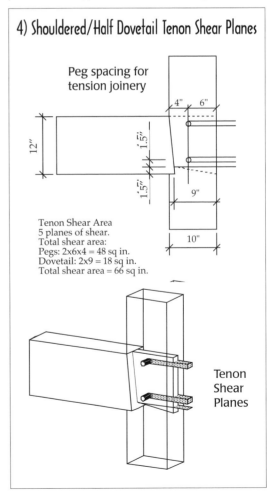

4) Shouldered/Half Dovetail Tenon Shear Planes

Peg spacing for tension joinery

Tenon Shear Area
5 planes of shear.
Total shear area:
Pegs: 2x6x4 = 48 sq in.
Dovetail: 2x9 = 18 sq in.
Total shear area = 66 sq in.

Tenon Shear Planes

The wedged half dovetailed through tenon is an effective tension joint because it relies not only on the peg, but also on the shear strength of the tenon itself to resist shearing forces.

Equation to Determine Shear of Tenon

In our example the tenon is said to be in double horizontal shear (also called *block shear*), because two shearing surfaces (above and below peg) must shear simultaneously for failure to occur. To determine the safe working force in horizontal shear (Z) at each peg we can use the following equation: $Z = H(wl)$

In which: H = working stress in horizontal shear, psi.

w = width of tenon, inches.

l = length of tenon from center of peg, inches.

In our example w = 2 inches, l = 6 inches, and H = 120 psi. To solve the equation: 120 x (2 x 6) = 1440 pounds for each shearing surface, or 2880 pounds for each peg in double shear. If we have two pegs in this joint, the tenons total safe shearing load is 5760 lbs. To determine shear on the dovetail portion of the tenon: $Z = H(wl) = 120(2x9) = 2160$ pounds. The total safe load for the tenon considering pegs and dovetail = 7920 lbs.

The safe working stress (also known as basic stress) for white pine in horizontal shear is considered to be from 100 to 120 psi, depending on the source. Maximum strength in horizontal shear for white pine is 680 psi for green wood, and 900 psi for dry wood. A reduction factor, or factor of safety, of between 6 to 8 is generally used for determining safe working stress in horizontal shear. Table 1 below shows the safe (basic) stresses for a few common timber framing woods.

It should be noted here that large timbers do not increase in strength as they dry in the same proportion that small clear pieces do. This is because timbers tend to have defects (knots, grain slope, etc.) that can increase adversely with drying, offsetting partially or wholly the increase in the strength of the fibers. Therefore, the values for green would should always be used when designing timbers.

Equations to Determine Strength of Pegs

The pegs in this situation are in double vertical shear (perpendicular to the grain). Values for strength in shear vertical to the grain are generally not published because failure of a beam rarely occurs due directly to vertical shear. Strength in vertical shear is closely related to *side hardness*, and *compression perpendicular to the grain,* so these values are often used to determine safe values for vertical shear. This results in assumptions for safe working strength in vertical shear that commonly range from 2 to 5 times that of shear parallel to the grain.

Table 1) Safe Stresses for Clear Wood under Long-Time Loading

Species	Extreme fiber in bending, or Tension Parallel to Grain psi (R)	Maximum horizontal shear, psi (H)	Compression perpendicular to grain, psi (S_L)	Compression parallel to grain, psi (S_P)	Modulus of elasticity in bending, 1000psi (E)
Doug. fir, coast region	2200	130	320	1450	1600
Hemlock, eastern	1600	100	300	950	1100
White pine	1300	120	250	1000	1000
Red pine (Norway)	1600	120	220	1050	1200
Southern yellow pine	2200	160	320	1450	1600
Spruce	1600	120	250	1050	1200
Oak, red and white	2050	185	500	1350	1500

From Recommendations for Basic Stresses, Forest Products Lab., Rept 1715, Supplement 2 to U.S. Dept. Agr. Misc. Pub. 185

Pegs in Double Vertical Shear

In one of my old Audels Carpenters and Builders Guides, there is a chart of *Safe Shearing Stresses* for a few species of timber both parallel and vertical to the grain (Table 6, pg. 231). This table gives a vertical shear factor for red oak of 1000 psi, which is 5 times what it gives for horizontal shear. This equates to the same value given in Table 7 (pg. 236-7) for the *side hardness* of green red oak. Table 7 also gives a value for *compression perpendicular to the grain* of 610 psi. This is slightly higher than that given in Table 1. To be conservative, let's use the factor of 500 psi for compression perpendicular to the grain as listed in Table 1 as our factor for safe vertical shearing stress in red oak. This is 2.7 times that listed for horizontal shearing stress. The formula to determine the vertical shearing stress using these factors is: $Z=SA$

In which:

Z = maximum vertical shear force (shear perpendicular to grain)
S = safe shearing stress, psi; A = shearing surface, in^2.
For a 1 inch oak peg we have 2 shearing surfaces so the value for A is:
$2 \times \pi D^2/4 = 2 \times \pi(1^2)/4 = 1.57$ in^2, where D = peg diameter.
We therefore have: $Z = 500 \times 1.57 = 785$ lbs each peg.
For a 1-1/4 inch peg: $Z = 500 \times 2.454 = 1227$ lbs each peg.

This is a rather straight-forward equation to determine peg strength. However, it relies on an arbitrary assumption of a safe vertical shearing stress factor so the results can vary based on how conservative you want to be.

Peg Bending

Another method is to determine the strength of the peg in bending using equations for horizontal shear. In this equation we avoid arbitrary assumptions by using the statical moment of the area (Q), the moment of inertia (I), and the maximum strength in shear parallel to the grain (H) to find the allowable maximum vertical shear (Z) on the peg. The equation becomes:

$Z = HI/Q$; where: H = Shear parallel to the grain, maximum strength, psi (see Table 7, pg. 237).

For circular cross sections: $I = \pi r^4/4$; $Q = 2r^3/3$; where r equals radius.
For a 1 inch peg:
$I = \pi(.5^4)/4 = 0.0491$; $Q = 2(.5^3)/3 = 0.0833$; and H for red oak = 1210 psi;
Therefore: $1210 \times 0.0491 / 0.0833 = 713$ lbs.

The peg strength in this example is 713 lbs for each peg. This is in the same range as that in the previous example, so we know we are on relatively safe ground. When one faces this situation, always use the lower value.

In our example we are using two pegs and have a dovetail shear plane, making the total shear force on the pegs 2340 lbs (4,500 - 2160 = 2340). This exceeds the allowable shear of 1426 lbs for two pegs. This is obviously not sufficient to resist the load. To gain additional strength, we can do one of three things: 1) *add additional pegs*; 2) *increase the diameter of the pegs*; or 3) *add additional members within the bent to transfer loading, therefore alleviating a portion of the horizontal load on the posts.*

I would tend to choose the latter and add additional members, thereby reducing the load on the post. However, for the sake of understanding the dynamics of the pure joint, let's continue our examination without additional members.

The joint above, with a wedged dovetail and 3 pegs, has 7 shear planes resisting the shearing forces—one plane for the wedged dovetail, and 2 planes each for each peg. Greater resistance is obtained due to increased friction from the compressive force placed on the dovetail tenon shear plane by the wedge.

Horizontal Shear Stress Formula $H = VQ/Ib$

To determine the shear stress on round pegs you can use the horizontal shearing stress formula: where; H = horizontal shearing stress, V = vertical shear load, pounds, Q = statical moment of the area, I = moment of inertia of the section, inches^4, and b = width of beam (diameter) at the neutral plane. In our example we have a total load of 2340lbs, or 1170lbs load on each peg. $V = P/2 = 1170/2 = 585$lbs. $H = 585 \times .0833 / .0491 \times 1 = 992$psi. This exceeds the pegs capacity to resist the load, so we must find a way to gain additional strength. This formula can be simplfied to: $H = 4V/3A$; $H = (4 \times 585) / (3 \times .785)$ $H = 2340 / 2.355 = 993$psi.

Before adding more pegs we first need to consider any additional joinery in the post, such as mortises for connecting members, to make sure there is sufficient area and relish remaining to add more pegs. Peg location and spacing can be determined by using the ratios for peg spacing in Diagram 5.

In our examle the total load on the pegs is 2340 pounds. This is a reduction of the total 4500 pound load because the shearing surface of the half dovetail tenon can carry 2160 pounds of the total load. If we use the lesser of the two figures for peg strength in horizontal shear, 713 pounds per peg, and use three pegs, we find the total load capacity of the pegs to be 2139 pounds. This does not quite meet our requirements, so we can either increase the peg size or add additional members to further distribute the load. Adding more than three pegs would not work in this situation because it would exceed peg spacing requirements. We could increase the peg dimension, even to 1-1/8" and surpass the load force in strength, but this would still be pushing our

Pegging scissor arches joining to principal rafters in an arch braced truss. In this situation the I usually space the pegs 6 times the peg diameter.

Pegging spacings are based on the ratio of peg diameter to distance. Tension joints should have pegs spaced 4 times the diameter from the loaded edge, with the distance from the end of tenon (relish) from 6 to 7 times peg diameter. From the unloaded side edges of timbers the standard is 1-1/2 times peg diameter. Compression joints are less critical, but it is common to use 2 times the peg diameter from the compressed edge. Often what appears to be a tension joint is often load neutral or minimally in tension due to other members redirecting load forces to other members of the frame. In this case, the pegs may be offset to be within 2 to 4 times the distance from the loaded edge. A good example of this is the photo on the previous page of a pegged half dovetail tenon joint.

5) Peg Spacing for Joint in Tension

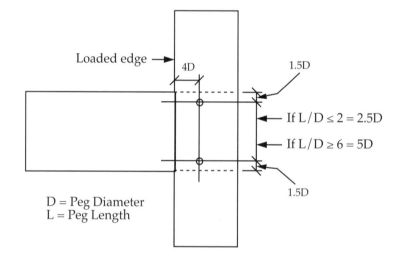

Loaded edge →
4D
1.5D
If $L/D \le 2 = 2.5D$
If $L/D \ge 6 = 5D$
1.5D

D = Peg Diameter
L = Peg Length

Determining Critical Length of Pegs

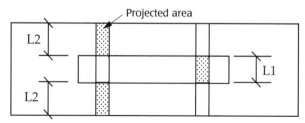

Projected area
L2
L1
L2

Critical length for Tenon = L1
Critical Length of Mortise = L2 + L2
If mortise sides (L2) are less than 1/2 tenon width
(L1), critical length for tenon becomes L2 + L2.

safe long-term loading requirements. The logical and most efficient approach would be to add additional members to distribute the load, thereby reducing the thrust on the post/tie beam joint.

Equation to Calculate Strength of Mortise

The final step is to determine the bearing strength of the mortise cheeks by calculating the shearing stresses perpendicular to the grain in the mortise. This is a little trickier than the previous calculations because determining the actual cross-sectional area resisting the force is not clear-cut. Therefore, empirical evidence and repeated testing of joint variations are relied upon to evaluate working stresses.

In the example of an English tying joint, as above, the joint is a pure compression joint as all of the force loads are acting to compress the members together. The rafter joining directly to the tie beam alleviates any bending forces on the post, and is by far the most efficient way to resist the horizontal thrust due to the roof load forces directly. The critical point in this design is the amount of material (relish) in the tie beam resisting the rafter tenon's outward thrust, and the number of pegs.

Until recently, most of the testing and engineering data available has been carried out using steel bolt connections, though in recent years new testing on pegged connections has been carried out (see pg.103). Steel bolt connections differ from pegged joinery because the compression, and subsequent friction, of the tightened bolt adds additional strength by creating a more uniform force on each face of the mortise. The addition of steel washers or plates helps to further dissipate or distribute the forces, making the two faces of the mortise act more as a single unit. However, comparisons can be made.

When designing steel bolt connections there are two factors which must be considered. The first being that it is assumed that the bolt is 1/16th" smaller than the hole size. Because of this, there is a reduction in the total shearing area because the bolt does not make complete contact with the hole. This differs from pegged joinery in that the peg *does* make complete contact.

The second is that when determining loads acting perpendicular to the grain using bolts a *diameter factor* (v) is used in the equation that essentially increases the strength of the bolted joint due to the compressive forces of the plates, washers and bolts. For a one inch bolt this factor is 1.27—an increase of 27% in the strength of the bolt. Since we are not dealing with bolts, but wooden pegs, it seems logical that if we leave this increased diameter factor out of the equation for pegged joinery then a comparison between bolts and pegs can be safely made. Let's see what we come up with.

Table 2: Basic Stresses for Bolted Joints

	Basic stresses Parallel to grain (S_P)	Basic Stresses Tension Perpendicular to grain (S_T)
Red oak	1350	500
Eastern white pine	1000	250
Southern yellow pine	1450	320
Douglas fir	1450	320

From "*Factors for calculating the allowable strength of mechanical fastenings (permanent loading basis) in seasoned wood.*" Published in, Wood: A Manual for Its Use As A Shipbuilding Material, Dept. of Navy, Bureau of Ships, 1957, page 238-239. Reprinted by Teaparty Books, Kingston, MA 1983.

Tension Joinery

All mortises are pre-drilled prior to assembly. Once assembled, peg holes in the tenons must be drilled using the modified draw- bore method.

Pegging a tongue & fork rafter peak.

Through the process of repeated testing, ratios between bolt diameter, length and the spacing have been determined. By utilizing these spacing ratios in further testing, factors for the allowable strength of mechanical fastenings for a variety of timber species have been determined. These factors are relevant only if correct bolt spacings (or in our case, peg spacings) are used. The working (safe) stress values for four common timber framing woods are found in Table 2. It should be noted that this table gives safe shearing stresses in tension perpendicular to the grain. In this case it is used to denote the strength as if the fibers were being pulled apart, as in a mortise cheek failing. This is similar to cleavage.

As mentioned, the strength of the joint is based on proper pin spacings in relation to the ratio of the pin length to dimension, L/D (see Dia. 5). When determining the strength of the mortise the effective pin length is equal to the total width of both sides of the mortise. The basic stresses in Table 2 have been determined based on these ratios. When the ratio of L/D exceeds 5:1, a factor known as *the percentage of basic stress* comes into play. When L/D is less than 5:1, the percentage of basic stress from Table 2 is 100%. A ratio of 6:1 falls to 96.3%, and 7:1 falls to 86.9%. In general practice it is unlikely that the L/D ratio will go beyond 7:1, however, if it does, additional research must be made. In our equation, the percentage of basic stress is represented by r.

Using the following equation we can find the allowable unit stress (Sa):

$Sa = S_T(rv)$

S_T = basic tensile stress perpendicular to the grain, psi (Table 2).

r = percentage of basic stress.

v = diameter factor.

This is the equation if a bolt were used. In our case we are considering r to equal 100%, and v to equal 1 as described earlier. Therefore, we find the equation can be expressed simply as: $Sa = S_T$

In Table 2 we find that S_T for white pine is 250psi, therefore, Sa = 250.

To find the allowable load on each pin (Z) use the equation: $Z = Sa \times A$

Where A = the net projected area of the pin, A = length (L) x diameter (D).

$A = L \times D = (2.5 + 2.5) \times 1$ inch diameter = 6.25 in².

We've determined that the allowable unit stress (Sa) in our example is 250psi, therefore:

6.25 x 250 = 1562.5 lbs x 2 pegs = 3125 lbs total safe load.

This exceeds our required 2340 pound load on the pegs, so we are in good shape. However, we find that the pegs in vertical shear and in bending fall short are our weak links.

In Review

In completing the calculations we find the capacity of each failure mode using two pegs to be: 1) tenon bearing shear 7920lbs, 2) pegs in double vertical shear 1570lbs, 3) pegs in bending 1426lbs, 4) mortise bearing shear 3125lbs. The weak link is the pegs in bending, though this is very close to pegs in double vertical shear. We could add an additional peg to increase the resistive strength to 2139 lbs, but this still falls slightly short of that required to safely resist the load. It is time to add more members. By adding a collar tie and queen posts, we'd be just fine.

Current Testing and Joinery Analysis

I previously mentioned that until very recently most of the testing on pinned joints had been carried out on bolted connections. The equations and the approach that I have used on these pages were all developed by researching the various information and testing analysis that was available in the early 1990's. Through extrapolation, association and number crunching, I concluded that the equations published here could be applied to pegged timber frame joinery with accurate results. I still feel this to be the case, however, it is always good when new testing results become available.

In the past few years the *Timber Frame Engineering Council* (TFEC), building upon Ben Brungraber's pioneering work beginning in the mid 1980's, began to carry out comprehensive analysis based on physical testing and numerical modeling of pegged timber frame joinery. The TFEC's efforts have resulted in *Standard Design Models* for four failure modes of pegged joinery, culminating in the publication of Technical Bulletin No. 2009-01, titled *Capacity of Pegged Connections*, in November 2009. A brief overview of this testing results with formulas for the *four failure modes* can be found in the appendix (pg. 239). A further overview of this can be found on page 224.

The rafter foot joined directly to the post places the tie beam to post joint in tension. For bents 16 feet or less in width, the wedged half-dovetail joint with three pegs may be sufficient to resist the total load forces. For spans over 16' additional framing members will most likely be required to redirect the force loads on the joint more evenly throughout the frame.

Designing Tension Joinery

Engineering is an extremely complex science based on many assumptions and theories that are not always absolute. Wood, for instance, has so many varying characteristics that no two pieces are ever guaranteed to act, or react, the same way twice. Available information on the mechanical properties of wood are based on repeated testing intended to find the average properties within a specific species. Assumptions as to the actual quality of timbers, the grain characteristics, knot patterns, etc., that can affect the structural integrity of the structure often have to be made in the field. This is why conservative estimations are imperative.

The information herein is by no means a complete analysis of all the possible considerations when designing timber frame joinery. It is intended as an overview only, and should *not* be relied upon as a definitive source. In writing about tension joinery I have attempted to present in a simplified manner what is most definitely a difficult subject. Use it for fun, test yourself, but it is absolutely necessary to confirm your results with a licensed engineer before you cut the frame. Hopefully, it sparks a bit of curiosity to investigate these engineering principles further. If so, then it has been time well spent.

Student flushing off the pegs in a hammer beam with a Ryoba saw in the Fall 2004 workshop.

Top: In a properly designed hammerbeam bent all joints will be in compression. This frame shows the proper pegging pattern. When 3 or more pegs are used in one joint, offset pegs so they are not all in one shear line. Left: A wedged half-dovetail joint with 3 pegs. Braces use 2, 3/4" pegs. Above: Pegging collar tie to rafter. All joinery above cut by students.

Chapter 6
Roof Framing & Truss Design

Arched brace truss with 32 foot clear span.
Red oak timbers. 1981, Freeport, Maine.

Clear-Span Truss Design

Clear-span hipped roof hammerbeam frame with diagonal spans of 64 feet. Douglas fir. North Conway, New Hampshire, 1985.

Examples of the many styles and designs of mediaeval European timber frame trusses survive in abundance throughout Great Britain and Western Europe. While there are a considerable number of discernible truss styles and many unique regional variations, overall, the designs may be broken down into two general categories: *Tie-Beam Trusses*, those having a continuous tie-beam, and *Vaulted Trusses*, those without a continuous tie-beam.

Tie-beam trusses were predominantly used in domestic house construction and buildings requiring relatively short clear-spans. Some of the more unique examples are found in community halls, churches and public buildings throughout England and Europe, dating to the early 13th century. The principal truss elements were often incorporated in the makeup of vaulted roof trusses, and it was also very common to combine elements of more than one design in a single tie-beam truss.

Due to the many different styles and individual variations, it's difficult to separate tie-beam truss designs into specific categories, however through all of the variations, three designs stand out: the *King-post*, *Queen-post* and the *Crown-post* truss. The structural nature of these designs in timber framing pose practical clear span limitations of about 32 feet. They can be designed to span greater distances, and often are, in conventionally built trusses, however in timber framing they tend to lose some of their aesthetic appeal and practicality. For longer spans, the likely move would be to a vaulted roof truss system.

Vaulted roof trusses were primarily used in the construction of churches, cathedrals and community halls, with the earliest examples dating back to the late 12th and early 13th centuries. While, again, there are a number of variations in designs and styles, there are three predominant designs common to all regions throughout Europe: the *Arched-Brace truss*, the *Hammerbeam truss,* and the *Cruck truss*.

Trusses are usually named after their dominant components or principal members. Many times, a variety of elements are incorporated into a single truss, resulting in names like *Arch-braced King-post truss*, *Hammerbeam Scissor truss*, etc. How and why this comes about is due in large part to the individual creativity of the framer or designer. To reach a creative peak, however, the ground rules and principles of truss design must first be understood.

The hammerbeam truss is an extremely efficient clear-span truss design. Spans of 30 to 50 feet can be obtained using timbers as short as 8 to 12 feet. Arch braced trusses, below, are another efficient design, requiring few timbers to span great distances.

I have always considered proper design to be the simplest and most direct method available to satisfy the requirements at hand. I also believe that the purest structural forms, uncluttered with unnecessary components or embellishments, stand out as the most beautiful in the end result. Like good music, it's not always the notes that are played, but often the space between the notes, that create the magic. With music, you can't always express why you like a song, it's all in the feeling you get. I believe we respond to architectural forms in the same way. There is something innate within our souls that recognizes and responds to proper design. While we may not be able to express it, when we see it, we can feel it and acknowledge something special.

Traditional timber frame designs by their nature seem to capture this unspoken quality, but none do it so cleanly and purely as does the king-post truss. A timber framed king-post truss represents the most fundamental structural form. Few will dispute its inherent beauty or that its simple, straightforward lines create an impact that greatly exceeds its complexity. And when we look at it, it makes perfect sense.

Haunched king post detail.

King-post Truss

A king-post truss represents a basic *simple truss,* and is perhaps one of the most common of all structural forms. It is utilized in a wide range of structures, from bridges to those wiry trusses you often see rambling down the highway with a 'wide load' banner beckoning from the Datsun pickup trailing behind.

The structural nature of the king-post in timber framing on one level is very similar to that of the keystone of an arch. The upward thrust of the rafters imposes a compressive force on the king-post equal to the total vertical load at the peak—just like a keystone. Fortunately, compression joints are the strongest, so we can use this to great advantage and rely on king post trusses to be real workhorses.

This upward thrust of the rafters in effect is lifting the king post, thereby placing it in tension (which is precisely what makes it a very stable truss). This enables it to resist a significant portion of both the roof load, and the secondary floor load if the lower tie is loaded. Its resistive strength is limited only by the tensile strength of the king post itself, which is a factor based on its dimension, and the joinery employed at the roof peak and at it's foot where it joins to the tie beam. Diagrams 6.1 and 6.2 show two if the common joinery details.

As with all truss forms, the ultimate strength of the design is measured by the nature and makeup of the joints. While all of the joints ultimately must share an equal portion of the load, the design of the king-post-to-rafter joinery deserves special scrutiny because the brunt of the force must be taken by a relatively small cross section of timber as illustrated in diagram 6.1. To satisfactorily resist the upward thrust of the rafters, the cross-sectional area remaining behind the mortise must be of sufficient area to resist the horizontal shear force (H) imposed by the tenon. This can be determined by using the equation $S_P = P/A$; where S_P is the horizontal shearing stress, P is the load and A is the sectional area. There is also a considerable amount of friction from the surface contact of the members, increased significantly if the shoulders are haunched, but this should be considered only as a bonus.

In order to determine appropriate joinery design, the forces acting on the joints must first be analyzed. To formulate a clear picture of what is happening, it's helpful to think of the forces in relation to how they are acting on the joint, as opposed to the members. In a common force diagram, the arrows illustrate the type of force (compressive or tensile) as it affects the member. Unless other internal forces in the truss are at play (such as a floor load on the tie beam), a force imposed on one beam will produce an equal and opposite reactionary force that will be imposed on the joint. The reaction force of a member in compression is to push against the joint and its adjoining members. In a tension member, it is to pull.

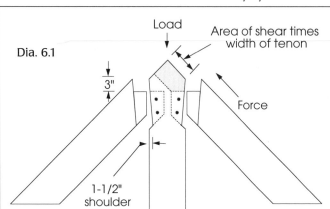

Dia. 6.1

Load

Area of shear times width of tenon

3"

Force

1-1/2" shoulder

Shouldered King Post/Rafter Joinery

Determine the area of shear by multiplying the width of mortise by the length of the remaining section. The total area of shear is then multiplied by the appropriate shear properties of the species of wood used, adjusted by the angle of force to the grain.

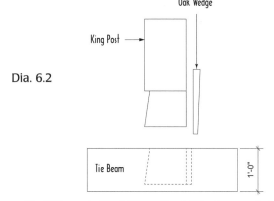

Oak Wedge

King Post

Dia. 6.2

Tie Beam

1'-0"

Half Dovetailed King Post/Tie beam Joinery

This is the only joint in the truss in tension, all others are in compression and will tend to tighten under loading. A common practice is to cut a half dovetail on the tenon with a corresponding mortise cut 1-1/2 to 2 inches oversized so the tenon will drop in, and then wedged tightly with an oak wedge.

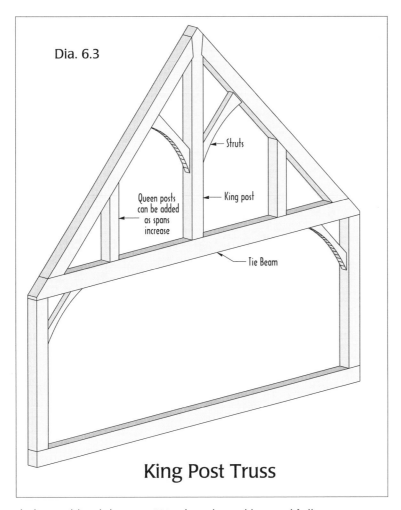

Dia. 6.3

Struts

Queen posts can be added as spans increase

King post

Tie Beam

King Post Truss

In mediaeval timber frames the king-post struts were generally placed to support side purlins and not necessarily for trussing action. For spans under 24 feet, it's possible to do away with struts completely, as long as the timbers are sized appropriately (and assuming there is no live load on the tie beam). As spans increase, the struts become much more necessary and should move lower on the king-post, and closer to the mid-point of the rafters. Queen-posts can be added from the lower third point of the rafters to the tie beam for additional stiffness on longer spans. In this case the upper struts should join the rafter at the upper third points, as in the illustration to the left.

Haunched king post to rafter detail with ridge beam mortise.

The king post truss below spans 32′ and was designed to exemplify the maximum span with the most efficient use of material. This was cut in Fox Maple's Spring 2004 worksop. The photo at right shows the joinery detail of a rafter to haunched king post with ridge beam mortise.

32 foot clear-span king post truss. King struts and queens join at 3rd points on the rafters.

King Post Truss.
This 32 foot clear span truss was designed to provide the greatest amount of space with the least amount of materials and labor per square foot. The king post truss is the most efficient truss design. Clear-spans up to 36 feet can be reasonably and economically designed. June 1994 Workshop Project.

King posts are like the keystone of an arch, a fundamental structural element used for thousands of years. They are also ideal for polygons, such as the octagon below with half-dovetail & wedged struts cut in the Spring 1992 Advanced workshop.

Designing king post joinery to safely resist the load forces in a king post truss is not a difficult process. The traditional king post joinery details work as well today as they did in mediaeval Europe. The only variable is the proportional area of the bearing surfaces based on the load forces. By first determining the amount of force or thrust imposed on the joint, the cross-sectional area required to resist these forces can be determined. The same steps must then be taken for all other joints in the truss.

Understanding how the forces are acting within the framework is essential if one is to design a proper truss. Traditional joinery details provide proven approaches, and in most cases will result in adequate strength if followed in the proportional scale. This requires a general familiarity with traditional joinery. As your frame designs become more sophisticated, and you begin to encounter situations that are stretching the limitations of historical, documented joinery, the more important it becomes to gain a strong understanding of the nature of force systems within a structure.

Queen-post Truss

Traditional queen-post roof and truss designs come in a number of variations. For the most part, queen-posts were commonly used as an element within a truss or structural framework and not as a principal truss member—or truss—itself. In many traditional frames, queen-posts were used to support side purlins. Side purlins, which run along the mid-span of the common rafters, were used to transfer up to half of the common rafter load to the principal rafters. The dynamics as a clear span truss are significantly altered in this case. In this case the queen-post is required to support what is essentially a point load, and transferring these loads directly to the tie beam. In this capacity, the queen-post is acting simply a column supporting a concentrated point load, relying on the tie beam for support. While this design is common, and a practical approach in timber framing, it is not considered a truss because it lacks the necessary components which define a simple truss (a truss must have at least five members and four joints, see *The Makeup of a Truss*), relying instead on the inherent strength of the tie beam and additional support systems. Due to the load transfer—and no trussing action—the tie beam in this design is usually supported by one or more posts on the first floor. Without supports under the tie beam, this design would be appropriate for short spans of no more than 20 feet, and tie beam could not be expected to carry a floor load.

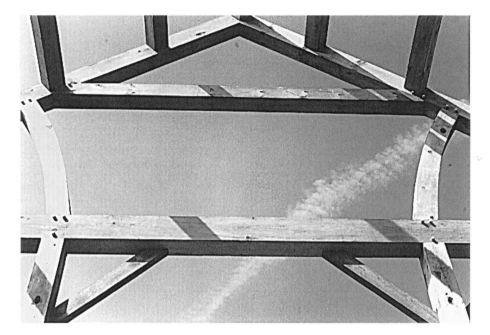

Queen-post trusses are often a misnomer, as they are usually not true trusses, but rather, simple structural frameworks. Queen-posts are usually designed to be a component of a compound truss. In timber framing, queen-post frameworks like this one can be designed to clear-span 30 to 32 feet, so long as they carry no floor loads.

To create a true clear span-truss, it becomes necessary to introduce additional members, such as a collar tie within the middle third of the rafters to oppose the bending load on the rafters, or a king-post, which would stiffen the tie-beam allowing it to carry a greater load. The collar tie effectively relieves a portion of the load transferred by the queen-post to the tie-beam and transforms the queen-post from a *compression member* to a *tension member*. In this way, the truss could be designed for clear-spans up to 30 feet.

Another alternative would be to make the vertical wall post a part of the roof truss. This is easily accomplished by placing a strut from the lower third point of the post to the tie beam, directly below the queen-post, which would be placed at the lower third point of the rafter. This creates a compound truss, and could be designed for spans of 32 feet or more. In this approach, the queen-post begins to resemble and serve as a hammer post. The queen-post should join at the lower third to mid point of the rafter, and fall where it may on the tie-beam. This is a very common method in traditional timber framing, and begins to resemble the dynamics of a hammerbeam truss, which we'll discuss later.

The Queen post trusses in the frame above and below span 30 feet, making a dramatic cathedral ceiling. Plattsburg, New York, 1982.

There are a number of bent framing and truss designs that use queen-posts as primary and secondary components. Some of which can be designed to clear-span 20 to 30 feet. Most often, however, these begin to stray from the concept of a true queen-post truss, which by definition consists of the rafters, tie beam, queen-posts and collar tie, as illustrated in the pictures on this page.

Arch brace joining post to tie beam.
Below; Arched scissor truss.

Below: Setting 30' arch braced truss of red
oak. The 4 arches were joined to the rafter,
collar, post and tie beam. All horizontal thrust
is transferred by the arches to a vertical load
at the tie beam. Freeport, ME, 1981.

Vaulted Trusses

While tie-beam trusses rely on the tie-beam joined directly to the rafter feet (or top of the post) to resist horizontal thrust, vaulted trusses must rely on an immovable abutment to resist spreading. This may be masonry, as was common in mediaeval Europe, or timber framework. In the case of timber framework, the course usually taken is to direct the force to the foundation by making the wall post part of the truss—in essence, relying on the ground floor or second floor tie beam as its structural tie. Just how this can be accomplished for a variety of designs will be discussed.

Arch-braced Truss

The structural attributes of arches have been well known to builders, stretching back well before the Roman Empire. While understanding these benefits may have partially formed the reasoning behind introducing arched timber roofs in mediaeval Europe, many historians believe that it had as much to do with style as structure. The common designs of cathedrals included arches, so why not retain the flavor and build them out of timbers as well. In analyzing the distribution of the forces in arched-braced trusses, it becomes clear that straight timbers would perform just as well, and in many cases, perhaps better.

Arched-brace trusses come in a variety of forms, however most begin as a simple set of rafters with a collar tie located from the midpoint to the upper third points of the rafter, with the arches extending down to, or near, the rafter feet.

Structurally, the arches are acting as struts, laid out in a fashion to create a combination of *simple trusses* to make a *compound truss*. Additional strength is gained from the relatively long surface contact of the rafters and the arched braces. This stiffens the rafter considerably by compounding its own strength properties (we're adding dimension to the rafter). In essence, each joint is acting as a *gusset plate* of enormous strength. This is a critical joint, and should consist of a *fully housed tenon*, at least 2 inches wide by 5 inches into the rafter. When pegged at intervals of 6 inches, the force is spread evenly over the total contact area, giving little chance for withdrawal, and significantly increasing the strength of the rafter.

The single, upper arched-brace design (see dia. 6.4), where the brace joins to the rafter feet and collar tie only, is limited to fairly short spans of about 20 feet. On larger spans, it is best to use the double arch design, as in the photo to the left, with the lower arches joining directly to the post and the tie beam at the tie beam level. By directing the force directly to the tie-beam level, spans of up to 36 feet become reasonable.

Arch braced trusses gain strength by joining arches to rafter, post and tie beam directly. The arched scissor truss below was used for a gabled dormer. This design could span up 20'-24' with no additional members.

This arch braced roof to the left used a scissor truss to make the upper arch. Tim Bickford is waiting for a purlin to be flown in. The arch truss in the top left photo used a collar tie. Above, ripping the arch. Note the full length 5 " tenon.

For design purposes, it is easy to assume that the arches will perform as designed. In practice, however, *the design is only as strong as the materials used for the arches*. The ideal arches would be cut from trees that grew with a natural sweep equal to the arch you desired, as was common practice in mediaeval times. Today, this may not be so easy to do. Unless you have a several hundred acre wood lot in which to roam about looking for the right tree, and the time to spend doing it, you may be hard-pressed to find the right trees to fit your design. It is possible to steam bend the timbers, but this is difficult, time consuming and expensive. This leaves us with the most practical and available method, which is to shape the arches out of straight timbers.

Shaping arches from straight timbers requires that the timbers be of considerable depth. (In most cases a minimum of 16 inches.)

The arches in this frame were made up of four sets of sawn oak with full tenons along contact plane. The lower arches were set as the upper rafter/arch assembly was lowered with a crane. Note the key tenon joining the ends of the arches. Don Morrison, myself, and Mike Sandman are directing the set. Freeport, ME 1981.

Below: Arch braced scissor truss, 32 foot clear-span. Spruce and white pine. Strong, ME, 1990.

In making arches this way, there are a few ground rules that should be followed.

1) *The sweep of the arch should never be cut so as to take more than 30% of the depth of the straight timber at its deepest point, leaving 70%.* (The equation would be; Depth of timber x .3 = depth of sweep.) This can be rounded off to the nearest whole inch. For instance, on a 12 inch timber, the sweep should be no more than 4 inches deep, leaving 8 inches at the narrowest point of the arch. For a sixteen inch timber it would be 5 inches removed, leaving 11 inches, etc…

2) *Avoid cutting the sweep of the arch into the heart, or pith, of the timber.* Always lay out the arch from the side furthest from the heart or pith. If the arch is cut beyond the heart, the arch will tend to check or split on this line, potentially weakening the strength of the arch.

3) *Always assume that the effective size of the arch is equal to its depth at its narrowest point.* If you cut 5 inches out of a 16 inch beam, the whole timber is considered to be 11 inches deep for load calculation purposes.

4) *Survey and choose your arched timbers wisely.* Avoid any timbers with signs of shake or grain run out, and make sure there are no knots or knot clusters near the narrow point of the arch. Look for any visual defects that you feel may affect the stability of the arch, now or in the future. Avoid center-cut timbers. If free-of-heart timber is unavailable, use well sawn, boxed-heart timbers.

Since the arches exert a significant upward thrust on the collar tie, longer spans may require struts, or a king-post above the collar tie.

Arch Braced Trusses

Dia. 6.4

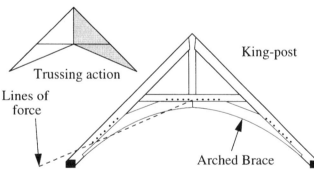

Trussing action

Lines of force

Arched Braces

Double Arched Brace Truss

Trussing action

Lines of force

King-post

Arched Brace

Single Arched Braced Truss

The primary design function of all vaulted roof trusses is to resist horizontal thrust. Structurally, Arched braced trusses rely on a combination of simple trusses (formed by the braces) to form a compound truss which will effectively resist horizontal thrust. The joinery details of the braces to the rafters and collar tie, are the most critical points of the design. The tenons on the braces should be at least two inches by five inches long, and the full length of the angle cut, and pegged from 5 to 6 inches on center along the full length of the tenon. Done in this way, the stress imposed on the joints will be distributed evenly over a rather large area, significantly reducing the likelihood of pull out. On double arched roofs, the collar tie should be placed at the upper third points of the rafters, and the arches should meet at the lower third points of the rafters. On single arched braced trusses, the arches should join no further than 2 feet from the foot of the rafter. This is an extremely critical joint, subjected to virtually the full force of the truss load. The bending loads at the point of the lowest peg should be analyzed carefully to assure that the rafter is deep enough to resist deflection.

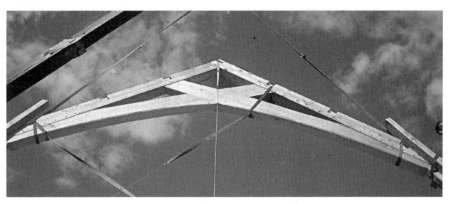

An arched braced scissor trusses like the one to the left can be designed to span 20 to 24 feet with just the 2 piece arch.

Hammer beam, post, arch detail.
Recycled Douglas fir.

Hammerbeam gable bent with sleeved
collar to receive upper arches. Red Oak,
North Berwick, ME, 1984.

Hammerbeam Trusses

The most popular vaulted roof truss, no doubt, is the *hammerbeam truss.* Its visual impact is dramatic, but following a few basic guidelines it is relatively easy to lay out and execute the joinery, and requires short, reasonably sized timbers. It is a compound truss basically made up of two separate trusses, inclined and joined, or hinged, at the peak.

With no continuous tie beam (replaced with intermediate hammer beams) at the top plate level, it is extremely important to address and counteract the issue of horizontal thrust. This force must be redirected to a solid immovable point. (I have seen many photographs of hammerbeam truss frames, some of considerable span, which appeared to overlook its actual effect.) In the absence of a masonry buttress, the traditional method is to divert the thrust to the foundation by making the post a part of the truss. For the design to work, this is absolutely imperative.

This is accomplished by running the lower strut from the hammer beam (directly below the line of force of the hammer post) to the bottom third point, or lower, on the post. In this way we are actually relying on the lower tie, or floor system, to act in the place of a continuous tie beam, in essence, making it a part of the truss also. This approach effectively transfers the load to an immovable, fixed point, and subsequently to a vertical load on the foundation.

On spans under 28 feet, the collar tie should join at, or near, the mid point of the rafters with the hammer post joining no lower than the lower third point of the rafter and resting on top of, or joined to the end of the hammer beam. *The length of the hammer beam should be equal to two thirds the length of the post.*

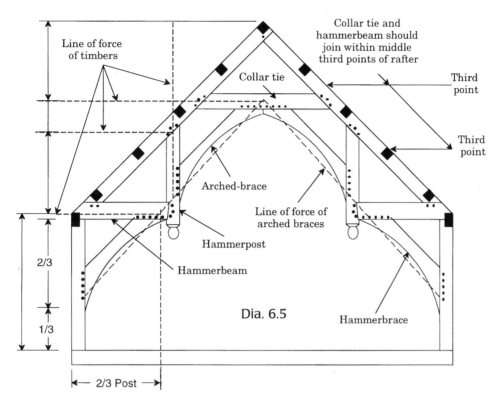

Line of force of timbers

Collar tie and hammerbeam should join within middle third points of rafter

Collar tie

Third point

Third point

Arched-brace

Line of force of arched braces

Hammerpost

Hammerbeam

Dia. 6.5

Hammerbrace

2/3

1/3

2/3 Post

A hammerbeam truss relies on the lower arched brace to resist horizontal thrust. The lower brace should join to the post at the lower third point or lower. The hammer beam should be 2/3 the length of the post. The upper braces should be relative to the angle of the roof pitch. The lower arched braces, in essence, are acting as a secondary set of rafters so they must maintain a continuous line of force. The collar tie and hammer post should fall within the middle third of the rafters. Let the ratio of the hammer beam to post dictate the placement.

Hammerbeam Truss

On longer spans, the ratio can be adjusted so that the collar ties and hammer post join to the third points of the rafters. There is some flexibility in this placement depending on the size of the timbers and the span, however, as a rule-of-thumb, these general locations should be your starting point for design considerations. In doing so, a well proportioned, attractive, and most importantly, sound truss will result.

The upper arched braces should be at an angle relative to the rafter pitch and should form a continuous line of force. These arches may be looked at as making up a secondary set of rafters. It is this interior, secondary rafter system, that transfers the force to the lower ties and subsequently resists the horizontal thrust.

Each side, or braced rafter system, of the hammerbeam truss is acting more or less as an independent truss. The timber sizes can be relatively small because there is rarely a need of any spans between joints of more than ten feet, even in wide spanning frames. Following these proportional guidelines, a truss could be designed to span virtually any distance by simply using multiple tiers of hammer beams as necessary, based on the ratio that each hammer beam should be two thirds the length of the post.

Hammerbeam bent truss with proper proportions to direct loads to post feet. The deck sill plate essentially acts as the lower chord of the truss.

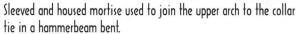

Sleeved and housed mortise used to join the upper arch to the collar tie in a hammerbeam bent.

Upper right: In a hammerbeam truss the hammer posts can rest on top of the hammer beam or pass by. In this frame cut in the 2004 workshop at Fox Maple, each type is used. Right: Rick Gardner and Tim Bickford preparing to assemble a red oak hammerbeam bent, 1990. Bottom left: Hammer beam with Dutch tenon. This frame was built by Ed & Mary Toole, in Chestertown, Maryland. They had no previous building experience until participating in the Waldoboro, ME, 1994 & Sylvatus, VA, 1995 workshops. Bottom right: Hammer post to hammer beam detail with drop.

Crown-post

The term 'Crown-post' actually refers more to a roof system than it does a truss, although there is trussing action at work. Basically, a crown-post is an upright in a principal truss, ending at a collar tie. The crown-post supports a collar purlin, which in turn supports a series of common rafters by their collar ties.

The principal rafter trusses are generally spaced from 10 to 16 feet apart, and the sets of common rafters, from 2 to 4 feet, in bays formed between the principal rafters. With the collar purlin supporting the common rafters (itself being supported by the crown-post), the principal bent is subjected to considerable loading that is equal to the roof area of the bays, and must therefore be designed accordingly.

The common rafters are simple rafters, not trusses, so they can be of substantially lighter timbers, with the key structural element being the collar ties. It is at the collar tie that the rafters are essentially picked up and supported (therefore preventing horizontal thrust at the top plate). For this, the collars must be of substantial depth to resist the deflection under the roof load. In most traditional designs, the common collar ties are located very near the peak—usually within three or four feet vertically to reduce the bending force. The photo to the right shows a very common medieval crown-post roof design that has no principal rafter. Struts join from crown-post to collar, with struts below collar joining to the posts (see photo following page). Braces usually extend from the crown-post to the collar purlin, at or close to the third points of the span for added support. With the addition of side purlins, located in one or more places along the principal rafter, the loads on the common rafters are further distributed, allowing for smaller members or greater spans.

In general, crown-post roofs are limited to spans of less than 30 feet. However, with additional truss elements, such as arched struts below the collar beam and lower tie beam, longer spans can be reasonably achieved.

Quite often, crown-posts are found as elements of other roof systems. There are many examples of crown-posts above the upper collar ties of arched-braced and hammerbeam trusses. In these cases, with the hammer beam and arched braces supporting the lower roof framing, the crown-post is only required to support the upper common rafters.

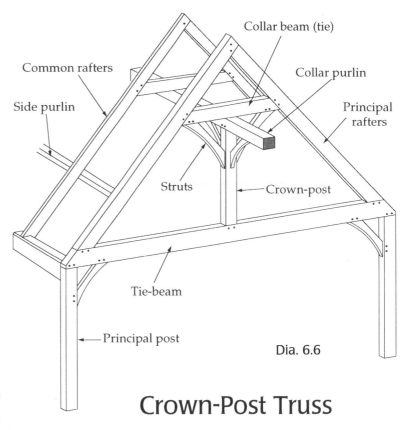

Collar beam (tie)

Common rafters

Side purlin

Collar purlin

Principal rafters

Struts

Crown-post

Tie-beam

Principal post

Dia. 6.6

Crown-Post Truss

Crown Post roof in the 12th century Tithe Barn at Brook, Kent, England.

While not a true cruck, this 12th century English Tythe Barn at Brook, Kent, is a cruck-like structure with elements of the upper cruck design.

Cruck Trusses

Cruck trusses are one of the earliest forms of joined timber construction. They were developed as early as the 8th century in England, and used primarily in the construction of primitive dwellings and barns. The oldest surviving examples date back to the early 13th century. They were common throughout most of Great Britain, with numerous examples surviving which date back to the early 13th through the 15th centuries.

Cruck trusses are essentially pairs of opposing inclined timbers, known as *blades*, in the shape of an "A", to form an inner framework to support the roof and/or walls of a structure. Traditionally, the blades were formed by splitting a curved tree down the middle to create two mirrored timbers, however, straight timbers may also be used to form the same structural concept.

As with most mediaeval truss designs, there are variations in design, but the most common are as follows: *Full Crucks*, the blades of a full cruck rise in one piece from the ground level to the peak, forming the supports for the walls and roof rafters; *Base Crucks*, when the blades rise from the ground level to a collar beam which supports the upper roof trusses, as well as the walls; *Middle Crucks*, when the blades rise from the mid point of a wall (traditionally masonry) to a collar beam supporting the upper roof trusses; *Raised Crucks*, when the blades rise from the wall, as in a middle cruck, but continue to rise to the peak in one piece; *Jointed Cruck*, when the blades are formed by joining more than one timber together. In this design the lower blades usually act as a wall post with the upper blade joined at the wall plate level and rising to the peak, and; *Upper Crucks*, when the blades are supported by a tie-beam and rise to the peak.

All cruck trusses share the same structural purpose by forming an underlying framework to support an outer, non-structural, shell. However, they differ in the fact that while full crucks and base crucks formed the basis of support of the whole building, requiring non-load bearing walls and scantily framed rafters, the other forms (often referred to as *Cruck-like* trusses) relied on masonry walls, and in the case of an upper cruck, timber tie-beams for support. These types share many similarities to arched-brace trusses, differing primarily in the fact that arched-braced trusses were generally joined to rafters and didn't support the purlins directly.

Traditionally, cruck frames, especially full crucks, were used on frames of relatively short spans because they are limited by the length of a single blade. Base crucks, middle crucks, upper crucks, and jointed crucks could be designed to span greater distances, but it is rare to find mediaeval cruck trusses of any style spanning much over 25 feet, with the majority being about 20 feet.

Dia. 6.7

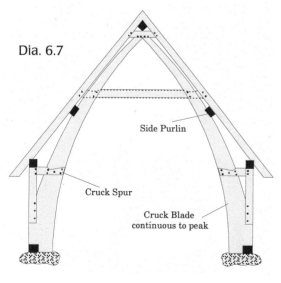

Side Purlin

Cruck Spur

Cruck Blade continuous to peak

Full Cruck

Crucks

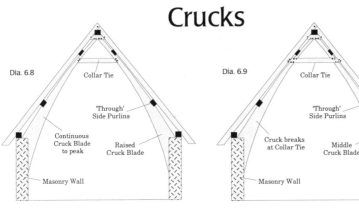

Dia. 6.8

Collar Tie

'Through' Side Purlins

Continuous Cruck Blade to peak

Raised Cruck Blade

Masonry Wall

Raised Cruck

Dia. 6.9

Collar Tie

'Through' Side Purlins

Cruck breaks at Collar Tie

Middle Cruck Blade

Masonry Wall

Middle Cruck

English full cruck frame.

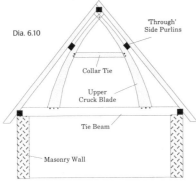

Dia. 6.10

'Through' Side Purlins

Collar Tie

Upper Cruck Blade

Tie Beam

Masonry Wall

Upper Cruck

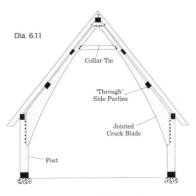

Dia. 6.11

Collar Tie

'Through' Side Purlins

Jointed Cruck Blade

Post

Jointed Cruck

The structural elements of a cruck can be seen in the way the arches of the hammerbeam truss below transfer the load forces to the foundation.

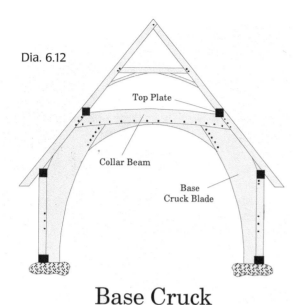

Dia. 6.12

Top Plate

Collar Beam

Base
Cruck Blade

Base Cruck

In full and base crucks, the walls were framed by joining a short spur, known as a *cruck spur,* at the wall plate height to support a wall plate. The wall studding was then joined to this plate and the sill. One or more 'through' side purlins were then joined to the blades with a ridge purlin at the peak. Common rafters were joined to the wall plate, usually with a simple bird's mouth, then laid on and pegged to the side purlins. Some larger designs had a tie beam joined at the mid point of the cruck and extending beyond the blades to support the wall plate. Another collar tie was joined to the blades at a point approximately two thirds up from the base.

The major support in the cruck truss is gained primarily from the steep pitch of the blades, coupled with their relatively large dimension. Aside from a short collar tie near the top of the blades, there is rarely a necessity for any additional ties or struts. Since the feet of the blades are joined to either masonry walls, or directly to sills in a vertical position, outward thrust is virtually eliminated.

Inspired

Our predecessors have left us an enormous legacy in their many examples of fine timber framing. In seeing their works, we are inspired by the integrity they possess, and motivated to raise the level of our own work in the hope of gaining only a portion of their success. In years to come, *our success, too,* will be measured by the integrity with which we approached our craft. And if we are successful, it will be evident in the works that we leave behind, and measured by the onlookers of some future generation through the inspiration we're able to bestow upon them.

The `cruck-like' frame to the right was designed to support the middle bent post to create an open area below a cantilevered floor. Sag Harbor, NY 1989.

The Make-up of a Truss

Webster's dictionary defines a truss as, *"an assemblage of members (as beams) forming a rigid framework."* By structural definition, a rigid framework consists of three members connected so that the three pinned joints do not lie along a straight line. This of course forms a triangle. By itself, a single triangle is not considered a truss.

A truss is formed by adding at least two more members which are joined to each other, and to two of the joints of the original triangle (see Dia. #1). The two existing joints and the new joint cannot fall in a straight line. This forms what is called a *simple truss. A simple truss must contain at least five members and four joints.* More members are not required, and fewer would result in an unstable truss. For design purposes, each leg between joints is considered a separate member, regardless if it is a continuous member or not.

By adding two or more simple trusses together in a single framework, we create what is known as a compound truss. All trusses, no matter what form they may take, are essentially nothing more than an assemblage of simple trusses formed to create a single compound truss.

Theory of Truss Mechanics

The purpose of a truss is to redirect the force loads acting on a framework uniformly throughout its members and joint systems to its foundation, as if it were a single beam. In order to do this successfully, the framework must maintain a state of *static equilibrium* between all members and joint systems.

Newton's theory stating that *for every action, there is an equal and opposite reaction,* forms the scientific basis for the structural principles governing truss design. The goal of the designer is to determine the force systems acting under loading both *externally* (action) and *internally* (reaction), and counter them by creating additional force systems within the framework. The makeup of a simple truss is a pattern which practically addresses these forces and may be duplicated and combined to create a *compound truss* for virtually any design situation, without having to change shape under varying load conditions. In this way, a truss could be designed to bridge any conceivable span, with the capacity to redirect any system of joint loads to any given set of supports.

View of the upper scissors in a hammerbeam scissor truss that oppose the longitudinal truss on the opposite page.

1) Simple Trusses

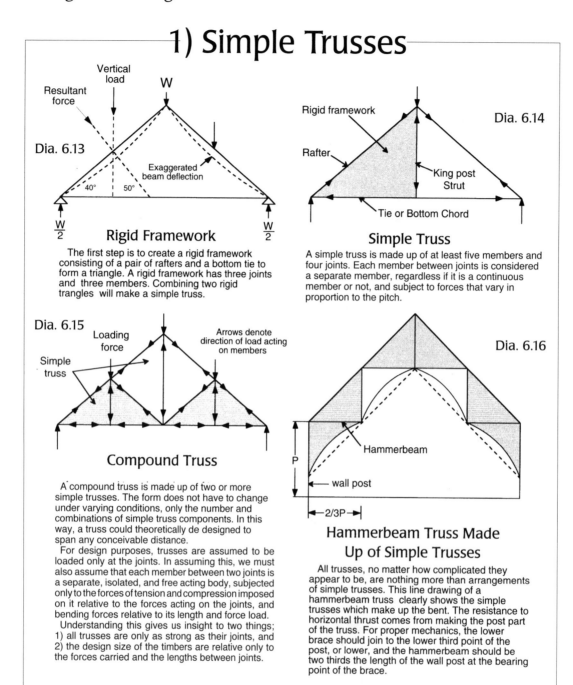

Rigid Framework

The first step is to create a rigid framework consisting of a pair of rafters and a bottom tie to form a triangle. A rigid framework has three joints and three members. Combining two rigid trangles will make a simple truss.

Simple Truss

A simple truss is made up of at least five members and four joints. Each member between joints is considered a separate member, regardless if it is a continuous member or not, and subject to forces that vary in proportion to the pitch.

Compound Truss

A compound truss is made up of two or more simple trusses. The form does not have to change under varying conditions, only the number and combinations of simple truss components. In this way, a truss could theoretically de designed to span any conceivable distance.

For design purposes, trusses are assumed to be loaded only at the joints. In assuming this, we must also assume that each member between two joints is a separate, isolated, and free acting body, subjected only to the forces of tension and compression imposed on it relative to the forces acting on the joints, and bending forces relative to its length and force load.

Understanding this gives us insight to two things; 1) all trusses are only as strong as their joints, and 2) the design size of the timbers are relative only to the forces carried and the lengths between joints.

Hammerbeam Truss Made Up of Simple Trusses

All trusses, no matter how complicated they appear to be, are nothing more than arrangements of simple trusses. This line drawing of a hammerbeam truss clearly shows the simple trusses which make up the bent. The resistance to horizontal thrust comes from making the post part of the truss. For proper mechanics, the lower brace should join to the lower third point of the post, or lower, and the hammerbeam should be two thirds the length of the wall post at the bearing point of the brace.

Joint Systems

For design purposes, trusses are assumed to be loaded only at the joints, and the members are assumed to be under no bending loads, the only variable being the magnitude of the direct forces on the members. Therefore, the ideal truss should be looked at as a system of joints, with members only subjected to *tensile* and *compressive* stresses.

In reality, bending forces do exist, and it is in determining the bending moment of each member that we arrive at the number and layout of joint systems required in a given truss so that it will work as a single beam (in essence, a truss is merely duplicating the force systems inherent in a single beam).

When a specific force load, or combination of force loads, proves to exceed the design limitations of any single member or joint, equilibrium can be regained by adding additional struts to create new joint systems, thereby distributing the forces more uniformly.

If one or more members is allowed to deflect under loading, a secondary force system is created, producing an unbalanced strain on the joint in the form of buckling or rotation. If the rotational forces exceed design limitations for the joint, the joint system, and therefore the complete truss, will no longer be in equilibrium. For the truss to work, *all joints must be in a state of static equilibrium.* This implies that all members must be loaded uniformly and within their safe design load capacity. A truss is only as strong as its weakest joint. If one fails, the complete structure will fail.

By relying on the joint systems as the key factor, trusses can be designed with smaller timbers to carry greater spans. In fact, it is generally accepted that the smaller the members, the stronger the truss, because the dead load is kept to a minimum.

Balancing Structure and Aesthetics

If we are relying on the size of the timbers to resist the forces alone, we, in effect, may not be creating a truss, but merely a stiff rigid framework. In timber framing, we rely on this quite frequently, and with just cause because: *Trussing is only necessary when we are attempting to create structures that exceed the design limitations of the material at hand.*

In timber framing, our goals and priorities are somewhat different than in conventional framing, where 2 by 4 trusses with metal gusset plates serve the purpose just fine. In these cases, the number and arrangement of struts is of little significance aesthetically. The only consideration is the strength of the truss.

Timber framers, on the other hand, must be concerned with a subtle balance of structure, proportion, and visual appeal. As the dominant feature of the completed home, most trusses remain in view throughout the life of the building and often lend the subtle nuances that add, or detract, from the overall effect. And while timber frame trusses are quite often overbuilt to the point that many of the members serve more as decorative elements than as design essentials, we also do not want to muddy a design by adding members that will take away from the visual impact. It is a fine line, but in achieving this end we may be more inclined to adjust the timber dimensions in a given frame to achieve a structural balance (therefore reducing our reliance on truss dynamics) over choosing to add additional struts. Because of this, what we may presume to be a truss, in some cases may not be, in that the members themselves (or other support members in the frame) may be carrying loads that are presumed to be carried by the truss design. In such cases, the actual members are acting as a truss unto themselves in that they are capable of maintaining static equilibrium due to their own particular strength properties, just as a simple joist does, for instance. This is completely acceptable, however the design decisions should be based on true truss mechanics, and not just on our whims.

A hammerbeam truss is a true compound truss, so long as the proportions and proper truss mechanics are followed. It is critical that the post actually is a part of the truss and that the post feet are fixed. In the bent above, the lower tie beam has through tenons into the posts, which addresses this issue directly.

The frame below may be considered an aisled double hammer beam, in that aisle posts were used above the lower hammer beams to support the upper hammer beams.
Appleton, WI, 1991

Types of Force Systems

As already mentioned, there are two types of forces acting on the truss: *external loading forces* and *internal loading forces*. External forces are the result of the total roof load imposed by both *live load* (the working load on the roof such as wind, snow, etc.) and *dead load* (the actual weight of the materials making up the roof). The internal forces are those created within the framework, member to member and joint to joint, in direct response and proportion to the external loading forces.

The effects of any force acting on a framework can be determined by analyzing the characteristics of: *magnitude, direction* and *point of application*. By quantifying these characteristics, we can then determine the appropriate size of timbers, the placement of struts, and the joinery requirements.

Member Stresses

Stress is the result of internal resistance to external forces, and is measured as the amount of *force* per unit of area. The equation used to determine the amount of stress is; $S = P/A$. In which: $S = force per unit area$, $P = applied load$, and $A = cross-sectional area$. The amount of force imposed at any given point along all horizontal members under a uniformly distributed load is measured by using the equation: $W = lw$; *where W is the accumulated load (lbs), l is the horizontal length (ft), and w is the distributed load (lbs/ft).* As the accumulated load on the timber increases along the length of the

beam, the bending stress will also increase reaching a maximum at the center of the span. This point denotes the resultant center of pressure. In members with depth and width (actual material), it is known as the *center of gravity* or *bending moment* of the body. When dealing with theoretical geometric areas for purposes of determining force loads, it's known as the *centroid of an area*.

Since a truss is, in essence, acting as a single beam, this equation is used to calculate the total truss loading. The rafters are also being subjected to a distributed bending load both vertically (the result of snow and the dead load) and perpendicularly (the result of wind) to the rafters. For vertical loading, the force of the load is based on the length of the horizontal span, not

2) Load Distributions

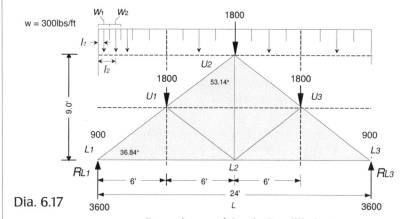

Dia. 6.17

Equations of Static Equilibrium

To determine if equilibrium exists, the known loads must first be attributed as follows:
Trusses spaced 10 feet, roof loaded at 30psf = 30 x 10 = 300. $w = 300$lbs. per lin. ft.
Equation to determine total load on truss: $W = Lw = 24 \times 300 = 7,200$ lbs.
L = total length; l = unit length, w = unit load, W = total load.
Determine loads at joints from L_1 to center and L_3 back to center.
Load at $L_1 = 3 \times 300 = 900$; $U_1 = 6 \times 300 = 1,800$; Load at $U_2 = 6 \times 300 = 1,800$;
load at $U_3 = 6 \times 300 = 1,800$; Load at $L_3 = 3 \times 300 = 900$.
For a body to be in equilibrium the sum of all forces must equal zero. This can be determined by using the *Equations of Static Equilibrium* as follows: Horizontal plane equals; $\Sigma F_x = 0$;
Vertical plane, $\Sigma F_y = 0$; Moment of forces, $\Sigma M = 0$ (Σ = sum of). Moments (forces tending to cause rotation about a given point) are determined based on distance and magnitude of load and can be used to determine unknown reaction forces. To find reaction loads at RL_1 and RL_3 use the equation for Moments of Forces. Loading is calculated at joints. In our example the equation is:

$$\Sigma M\,L_1 = 0: \ (6)(1800) + (12)(1800) + (18)(1800) + 24 \times 900 - 24RL_3 = 0.$$
$$86,400 \div 24 = 3,600: \ RL_3 = 3,600.$$

To find RL_1, reverse order of equation. To check solve for $\Sigma F_y = 0$:

$$\Sigma F_y = 0: \ 3600 - 900 - 1800 - 1800 - 1800 - 900 + RL_1 = 0: \ RL_1 = 3,600$$

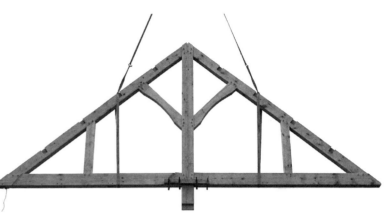

the length of the rafter. For perpendicular loading, it is based on the length of the rafter, as if it was a horizontal member.

To determine the maximum bending moment of the rafter itself, isolated from the truss, the equation *WL/8* is used. This equation is used to determine strut requirements and placement in the truss.

It is unlikely that maximum loading of all types will occur at the same time, so for design purposes it is generally assumed that the total loading at any given time will consist of the total dead load, plus partial snow and wind loads (live loads). Building codes have taken this into account and created standard acceptable live roof loads for various types of building in all regions of the country. For residential houses this ranges from 10 pounds per square foot (psf) in southern areas, to 90 psf in northern areas. A figure of 50 psf for combined roof loads is commonly used for residential houses in many regions of the country. Your local building inspector can give you the acceptable combined roof loads for your area.

The king post truss design above is by definition a simple truss, and therefore a good example to use to understand how to determine force loads within a truss, and a simple framework.

Determining Force Loads

Determining force loads is somewhat of a complex subject, entailing quite a number of considerations. While a full discussion is impossible in this chapter, there are a few equations that are worth being reviewed.

The purpose of a truss is to distribute the forces evenly throughout all the joint systems. This is accomplished with an arrangement of struts. Strut placement in a timber frame truss should be chosen for optimum trussing action, balanced with actual timber design load capabilities. To begin the process, the first step is to quantify the *magnitude*, *direction* and *point of application* of the force loads.

The forces acting on a truss can be categorized as: *known applied forces*, and *unknown reaction forces*. The known forces are the result of external roof loading. For these we have known (or assumed) values of weight, distance and area. To find the unknowns, these known values must first be attributed to the framework. By using the equation for member stresses in distributed loads, $W = lw$, the total roof load can be calculated. Since loading is only assumed to be on the joints, the equation is calculated at all joint locations on the rafters. This gives us the vertical load distribution on the truss. From this we can determine subsequent loads transferred to all other joints (see dia. 2).

Because every action must have an equal and opposite reaction, there is also a reaction force in the form of upward thrust at the supports, which equals the total truss load. On symmetrical structures, the thrust would be equal on both supports. If the truss had struts in an asymmetrical layout, or the peak was not centered on the span, the distribution would vary, requiring a strut layout that would balance the forces. To determine the distribution we use the *Equations of Static Equilibrium*.

The white oak frame below used a collar tie and queen posts with cantilevered hammer beams with English tying joints to address the thrust at the eaves. In this design the upper queens are acting more like aisle posts. The cantilevered hammers were intended to create an overhang for straw bales. Oskaloosa, Kansas workshop project, 2002.

3) Determining Resultant Forces

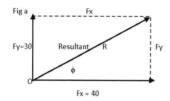

Fig a

Given: Fx = 40 and Fy = 30; Find R
Using the Pythagorean Theorem: $c^2 = a^2 + b^2$
$R^2 = Fx^2 + Fy^2$; R = 50
The following are useful for right triangles:
Sinϕ = opposite/hypotenuse = Fy/R
Cosϕ = adjacent/hypotenuse = Fx/R
Tanϕ = opposite/adjacent = Fy/Fx
To find the angle ϕ use:
Tanϕ = 30/40: $\phi = \tan^{-1}(3/4) = 36.87°$

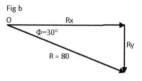

Fig b

If we are instead given R and ϕ the rectangular
components: Rx and Ry can be found using:
Rx = R Cos ϕ = 80 Cos 30° = 69.28
Ry = R Sin ϕ = 80 Sin 30° = 40
If we have a structure that has multiple forces
acting on it the Resultant of the forces can be
found by first breaking all of the forces into
their Fx and Fy components using the method
shown here.
Then: Rx = the sum of all of the Fx values and
Ry = the sum of all of the Fy values.

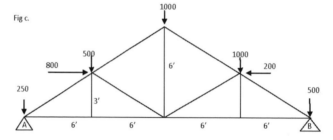

Fig c.

The given rigid frame has a mix of vertical and horizontal loads. Find the Resultant force.
From Fig b:
Rx = sum of Fx's = 800 – 200 = 600 lbs to the right.
Ry = sum of Fy's = 250 +500 + 1000 + 1000 + 500 = 3250 lbs down
From Fig a:
$R^2 = 600^2 + 3250^2$; R = 3305 pounds
$\Phi = \tan^{-1}(3250/600) = 79.5°$ as shown at right:
R represents the total force on the frame and ϕ is the angle at which it acts.
Knowing Rx and Ry is very useful since they represent the total horizontal and vertical force that the structure
below the frame must resist. Posts at A and B must support the 3305 pounds while the horizontal 600 pound
force will cause the structure to rack (typical of wind loads) and must be restrained by proper sizing of the
knee braces or by the sheathing (see Braces and Bracing section). To find the values of A and B the Moments
about A must be solved. Denoting clockwise as positive and counterclockwise as negative we get:
250(0) + 800(3') + 500(6') + 1000(12') + 1000(18') - 200(3') + 500(24') - B(24') = 0. B = 1950lbs.
Since A + B = 3305, A is then 3305-B = 1355lbs. This type of loading can occur with windblown snow loads.

Equations of Static Equilibrium

Static equilibrium is the *"state of a body, initially at rest, which remains
at rest when acted upon by a force system."* Equilibrium exists when the net
sum of the force systems equals zero. The equations of static equilibrium
are used to determine if this state exists in both the vertical and horizontal
planes, as well as for the moments of all forces about any axis, to the plane
of the structure. The equations are:

Horizontal plane: $\sum Fx = 0$
Vertical plane: $\sum Fy = 0$
Moments of joints: $\sum Mz = 0$

In plain English, this means that the sum of all the forces acting on the
truss (Horizontally, Vertically and Rotationally) equals zero, the structure is
perfectly balanced. Diagram 6.17, page 126, illustrates how this is approached
mathematically with an example for all three equations.

Determining Resultant Forces

The direction and magnitude of forces acting within the truss must next be determined to find out what stresses are acting on the joints. From this we can determine appropriate joinery design and strut layout.

When two forces intersect (known as concurrent forces), a resultant force is created which produces the same effects as the forces it replaces. By determining the resultant force, and its angle in relation to the primary forces, we can determine the distribution of loads within the truss. When two forces are at right angles, the resultant force can be found by using the Pythagorean theorem (see Dia. 3). When they are not at right angles, the resultant can be found by way of the cosine law;

$$a^2 = b^2 + c^2 - 2bc \, cos\emptyset$$

In which: a = resultant force; b and c = lines of force origin, and $\emptyset$ = the intersecting angle of forces.

Forces not acting in a purely vertical or horizontal direction can be determined by creating rectangular components. The relationship of all forces to one another are constant, regardless of how the loads may vary. Since all actions have an equal and opposite reaction, the forces determined for one condition will share the same proportional characteristics in all opposing conditions. The principle states: *The point of an external force acting on a body can be considered to act anywhere along its line of action without changing the other external forces acting on the body.*

Using trigonometry, you can determine the resultant of any concurrent force if you know the magnitude of only one force and the angle, direction or point of application (*see Dia. 3*).

These few examples by no means represent all of the conditions or considerations for designing trusses. However, they may help in giving a basic understanding of how forces are acting within a truss, allowing one to determine loads on the joints. Understanding that will allow you to design joinery with more confidence. Anyone willing to spend just a little time to apply these principles to some examples of their own may find that it is a relatively simple process. In doing so, the results may mean more flexibility and creativity in your frame designs.

Scissor truss and valley system. The scissor truss was the upper part of a hammerbeam truss.

Understanding wood, and how to use it, is one reason the 17th century frames on these two pages have survived all these many winters and summers. Wood was a very expensive commodity to early builders, much more so than today. For the carpenters to be entrusted to transform trees from timber to structure, it was imperative that they understood the finer aspects of wood. This knowledge came from experience and was passed down from generation to generation, with each new generation accepting it with reverence, while adding new knowledge along the way. Much of this natural knowledge learned from human experience has been lost in modern times, but it can be regained piece-by-piece, if only we pay attention to our work. The science of wood can only go so far. It is the duty of the craftsman to impart within their work the stuff that will make future generations feel the respect and reverence to maintain and preserve it. Without this respect, the lifespan of a building may be very much shortened.

Chapter 7
Timber & Wood Technology

Working With Timbers

One of the first considerations when building a timber frame is choosing an appropriate timber species for the project at hand. In doing so, three aspects need to be considered: 1) *the visual qualities and characteristics*, 2) *the mechanical and strength properties*, and 3) *the physical properties*. Many species have the visual and mechanical properties, but lack the physical properties required for timbers (a timber is considered anything over 4 inches in depth). Maple, cherry and beech are three that come to mind, but many other native hardwoods fall into the same category. When these species are milled into large timbers they are subject to extreme physical aging defects—checking, twisting, crowning and sweeping—exceeding acceptable limits. To narrow the field as to which species are most suitable, we can gain great insight by examining the traditional choices made by old-time carpenters.

Traditional Timber Framing Species

Carpenters, in nearly all cases prior to the Industrial Revolution, built with timbers that grew locally, or directly from the building site. By being restricted to the native timber supply, the traditions and common practices of curing, seasoning, and even joinery design, evolved for a variety of local wood species through experience. If the supply of premium timbers was not available, and as their preferred species became scarce, they adapted to new species and developed new sets of criteria. In Germany, oak was the timber of choice through the 16th century. By the mid 17th century, the oak forests in Germany (and most of Europe) were nearly depleted, so they adapted to pine and spruce. To the north, in the Scandinavian countries, the stave church builders of the 8th through 11th centuries had vast pine forests as a timber supply, hence the stave churches were built of pine. Pine was the predominant timber in this period, but by the 16th century spruce had become the dominant species throughout Scandinavia, and subsequent frames were built using spruce.

English carpenters, having fewer coniferous forests, preferred the oaks, and were forced early on to manage their forests well. When oak became scarce, they often turned to English elm as a second choice, but their choices were more limited than that of the continent. It was common practice in England to plant a grove of oak trees to replace those harvested for each new building. I have a short story concerning this.

On one of my trips to England in the early 1980's I was visiting with Richard Harris, the Research Director at the Weald and Downland Open Air Museum, and the author of the great little book, *Discovering Timber-Framed Buildings*, in a pub in London. We were discussing the English timber framing traditions over a pint, and I queried something about the use of crooked timbers as not being by choice. My understanding was that the English had depleted their hardwood forests by the 16th century making charcoal and tithe barns (so as to collect taxes), essentially forcing them into woodland and forest conservancy not by choice, but by need (as a result, the now centuries-old forest management and reforestation programs of England manage some of their forests on a 300 year rotation). This led to my questioning the purported claim that the English began to plant trees in equal number to that used for each new building they built.

Throughout most of Europe, oak was the preferred timber framing wood until it was depleted near the end of the 17th century due to unsustainable forestry practices. This oak frame, built in 1687 near Kommern, Germany, is an example of the oak that was available. By the mid 18th century most German frames were being built with softwoods, using much smaller timbers and crooked, natural curved braces became more prominent.

Harris responded that there was truth to both notions, and then began to recount what to me was a most amazing story .

A few months earlier, it seems, he had received a call from one of the deans at Oxford, asking him to come to take a survey of one of the timber framed chapels on the campus. The 200 year old structure was built with English oak timbers and they seemed to have problems with beetles. Harris arrived, and sure enough his survey proved the problem to be real. It seems that a common type of powder post beetle had infested the timbers, many of which, he deemed, needed to be replaced. The next question was where to get such timbers.

Just like most of the old estate manors in England had their own woodland forest, Harris new that the older institutions and universities had their own private forests as well. Upon looking into it he found

that Oxford did indeed have its own private forest land, bequeathed by the King when university was charted, and after a bit of research found the number of the forest keeper. Upon calling the man to explain his need, the forester responded, "I have been waiting for your call now for some time." Harris was a bit confused, but the forester went on to say, "It says here in our records that those timbers would be due for replacement some time in early 1980's, and yes, we have the trees here ready to harvest. We've been preparing for that day, so just tell me when you want them and we will manage the felling and delivery of the timbers."

It seems they kept very good records, and in the book it stated that this particular type of oak was prone to powder post beetle attack once it reached 200 years old, and that these particular timbers would need to be replaced within an extremely accurate time frame of the actual date. The detailed notes and prognostications for this building, and indeed, the plans for its refurbishing were made as they were building it some 200 year earlier in the 1770's. Furthermore, they had indeed planted trees sufficient to replace the building—and they were now mature, 200 year old oaks of a quality equal to or better than the original timbers. This is real forward thinking.

The early carpenters in New England built with oak and chestnut almost exclusively from the first settlement through the 17th century. These were English trained carpenters for the most part, and they hung on to their traditional ways. By the late 18th century, virtually all of the frames in New England were built with softwood timbers. Pine was more prevalent in house frames, and hemlock for barn frames. This was due in part to the abundant coniferous forests, and also because pine had been reserved for the Kings Navy prior to the Revolution. Once the revolution was won, these pines became available to the carpenter to build house frames. In the mid-Atlantic states, oak and chestnut remained predominant throughout the traditional timber framing era which lasted into the late 19th century. The carpenters in the South used yellow pine, oaks and chestnut. Throughout the east coast, carpenters would choose the most appropriate species growing in proximity to the building site. As the westward expansion began to increase in the late 18th century the poor fellows in the Ohio River Valley had to resort to using American black walnut to build their barns. Such were the problems of the New World, relegated to black walnut. They certainly would have preferred pine or oak—something they were familiar with—but who knew? God bless the fortunate.

This later German barn, built to the south of Dusseldorf in the late 1700's was framed with mere scantlings and used much smaller and shorter timbers. Hand hewn timbers were just squared to the largest dimension possible, so using smaller timbers implied smaller logs. Note the wedged dutch tenons extending from the posts. This is a common detail in Germanic timber frames. The photo below shows this detail in another German barn from the same region and time period.

North American Species

From the middle ages to the current day, four common wood species have been favored worldwide by carpenters to build timber frames above all others. These are the oaks, pines, spruces and firs. The vast woodlands of North America, with its countless variety of hardwoods and softwoods, offered numerable options to the early carpenter, but still, these species remained the most common due to their time-proven qualities, workability, stability and structural properties. The following are some of the general properties of the most common species in use today.

Red & White Oak are both beautiful and rich in texture and have great strength properties. Both red and white are relatively stable, as far as twisting and crowning, but both season slowly and are prone to considerable checking if dried too rapidly. Though oak is hard and heavy, both red and white work well with hand and power tools—green or seasoned—allowing clean, sharp cuts both with and across the grain. White oak is a closed grain wood, and therefore has a higher resistance to rot than red oak, which is an open grain wood. White oak is much denser and therefore much more difficult to chop than red. However, both are dense woods and after a day of chopping joints in either type you will know you've worked. Often times lesser quality oaks species, such as pin, black, swamp and burr oak will be mixed in with Northern red oak as if it is the same thing. Beware of this, as these species are not the same and only suitable for railroad ties and pallets.

Preferred varieties: Northern red and white oak. Traditional uses: all structural framing members, principal bent framing and secondary members, joists, purlins.

White Pine is light weight, reasonably strong, and one of the most stable of all softwoods, second only to redwood. It has very little tendency to twist or crown, and because it seasons fairly rapidly, checking is usually minimal if handled correctly. It works easily with hand and power tools in both grain directions. It can become brittle when dry, requiring a little care so as not to crush or chip cross grain or end grain cuts. A liberal splash of linseed & turps on the end grain will help to prevent chipping and crushing when chopping.

Preferred varieties: Eastern white grows from Maine to South Carolina and west to West Virginia. The best quality comes from northern New Hampshire, Maine and upper Michigan. The higher mountains of western North Carolina, Virginia and West Virginia and Pennsylvania grow a high quality white pine as well. Stay away from pine grown in wetter, lowland areas.

Traditional uses: all principal and secondary bent framing, joists 12 feet and under, purlins 16 feet and under. Many pine frames used spruce or hemlock joists and purlins.

Douglas fir combines the best qualities of pine and oak with its lightness and rich color, complemented with unmatched qualities of strength. Dense-grained, old growth, is quite stable, but fast grown second and third growth timbers can be lively, prone to twisting, sweeping and severe checking if the pith is in the timber. It seasons quickly, but can become quite brittle when thoroughly dry. This can make it difficult to work across the grain with hand tools.

Preferred varieties: coast, and interior varieties from Northern California through British Columbia. Traditional uses: all structural framing members, principal bent framing and secondary members, joists, purlins.

Spruce has the highest strength to weight ratio of any species. However, it has a very stringy grain, and can be difficult to work with hand cutting tools. It is prone to severe twisting, checking and spiral grain, and remains rather lively—even

Portable sawmills can produce quality timber, create less waste, and save money. This operator is sawing a boxed-heart timber from a white pine log. Note the variations between the sapwood and the heartwood.

after seasoning—when dimensions exceed 6 inches. Checking in some varieties can become severe, to the point that additional considerations should be taken when designing pegged joinery.

Preferred varieties: Sitka, Engelmann and white. Traditional uses: ideal for secondary framing members, joists, purlins, common rafters, and timbers 6 x 8 inches and under in dimension. Rarely used for principal bent framing, especially when pegged joinery is used.

Yellow pine is dense and heavy. Fast grown plantation varieties can check, twist and crown dramatically in smaller dimensions, but the older tight-grained timbers will remain fairly stable. Though it is very strong, it is also extremely elastic, therefore, it should be limited to short spans to prevent visible deflection. On the other hand, it is resilient and has shear properties nearly equal to red oak. It was the favored wood to build dance floors during the hay-day of ballroom dancing, the jitterbug and dance halls, because of its elastic and resilient quality.

It seasons slowly, and maintains a resinous feel even when thoroughly seasoned. This makes it somewhat rot resistant and easy to work with hand tools, especially when cutting across the grain, however, dense, tight-grained, timbers can become as hard as a rock and difficult to chop when thoroughly seasoned.

Preferred varieties: Longleaf, shortleaf, loblolly. Traditional uses: all structural framing members, principal and secondary bent framing members. Joists, purlins and common rafters when the width to depth ratio is not less than 1 to 2.

Hemlock has moderate strength properties, but is prone to a variety of aging defects that may affect its performance. It is difficult to grade properly, and for this reason is not approved for building federally funded houses, such as FHA mortgages. It is generally stable so far as twisting and crowning, but is extremely unpredictable. Shake and end checks can be problematic. It is very brittle and difficult to work in a green state, and almost impossible to work when thoroughly seasoned. Quite often, the prettiest timber will produce the worst aging defects. It does have a beautiful color when planed and oiled. Contrary to what many people seem to believe, hemlock is <u>not</u> resistant to rot, but rather rots quite rapidly if exposed to repeated wetness.

The hemlock of 200 years ago is a completely different beast than that grown today. It is the lowest priced and lowest quality of all possible timber framing woods and I would only recommend it in barns where animals are prone to chew and eat any other type of wood. Its best use may be in beams of 4 by's to 6 by's for floor joists.

Preferred varieties: Western, mountain, eastern. Traditional uses: all structural framing members, principal and secondary bent framing members, joists, purlins and common rafters. Common for barn frames because horses and animals will not chew it.

Ponderosa pine shares many similar traits to yellow pine and makes a very good timber for timber framing. It has strength properties on par with yellow pine but works more like white pine, though it is heavier and will tend to check a bit more. Ponderosa pine does have structural grading standards.

Traditional uses: all structural framing members, principal and secondary bent framing members, joists, purlins and common rafters.

These are only a few of the general characteristics of the species overall. Qualities can vary widely between varieties of each type, and the region grown.

Old growth Douglas fir timbers milled from logs salvaged from industrial logging waste in southern Washington State.

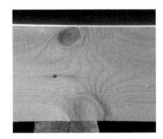

Isolated grain run out around knots have a greater negative affect when on edge knots than when the knot is centered within the face.

Strength Ratio

$$SR = 1-(k/h)^2$$

SR = strength ratio
k = knot size
h = width of face

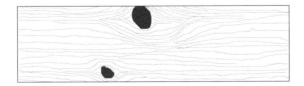 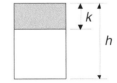

7.1) The formula for determining the strength ratio is based on the size of the knot in relation to the face of the timber. This same equation can be used for any defect that may cause interruption of the continuous grain fiber along the face of a timber, such as localized grain runout.

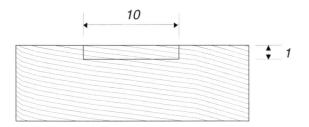

7.2) Grain slope relates to the angle of the grain in relation to the edge face of the timber. The example above depicts a grain slope of 1 in 10.

Visual & Structural Grading

The availability of structurally graded (or stress-graded) timbers suitable for timber framing is limited to Douglas fir, spruce and yellow pine. White pine and oaks currently do not have acceptable Stress Grade standards, and are therefore graded using only Visual Grading Standards (the same standards used for finish lumber). Therefore, you cannot go to the local mill or lumber yard and pick up white pine or oak timbers stamped *structurally select*. This has less to do with their mechanical properties than with the fact that prior to the revival of timber framing, these species were primarily marketed commercially as finish lumber and there was no need for industry to demand stress grading standards. It is private industry that funds all of the testing required to receive official stress grade standards for any given specie from the USDA. Work is currently underway to create stress grade standards for these species.

Visual grading standards do provide parallels to structural grading rules, and the mechanical and strength properties for these species are published. These can be used to provide accurate engineering data. However, most local mills sell their timbers as *mill run*, or ungraded. This leaves it up to the framer to do the grading in the shop, hence, the importance of gaining an understanding of the basic principles of wood technology.

Grading guidelines generally relate to grain slope, size and location of knots, the amount of sapwood and heartwood, and the presence of defects such as shake and end checks. While the technical information may be gained through study, there are other subtle aspects and nuances with wood that can only be understood through experience. Using timbers with a structural, or visual, grade stamp may tell us that it meets a certain standard, but it doesn't necessarily tell us how a particular timber may check, twist, or shrink over time. Learning to read these subtle qualities is something that only experience can teach. It should be the goal of all carpenters to understand both the scientific and the subtle properties of wood.

Table 3) Comparative strength of timbers with various grain slopes to strength of straight-grained timbers			
Maximum slope of grain	Modulus of rupture	Impact bending	Compression parallel to the grain—maximum crushing strength
	Reduction percentage		
Straight grained	100	100	100
1 in 25	96	100	100
1 in 20	93	100	100
1 in 15	89	100	100
1 in 10	81	99	99
1 in 5	55	93	93

Reduction values are shown as the percentage of strength. From Wood handbook: Wood as an engineering material. Agric. Handb. 72, USDA; rev 1987

Grading Criteria

The importance of structural grading is to determine the potential for physical defects to reduce the strength properties of a given timber. The four most significant defects that may cause a reduction in strength are *knots*, *cross grain* (excessive *grain slope*), *shake*, and *checks* or *splits*. The effect that these defects may have on a timber are quantified based on specific criteria to determine an appropriate *strength ratio*, or *reduction factor*. An overview of this criteria is as follows.

Knots—knots reduce the strength of a timber based on the size and location in relation to the direction of the load. Knots in the middle of the faces have less effect that those on the edges. Knots in tension have a far greater effect than those in compression. Determining the actual effect that a knot may have is strictly theoretical, based on the assumption that they are simply a hole in the timber. Assuming that a straight-grained, clear timber has 100% of the strength properties attributed to the given species, the presence of knots will reduce this strength in direct proportion to their size and location. The formula used to determine the theoretical reduction is known as the *strength ratio*. Graded timbers, structurally or visually, take no account as to how the timber may be loaded, therefore the strength ratio generally errs on the conservative side. In practice, if a knot, or knot cluster is placed toward the loaded side of a timber, so the knot is in compression, there is little or no reduction in the strength of the timber.

Grain slope—the slope of the grain is specified as the ratio of the distance of runout along the length of the beam over 1 foot. The reduction in strength for timbers of various grain slopes have been determined through repeated testing. The table below gives the reduction values—as a percentage of strength compared to a straight-grained timber—for a number of grain slope ratios. Severe grain slope is commonly referred to as cross grain. Cross grain is most often localized on the face of a timber, usually around knots or knot clusters. Cross grain, or grain slopes, with a ratio greater than 1 in 15 should be avoided for load bearing beams. Localized cross grain, and cross grain associated with knots can be treated as part of the knot, and the strength ratio determined in the same way.

Shake—reduction values for shake are based on the assumption that a timber with shake is essentially two or more timbers. This reduces the shear resistance, and is of greater concern if the timber is subjected to bending loads, such as floor joists, purlins, etc. Reliable strength properties can be determined by assuming that the cross section of the timber is only that of the interior section. Timbers with multiple shake layers, should be avoided. Shake is less of a problem when timbers are loaded endwise, in either compression or tension. It is best to avoid using any timber with shake.

Checks—checks or splits caused by impact and shear stress (improper felling or by mechanical means) cause a greater reduction than those naturally occurring during seasoning. In severe cases, reductions can be made based on the same assumptions as that of shaking. Surface checks may be insignificant, especially if they are not on the side face of a beam subjected to bending loads.

Through the experience of working with timbers a good carpenter will begin to understand and catalog specific qualities and characteristics that will form a basis for their own personal criteria and standards. In many cases, understanding the subtleties will come only after experience with timbers that have not quite performed up to our expectations. In other words, we must first face the problem before we can determine a solution. Studying the scientific properties of wood is essential to anyone serious about the trade. It would be foolish to ignore this data. However, the overriding goal should be to complement the existing data with the subtle, and often unspoken characteristics that we learn along the way through experience. Pay attention to details. Or as I say to my children, "Be aware of the world around you."

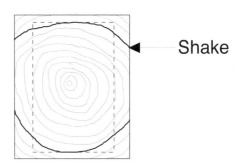

Shake

7.3) Shake is when the annual growth rings separate from each other (shown as the darker lines). When shake occurs, it is usually along the full length of the beam. Strength reduction is based on the net size of the timber within the outermost shake ring, depicted by dotted line.

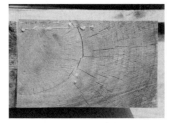

Shake is rare in white pine with the exception of what I call 'pond pine', as in the example above. This timber has a primary shake at mid timber, and a secondary shake near the right edge of the beam. The radial checking is normal for most timbers, but when it is accompanied with shake, it is highly likely that additional shake planes will result.

Isolated grain run out around knots should be considered part of the knot size when considering its effect on strength. If the knot and run out falls within the face, and takes up less than 25% of the face area, it will have little effect on the strength of the beam.

Determining Subtle Qualities

The fact is, all the data that is published about the mechanical and physical properties of wood is based on the *average* qualities arrived at through countless testing and experimentation of clear, straight-grained, wood. No scientific data can be presented that incorporates the specific location, micro climate or terrain that the tree was grown in, but these all have an impact on the actual physical qualities of every timber, individually. Traditional carpenters learned these subtle nuances through experience.

White pine is not just *white pine*. Pines from lowlands are tight grained, dense, and heavy, due to greater moisture content. We refer to them as *pond pine* in our shop. With experience, pond pine can be recognized by sight, but if this fails, the weight—about double regular pine—is a dead give away. Commonly the prettiest timber in a batch, they will tend to check, twist, warp, crown and even shake (a rare quality in white pine) much more than pine grown on hillsides and well drained soil. Oaks are best harvested from rocky hillsides. Low lying, sandy soils make oak porous and weak-grained, with a tendency to split and warp more dramatically. Boat builders in New England always preferred oak grown on the northern slope of rugged hillsides because it was more tenacious and stronger than those grown in the plains and flat lands.

By paying attention to the subtle qualities of the timbers during each production phase—lay out, chopping and raising—the better we become at reading the timbers, and in determining the best placement of each timber in the frame. Better frames will result. Follow-up examinations—after the frame has completely aged—will lend more insight, and further strengthen our understanding of these subtle qualities. Over time, you will begin to gain a bank of specific knowledge that will undoubtedly help in producing frames more efficiently, of higher quality, and with much more long-term satisfaction.

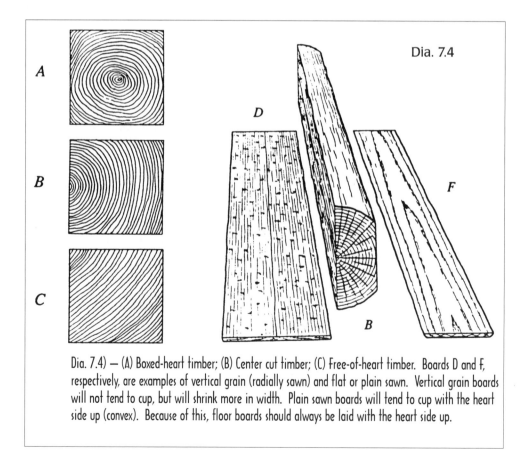

Dia. 7.4) — (A) Boxed-heart timber; (B) Center cut timber; (C) Free-of-heart timber. Boards D and F, respectively, are examples of vertical grain (radially sawn) and flat or plain sawn. Vertical grain boards will not tend to cup, but will shrink more in width. Plain sawn boards will tend to cup with the heart side up (convex). Because of this, floor boards should always be laid with the heart side up.

Working with Green Timbers

Of course, we all do our best work and walk away from the frame with perfectly tight joints and smooth, check-free, faces. We have plenty of photos, and memories of tight joinery and clean beams that will remain unchanged forever. But, if green timbers are used, no matter how perfect the joinery may be, or how well we surveyed the timbers, changes will take place. We must accept that the frame in its aged state is our real product. This is what we must sell, or live in, and find satisfaction in over the long term. Learning to recognize the subtle qualities of the timbers will help in predicting the long term effects of aging, allowing better joinery decisions to be made that may minimize any visual or adverse impact.

Unfortunately, aside from recycled or dead standing timber, timbers come to us from the sawmill in one state and one state only—green. There is simply no way to satisfactorily quick-dry a fresh sawn timber over 4x4 in dimension. When timbers are subjected to rapid, artificial drying, the fibers become brittle and difficult to work. In effect, case-hardening the surface fibers, making them brittle, and robbing a great amount of the strength naturally inherent in the wood fiber. Assuming that thoroughly dry timbers are virtually impossible to attain through standard sources, we should learn the best approach to working with *green timbers*. This begins with the curing, seasoning and handling.

Curing and Seasoning

When we consider drying timbers, our real concern should be curing and seasoning. These terms are often used interchangeably, but I view them as two related, but distinct, aspects of the drying process.

Curing occurs in the early stages of seasoning, and relates to the initial reactionary phase of the wood fiber to being felled and milled into timbers. Once the tree dies and is milled, the wood fibers begin to relax and take on their natural shape. There is usually an immediate reaction to being milled in the form of crowning, warping or twisting, resulting from the inherent tension in the wood, but no shrinkage will occur until all of the *free water* (moisture in the cell cavities) dissipates, and the *bound water* (moisture in the cell walls) begins to leave.

Seasoning is the longer term process of allowing the fibers to stabilize naturally as they slowly release the *bound water* within the cell walls. When the moisture content reaches equilibrium with the atmospheric moisture content (12% to 16%) a timber is considered to be fully seasoned. However, the positive effects of seasoning result prior to, and continue long after, the moisture equilibrium point is attained.

Drying is related directly to the reduction of moisture within the cell walls, and usually implies artificial means. Timbers dry once they are in an enclosed and heated house, or in a kiln. Curing and seasoning, more precisely, is the act of allowing the wood fiber to relax naturally, and to reach moisture equilibrium, without artificial means. Traditionally, builders were not overly concerned with

Log cants, or flitches, stacked for seasoning at a mill in the Black Forest, Germany.

Pine timbers need to be spaced with stickers on all sides for curing to prevent blue stain attack as in the photo above. Pine needs plenty of air. Hemlock and oaks, on the other hand, should be stacked tight to prevent sweeps and crowning. These woods milled into timbers need to relax more than anything for the first several weeks as a crucial part of their curing process. Packing tight, under weight or with straps will help in their long term stability. You want to keep hemlock wet until the day you start cutting it, or it will just fall apart due to its brittleness.

using dried timbers because the process is too lengthy (softwoods require one year per inch, and hardwoods one year per half inch). They were more concerned with properly curing their timbers and allowing them to season for as long as was practicable.

Living trees are subjected to a constant barrage of natural forces. Wind, gravitational pull, snow loading, etc. These forces place tremendous compressive and tensile strain on the grain fibers. To survive, the tree must create internal forces to resist and continue growing. The internal reactionary forces within the living tree create growth patterns that result in physical grain qualities and characteristics that directly affect the quality of the wood when cut. It's almost like their muscles are in a constant state of flex.

When a tree is cut, and dies, the living sap transforms and is replaced by water. After milling, a timber immediately begins to take on a relaxed shape, and any tension in the wood due to the forces, location, and conditions which it was grown under will begin to become immediately noticeable. These may be sweeps or crowns, twisting, shaking, etc. In most species, 90% of the deformations due to natural stresses will take place within six months, however, the first eight to twelve weeks is the most rapid curing stage. It is during these early stages that the most dramatic changes will take place. If a timber will have the tendency to take on a pronounced crown, twist, sweep, or shake, it will do so dramatically these first several weeks. Once fully cured, further changes in the timber will take place as it actually seasons and eventually dries, however these will be minimal compared to the changes taking place in the initial curing phase. These first few weeks can give great insight as to how the timber will rest in its final seasoned state, and where it may be best placed in the frame.

Tension & Compression Wood

A good example of how the natural forces imposed on a growing tree affect the quality and nature of the wood fiber in a milled timber is a tree grown on a hillside subjected to a great amount of wind. In this case, the tree will form its annual growth rings in an irregular manner. The growth rings on the windward side will be tight and close-grained (known as *tension wood*), while the rings on the leeward side will be relatively wide (known as *compression wood*). The greater the variation, the more unstable the timber will be. Both tension and compression wood are called *reaction wood*. It is reacting to the forces that were ever present on it during its growth.

Due to its weaker fiber, compression wood tends to shrink more in its length than normal wood. This can be as great as 10 times that of normal wood. All trees have both tension and compression wood to some extent, due primarily to the prevailing wind. This is what causes timbers and planks to crown. A timber with an excessive amount of compression wood will tend to sweep, bow or crown dramatically due to greater shrinkage of the compression wood to the normal wood in the same timber. Most often, we can use a crown to our advantage by placing it to oppose the direction of the load (floor joists, rafters, tie beams, always have the crown up). By allowing timbers to cure before working with them, any acute, or subtle, defects will become apparent, allowing us the opportunity to place them appropriately in the frame, or discard them altogether.

The curing and seasoning process can be facilitated by the way we handle and store the timber after milling. The following are a few things to consider.

Methods of Curing or Seasoning

During the turn of the century, logs on the west coast were customarily soaked in pools of saltwater before they were milled. This was due, in part, to the fact that they were run down the rivers into the ocean as a way of transport to the mill, but they were also then left in brackish pools for months, and sometimes years, before they were milled. This proved to have beneficial results because when salt is allowed to penetrate into the wood fiber it tends to hold moisture on the surface as the timber dries, allowing for a slower and more even drying process. The surface fibers of timbers under normal conditions dry much more rapidly than those on the interior. This variance is what causes surface checking. If the variance is too great, severe checks can occur. Aging defects will become more pronounced if timbers are allowed to dry too quickly. Timbers allowed to dry slowly and evenly will also have less shrinkage overall when fully seasoned. The practice of immersing logs and timber in saltwater is kept alive today among boat builders.

An alternative to soaking in saltwater used by old-time carpenters was to spread a layer of salt between courses of stacked wood and allow it to sit for about 3 days per inch of thickness. After this period, the salt was washed off with water and stickered for seasoning. This process is effective, but there is a possibility that the wood can become stained by the salt if it is left too long. Submersion in fresh water, though not quite as effective, also works to the same end. Whether using fresh water, saltwater, or salt, the goal is to slow down the drying process so that the outer surfaces dry more equally with the interior of the timber. Fast drying promotes checking, twisting and a greater amount of shrinkage overall. Hardwoods and hemlock can be stacked tight for long periods, but pine should be spaced with 1 inch sticking's immediately after milling to prevent blue stain.

Fewer defects will occur if the log is allowed to cure prior to milling. These hardwood logs at a mill in York, England, have been peeled of the bark, and will cure for up to a year or more prior to milling. Soaking the logs in a mill pond is great for the wood, but the best is to let the logs soak in the ocean for a year or 20. I have hauled redwood and red cedar logs out of the ocean on the coast of Oregon back in the 1970's that had been floating for up to 50 years. Once milled, the wood was like sweet cream.

Handling Timbers

The proper handling of timbers is an important aspect of the framing process. The following is a review of some of the important considerations.

1) Timbers should be ordered to allow a minimum of six week to eight weeks of curing before layout and cutting begins. This allows for the timbers to relax, allowing the initial tension to be released, and the natural crowns to become evident.

2) Pine timbers should be stacked and stickered with one inch stickings between layers, and one inch side-by-side so that there is an even air flow around each timber (stickings should be dry to prevent staining). This will prevent blue stain from attacking the sapwood. Blue stain can happen quickly, so be sure to keep plenty of air around pine at all times. Rows should be no wider than four feet, with the timbers stacked high to gain the benefit of the weight of the timbers themselves to resist twisting.

Oak timbers should be stacked tight (with no stickers) until just a day or two prior to working them, only to allow the surfaces to dry out, as it is hard to mark wet oak. Oak tends to crown, twist and warp much more dramatically than pine, so extra care should be taken when stacking and stickering. Blue stain does not affect hardwoods, and stacking tight restricts its ability to move. In the initial stages of curing, air circulation is not such a great factor for hardwoods as time, as it relaxes into a stable state with time through curing, not from drying. Stickers, if used, should be spaced every two feet for oak and the air space reduced to 1/2" between rows and side-by-side. Taller stacks are preferable, or banding should be run around the stack to help resist twisting. Protect all timbers from direct sunlight.

3) To achieve some of the beneficial results of soaking, water can occasionally be sprayed on them, or they can be left in the weather and rain, being careful only to protect them from direct sunlight. The stacks should be placed in a well ventilated area.

Applying a paraffin based end grain sealer to timbers while curing will result in fewer aging defects. All finished joinery should be coated prior to assembly as well. This is one of the best ways to preserve the quality of the timbers and the joinery by reducing shrinkage and checking. In visiting frames I have built after 10 to 35 years there is a remarkable difference in the timber's quality in those we end-sealed and those we did not. In the photo above the tenon entering an octagonal king post (and the pendant as well) is being coated just prior to assembly and raising. Doug Fir timbers, 1985.

4) Painting the end grain with a paraffin based end sealer will also help. Ninety percent of moisture evaporation in wood is through the end grain. Sealing the end grain slows the drying process down resulting in fewer long term aging defects. Sealing the end grain on all finished joinery prior to assembly is the best thing you can do to preserve a frames quality. U.C. Coatings makes a product named Anchor Seal, that is great for end sealing.

Timbers should be allowed to dry slowly, out of the sun and away from direct sources of heat. If timbers are laid out in the sun, even for a short period of time, the exposed surface will begin to check quite rapidly and you may also begin to notice pronounced bows or crowns due to the uneven drying. This is especially noticeable in hardwoods. If timbers must be laid out in the direct sunlight, it is wise to turn them frequently to allow for more even drying.

5) To help neutralize the pitch in the sapwood of pine timbers, and to reduce the surface pitch from oozing, a liberal coat of straight gum turpentine can be applied to the timbers upon delivery. Turpentine is a natural product extracted from pine trees. The effect is that it soaks into the sapwood and immediately breaks down the surface pitch. The pitch in a pine timber is only in the sapwood, the living fiber, and is usually only on the corners of a timber, and not more than a half inch to an inch deep. The heartwood does not produce pitch, and therefore, is not a problem. This process does not effectively dry the timber, but it does allow you to work without getting pitch all over your tools and self, and it also makes for easier sanding.

6) In the northeast acid rain has become a serious problem when handling timbers. Pine will begin to turn black after one rainstorm if not protected. In itself, it doesn't harm the timber, but it can add plenty of time to the clean up and finishing process. A liberal coating of a 50/50 mix of gum turps and boiled linseed oil will prevent staining for a few storms, but care should be taken to protect timbers from rain before, during and after cutting.

Quality Control

Curing, seasoning and handling are all extremely important aspects of cutting a fine frame. Proper handling will control some aspects, but eventually, it comes down to working with what we have. We do not always have control over the quality of the timbers that will be delivered from the mill. In most cases, we get what is called *mill run* timber. This is ungraded timber, coming from a random selection of logs the sawyer may have on hand. The timbers must be carefully surveyed for grade, appearance and obvious defects prior to the layout process. Determination can then be made as to the best placement in the frame—considering all of the conditions at hand. Of course, we may cull a few pieces out because of obvious defects, but for the most part we have to work with what we get.

The best way to assure quality timbers is to deal with a sawyer or mill familiar with timber framing. The timber order should clearly specify each timbers placement in the frame. If the sawyer isn't familiar with the components of a timber frame, educate him. If he understands the system, he can use his best logs for the most important members, and reserve his poorer logs for non-structural members such as sills, and members with little or no visibility in the frame.

Create a working relationship with one or two sawyers so they will become familiar with your criteria, and value you as a customer. Don't seek out the lowest price. This is extremely important if quality timbers are to be obtained, and many problems may be avoided.

Table 4) Shrinkage Values of Domestic Woods
Shrinkage from green to oven dry moisture content

Hardwoods				Softwoods			
SPECIES	**RAD.**	**TANG.**	**VOL.**	**SPECIES**	**RAD.**	**TANG.**	**VOL.**
Ash: black	5.0	7.8	15.2	Cedar			
Oregon	4.1	8.1	13.2	Alaska-	2.8	6.0	9.2
white	4.9	7.8	13.3	Atlantic white-	2.9	5.4	8.8
Beech, American	5.5	11.9	17.2	Eastern Red Cedar	3.1	4.7	7.8
Buckeye, yellow	3.6	8.1	12.5	Northern white-	2.2	4.9	7.2
Butternut	3.4	6.4	10.6	Port-Orford-	4.6	6.9	10.1
Cherry, black	3.7	7.1	11.5	western Redcedar	2.4	5.0	6.8
Chestnut, American	3.4	6.7	11.6	Douglas-fir: coast	4.8	7.6	12.4
Hickory, true				interior north	3.8	6.9	10.7
shagbark	7.0	10.5	16.7	interior west	4.8	7.5	11.8
shellbark	7.6	12.6	19.2	Fir: balsam	2.9	6.9	11.2
Honey locust	4.2	6.6	10.8	California red	4.5	7.9	11.4
Locust, black	4.6	7.2	10.2	noble	4.3	8.3	12.4
Maple				pacific silver	4.4	9.2	13.0
bigleaf	3.7	7.1	11.6	white	3.3	7.0	9.8
black	4.8	9.3	14.0	Hemlock: eastern	3.0	6.8	9.7
red	4.0	8.2	12.6	mountain	4.4	7.1	11.1
silver	3.0	7.2	12.0	western	4.2	7.8	12.4
sugar	4.8	9.9	14.7	Larch, western	4.5	9.1	14.0
Oak, red				Pine: eastern white	2.1	6.1	8.2
black	4.4	11.1	15.1	jack	3.7	6.6	10.3
laurel	4.0	9.9	19.0	loblolly	4.8	7.4	12.3
northern red	4.0	8.6	13.7	lodgepole	4.3	6.7	11.1
pin	4.3	9.5	14.5	longleaf	5.1	7.5	12.2
scarlet	4.4	10.8	14.7	pitch	4.0	7.1	10.9
southern red	4.7	11.3	16.1	pond	5.1	7.1	11.2
water	4.4	9.8	16.1	ponderosa	3.9	6.2	9.7
willow	5.0	9.6	18.9	red	3.8	7.2	11.3
Oak, white				shortleaf	4.6	7.7	12.3
bur	4.4	8.8	12.7	sugar	2.9	5.6	7.9
chestnut	5.3	10.8	16.4	Virginia	4.2	7.2	11.9
live	6.6	9.5	14.7	western white	4.1	7.4	11.8
overcup	5.3	12.7	16.0	Redwood:			
post	5.4	9.8	16.2	old-growth	2.6	4.4	6.8
swamp chestnut	5.2	10.8	16.4	young-growth	2.2	4.9	7.0
white	5.6	10.5	16.3	Spruce: black	4.1	6.8	11.3
				Engelmann	3.8	7.1	11.0
				red	3.8	7.8	11.8
				sitka	4.3	7.5	11.5
				Tamarack	3.7	7.4	13.6

From the Forest Products Laboratory. Wood handbook: Wood as an engineering material. Agricultural Handbook 72. U.S. Department of Agriculture; rev. 1987.

Physical Properties of Wood

Green or freshly cut wood is considered to be saturated with water. The water is held within the cells of the wood in one of two ways: 1) *free water*, or water within the cell cavities, and 2) *absorbed* or *bound water*, moisture within the cell walls. The free water in the cell cavities is the first to leave. When all of the free water in the cavities evaporates, only then will the water in the cell walls begin to evaporate. This point is known as the *fiber saturation point*. The moisture content of wood fiber at the fiber saturation point is considered to be about 30%. When the moisture content falls below this, the wood begins to shrink in direct proportion to the loss of moisture. The period of time that it takes the free water to leave may be considered the curing period.

Wood shrinks at variable rates based on its relation to the grain pattern and annual growth rings. It shrinks greatest in the direction parallel to the annual growth rings (tangentially). Shrinkage perpendicular to the growth rings (radially) is about one half of this amount, and shrinkage in the direction of the grain (longitudinally) is practically nonexistent except in some cases of reaction wood.

Understanding the way in which a timber will shrink, in relation to how it was milled, will help in determining the best placement of a particular timber in the frame, and also provide insight as to designing joinery to minimize the adverse effects of shrinkage. Diagram 7.7 on page 148 illustrates the type of shrinkage to expect from the three most common types of timber milling; boxed heart, free of heart, and center cut.

Referring to the formula used to determine shrinkage, earlier in this chapter, we find that eastern white pine and vertical grain Douglas fir are very close in their stability as far as shrinkage. However, boxed-heart Douglas

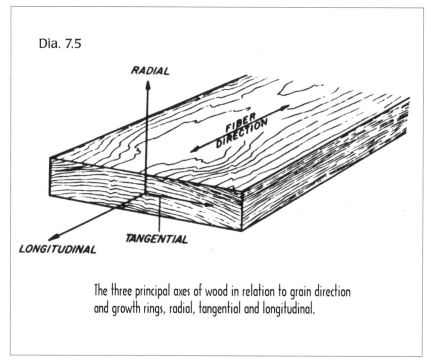

Dia. 7.5

RADIAL

FIBER DIRECTION

LONGITUDINAL

TANGENTIAL

The three principal axes of wood in relation to grain direction and growth rings, radial, tangential and longitudinal.

fir will shrink nearly as much as red oak, and quite a bit more than white pine. A quick review of the Table 4 on page 143 (Shrinkage values of Domestic Wood), shows that eastern white pine is, in fact, one of the most stable of all of the softwoods, second only to redwood. The radial shrinkage of eastern white pine is less than half that of coastal Douglas fir. Free of heart white pine (vertical grain) would be superior to Douglas fir in regards to shrinkage, however it is rare to find white pine trees that large. Volumetrically, it shrinks only 2/3rds as much as Douglas fir, and about half that of northern red oak.

Joinery Design to Minimize Defects due to Shrinkage

Twisting, warping, bowing and checking are the primary defects caused by shrinking. We will never totally control these conditions, but we *can* hope to diminish adverse effects by surveying timbers with some knowledge as to how a timber will shrink. With this knowledge, we can then lay out, position and design joinery that may diminish possible adverse effects.

It should be reiterated that, while the factors used in shrinking are generally accurate for any given species, the actual degree of change, or extent of defects, are greatly affected by the method and speed of seasoning or drying. Checks and splits, for instance, are caused in a timber or board when the surface of the wood is allowed to dry at a much faster rate than the interior wood. The greater the variance, the greater the chance for large, and sometimes, structurally damaging checks.

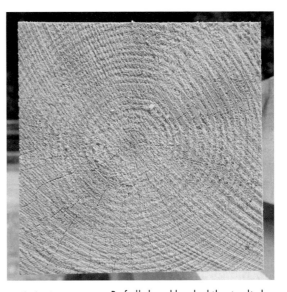

Perfectly boxed heart white pine timber with 35 annual growth rings perfectly and evenly spaced. This is the ideal timber and will remain stable after aging, with minimal checking or twisting.

Dia. 7.6

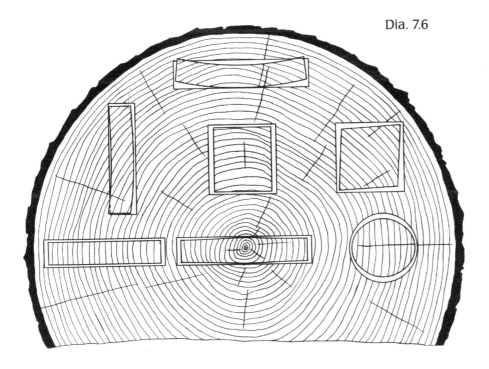

Probable shrinkage and distortions that may result from boards or timbers in relation to the growth rings. Understanding these characteristics will help in laying out and determining placement of timbers in the frame.

Formula For Determining Shrinkage In Various Species of Wood

By referring to the table of *Shrinkage values of domestic woods* prepared by the U.S. Forest Products Laboratory, we can quickly find the percentage of shrinkage for the various woods. From this, we can determine just how much shrinkage we are likely to have in a particular timber. By determining this, we may then begin to analyze our joinery connections and timbers with respect to how much shrinkage will occur. In doing so, we may be able to design joinery and make better use of our timbers, in hopes that the result will be fewer joints opening or, at least, the effect of the shrinking timbers will be minimized.

The equation to find the amount of shrinking is as follows:

C x M x W ÷ S = change in dimension in inches.

C = percentage of change in dimension from green to oven dry or 0% moisture content.
M = Change in moisture content. The equilibrium moisture content (EMC) is the point where the wood neither gains nor loses moisture when surrounded by air at a given relative humidity and temperature. The change is the percentage of difference from the fiber saturation point, 30%, to the EMC, in this case being the average humidity of the house environment (normally about 12%).
W = Width or thickness in inches
S = The fiber saturation point which is 30%.

If, by some chance, we are using timbers that have dried to some percentage below 30%, then the actual moisture content is used in this part of the equation. In this case, we will find the remainder of shrinkage likely.

Since most of our native timbers are sawn boxing the heart, let's run this equation for an 8" x 8" pine timber in which we consider that the shrinkage on both faces will be tangentially, and assume that the moisture content is equal to 30%. It must be understood, however, that a square, boxed-heart timber will shrink more on the faces than in the plane running radially through the center of the heart, to the center of the faces. To arrive at the correct shrinkage at this middle point, we would have to use the factor of shrinkage radially. This may be done, but for practical purposes, determining the shrinkage along the faces is all that is necessary.

Percentage of shrinking of eastern white pine at an EMC of 12%:

C=.061; M=18; W=8; S=30
.061 X 18 x 8 ÷ 30 = .2928

This timber will then shrink .2928" in each dimension or slightly more than 1/4" (9/32"). The final size of this timber will be just about 7 3/4" after all of its drying is completed.

Following this same process, we can determine the shrinkage for some of the other woods that are our likely choices in timber framing. These comparisons may help us in actually determining which timber species are likely to show the fewest adverse reactions or defects due to shrinking. The following are percentages of shrinking for 8" x 8" timbers milled from boxed-heart northern red oak, boxed-heart Douglas fir and free-of-heart Douglas fir, milled with vertical grain on all four faces. In this last case, we will use the percentage of shrinking radially since this is the case for direction of shrinking quarter sawn or vertical grain timbers.

Northern red oak:
.086 x 18 x 8 ÷ 30 = .4128"
or slightly more than 3/8"

Boxed-heart Douglas fir:
.076 x 18 x 8 ÷ 30 = .3648"
or slightly under 3/8"

Vert. grain Douglas fir:
.048 x 18 x 8 ÷ 30 = .2304"
or slightly under 1/4"

While sunlight and exposure to heat in the shop may have some effect on the timbers, by far, the greatest adverse effects due to fast drying is when the enclosed frame is quickly heated to room temperature, and allowed to stay that way for a continued period of time. I have noticed the greatest amount of checking, twisting and general defects in frames built with timbers felled in the summer, and inhabited in the following winter. This is, perhaps, the worst thing to do to a frame, but unfortunately, something that we may have very little control over in the real world of business and life.

Center-cut timber (left), boxed-heart timber (right). If the timber on the left had been cut along the dotted line, the lower portion would be considered free-of-heart-center (and vertical grain on four faces, the best cut of all). The way in which a timber is milled will have a great impact on how it will react as it cures, and the severity of aging defects. The best milling is free-of-heart-center, next is boxed heart, and third is center cut.

Ideally, trees should be felled in the winter months, when the sap is down. According to timber folklore, the best time is during the full moon in February. If at all possible, regardless of when the timbers were cut, the frame should be allowed to stand unheated (or marginally heated for working conditions) for the first full heating season. In this case, if the timbers are milled in the late fall or winter, cut and erected in late summer or fall, and are allowed to forgo blasting heat the first winter, much has been done to assure a slow and even drying process. In essence, this allows for almost two full years of slow drying before they are subjected to any artificial heat. If this is the case, virtually no checking or shrinkage will occur until the home is finally heated. Checking and shrinkage will soon take place, however it will be diminished quite noticeably compared to those that were heated in the first winter. As a customer, you may want to schedule your building plans to accommodate this. As a builder, you may want to bring this to the attention of your customer so that, if at all possible, a schedule may be worked out that will permit this to happen. Remember to seal the end grain on completed joinery.

Effects of Milling on Twisting, Warping and Bowing

The manner in which a timber is milled will have a great effect on the type of aging defects that may take place when it is thoroughly seasoned. The particular properties of the timber species should dictate, to some extent, the milling method that will result in the fewest adverse defects. It is the combined shrinkage, radially and tangentially, that dictates the type of defect that may occur. By analyzing these characteristics, we can better determine a preferred milling method for individual species.

When milling boards or planks (lumber usually less than four inches thick), there are basically two types of lumber that will result: *edge grain or vertical grain*; and *plain sawn or flat sawn*.

Vertical grain lumber is the result of sawing the log along the radial lines, exposing the radial surface (see diagram 7.4, pg. 138). Plain, or flat sawn lumber, is the result of sawing parallel to the annual rings and exposing the tangential surface. Often, both grains are apparent in a single board, but for the most part, only one is prominent. Vertical grain boards generally shrink less in width, but more in thickness, and tend to warp, cup or twist less than plain sawn lumber. In boards, it is relatively easy to determine which is which, and subsequently determine the effects that may come about with aging.

Timbers are a different story. Due to the greater dimension of the stock in width and depth, the likelihood of having each surface contain different, or even both grain patterns, is increased. Beyond the surface grain, there is just much more wood to deal with, implying that varying grain patterns exist successively throughout the timber. Because of this, we must consider a wider range of milling options than with boards. Basically, timbers are milled in one of three distinct methods: *boxed-heart*, *split* or *center-cut*, and *free-of-heart*.

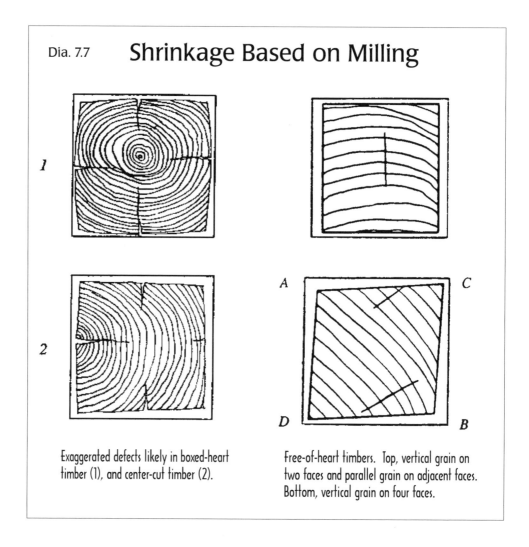

Dia. 7.7 **Shrinkage Based on Milling**

Exaggerated defects likely in boxed-heart timber (1), and center-cut timber (2).

Free-of-heart timbers. Top, vertical grain on two faces and parallel grain on adjacent faces. Bottom, vertical grain on four faces.

Boxed-heart—*A timber is said to be boxed-heart when the center or pith of the tree falls entirely within the four faces of the timber.*

Boxed-heart timbers are generally what naturally comes from second and third growth lumber of relatively small dimension. In most cases, this is what is preferred by timber framers when purchasing native pine and red oak in the northeast. For these species, boxing the heart provides the most stable timber in that there are relatively uniform forces acting on each face. In good quality pine or oak, a well sawn timber (that with the heart centered within the four faces) will have very little tendency to warp or twist since the effects of shrinking are more or less equal on all faces.

Boxed-heart timbers will shrink more on the outer faces than in the middle of the timber. This will make the faces take on a slightly convex shape as the timber dries. Checks, when they do appear, generally run along the length of the timber, and fall close to the middle of each face. In most cases checking will appear equally on all four faces. Boxed-heart pine, due to its relatively stable properties in regards to shrinking, will suffer fewer adverse defects from seasoning than either red oak or Douglas fir. From this standpoint, it is about the most forgiving and appropriate timber for timber framing of all the varieties native to the northeast.

Split or center-cut—*When the log is first sawn in half, exposing the center or pith of the tree on one surface.*

When logs are large enough, it is very common for the sawyer to split the log down the middle in order to get two timbers. This is not the preferred method of milling, for several reasons. One is that when sawn in this manner, the timber is subjected to unequal forces during the seasoning and shrinking process. The face with the exposed pith has the vertical grain exposed, and therefore, is subject to shrinking radially which may be about half that of the opposite and adjoining faces which have tangential surfaces exposed. The result may be a timber that takes on a trapezoidal shape (see diagram 7.7 opposite page). The larger the dimension, the greater the effect.

The center-cut face will also be subject to a greater amount of checking due to the fact that the pith has no strength, and as wood dries and shrinks, the checks and other defects take the path of least resistance. In many cases, the check may be so dramatic that the other three faces will not check at all. There is a net amount of checking that may take place in a timber. It may check slightly on all four faces, or dramatically on only one face. This is what will happen on a center-cut timber, but we can work this to our advantage in some instances as we will see.

Members within the frame that have at least one face exposed to the outside of the building, i.e., gable ends, front and back eaves walls, are the perfect placement for center-cut timbers. If the center-cut face is placed to the exterior of the building, the check will not be visible, and the remaining exposed surfaces may remain relatively free of checking. Center-cut timbers are also suitable, if not preferred, for all exterior braces (if free-of-heart timber cannot be had). In smaller dimensions and in hardwood, you will find virtually no

During the surveying process it is important to locate the areas where all of the joinery is going to go so as to assure the best location, free of knots or other defects. In this process you not only gain an understanding of the quality of the timbers, but as importantly you are essentially building the frame in your mind, which is a great benefit once you actually commit to the real layout process.

checking on any but the center-cut face of the timber. I do not recommend using center-cut timbers as interior timbers where the pith will be exposed. This is not a structural problem, it just won't be aesthetically pleasing after seasoning is complete. Center-cut timbers also have a tendency to sweep because the sapwood shrinks more longitudinally than heartwood. This is not a problem if other members tie into it along its span. If long center-cut timbers are used on open gable ends, there could become noticeable effects of the wall bowing.

Free-of-heart —*When the center, or pith, is nowhere to be found within the four faces.*

Free-of-heart timbers may or may not contain sapwood, depending on the size of the tree, however it does usually imply that the timber is all heartwood (the nonliving portion of the tree extending from the pith to the sapwood). In this day, it is a rare thing to find any type of timber large enough on the east coast that will allow cutting free-of-heart timbers. Free-of-heart timber is most commonly available in western timber species such as Douglas fir, redwood, western red cedar, and western hemlock. Old growth Douglas fir is, perhaps, the most available, as well as desired, by most users of heavy timber. It is still possible today to get 24" x 24" free-of-heart timber with vertical grain on all four faces, although these are only available from old growth trees that range from 400 to 600 years old. Sad to say, these trees are disappearing very rapidly, and I find it difficult to justify using such pristine timber in a frame.

Free-of-heart timbers may be milled from the tree in a variety of ways, or directions to the grain (see diagram 7.4, pg. 138). Because of this, the amount and direction of shrinking will vary in each case. Since we really have no control in milling, only preferences, we are apt to find just about every possible combination in every order that we place. The ordering of free-of-heart timbers does not mean that we are free of the task of analyzing our layout procedure. And, while generally much more stable than other timbers, they will still be subject to defects due to shrinking. The fact is that any fresh sawn timber will shrink and change shape to some degree. We must learn to understand how and why, and then attempt to minimize any negative effects through layout and placement in the frame.

In looking at what may happen to free-of-heart timbers, we can run through the procedures for determining shrinkage in relation to the grain, to determine just how a particular timber will react.

Diagram 7.7 shows two basic ways that a free-of-heart timber may be milled. One is with the annual rings parallel to two opposing surfaces and perpendicular to two opposing faces. The other being with the annual rings at approximately 45 degree angles to each face (vertical grain four faces). As the drawing depicts, the first example will result in a dried timber that will retain its square or rectangular shape. There will be more shrinkage between the faces that are parallel to the grain, but there will be virtually no change in the square of the timber. In the case when the timber is milled with vertical grain on four faces, the timber will tend to shrink to a shape that is more of a parallelogram. That is, the sides will be

Student chopping a brace mortise in a white pine beam of number one quality. In these timbers the knots were no larger than a quarter. I bet you'd like to know my sawyer, and my favorite fishing hole as well.

parallel to each other but not square. Just how much change can we expect? Let's take an example of each to see.

Following the formula for shrinkage on page 146, we find that in our first example—in the direction between the plain-sawn surfaces—we can expect a Douglas fir timber to shrink .3648" or a little under 3/8". In the direction between the vertical grain surfaces it would be .2304" or about 1/4". The shrinkage, in this case, would not affect the square of the timber. By running our calculation for the second example, we find that each face will shrink .2304" (the same as the vertical grain faces in example one). However, since the grain pattern from corner to corner is perpendicular to the grain in one direction and parallel in the opposite direction, there will be a much greater variance in the amount that each shrinks. The diagonal measure of an 8" x 8" timber is 11.313". Using the formula to calculate the shrinkage between A and B (parallel to the grain), we find that when thoroughly dried, the dimension will shrink down to 10.797", a change of .515" or about a half inch. In the direction from points C to D (perpendicular to the grain), we find a change from 11.313" to 10.987" or only about 5/16". This is a difference of nearly 1/4". It's clear to see that the timber, in its final dry state, will not remain square. This will be seen in the joinery when the timber eventually dries.

Just what the *actual* effect this shrinkage will have on our joinery is difficult to determine. But, by determining shrinkage beforehand, we may be able to design and lay out our frames in such a way as to accommodate shrinking with a minimum of adverse effects. Understanding the physical characteristics of wood shrinkage will enable us to make informed decisions, and hopefully, produce better, longer lasting, beautiful joined frames.

Some examples of just how we may design our joinery to accommodate shrinking and defects are worth mentioning.

Prior to scoring the actual layout lines, it is important to make sample layout lines in pencil, especially on angle layouts, to assure that you will miss knots or other defects. In this photo a student is testing out where to begin the layout to miss hitting the knot in a critical area of the layout.

Determining Timber Size and Joinery in Relation to Shrinkage

As timber framing has evolved, it has become a common practice to fully house connecting timbers, not because of strength considerations, but because of aesthetics (housing is essentially letting-in, or recessing the full dimension of a timber into a 1/2 to 1" routed *housing* into an adjoining timber). I have customarily housed purlins and joists, summer beams, connecting plates and braces. Without a doubt, the final results have been compelling due to the tight fits achieved. While housing may take a little more time to execute, it is actually easier to arrive at a perfect, completed joint, than by simply butting the joint to the next timber. However, the simple fact is that the adverse visual effects of shrinkage in many cases becomes more pronounced in a housed joint. This is due to the fact that timbers shrink greater in width and depth (tangentially) than in their length (longitudinally). Therefore, as the timber shrinks in the housing, gaps between the timber and the housing will result. Depending on the size of the housed timber, these gaps may be greater than those which may result from a butted timber.

Housed Joint

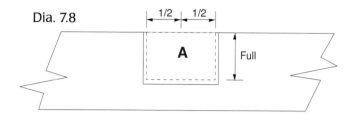

Dia. 7.8

Visible shrinkage around housing will be based on 1/2 the total shrinkage of the width of beam A, equally on each side. Visible gap at bottom of housing will be full amount of shrinkage of beam A, in its depth, as shown by dotted line.

Butt Shoulder Joint

Dia. 7.9

Visible shrinkage gap between joist and beam A, will be 1/2 of the total shrinkage of beam A. Dotted line depicts final shrinkage.

Shrinkage in a Housed Joint

The effects of shrinkage in both a housed and a non housed joint can be determined quite easily by using the shrinkage formula already explained. As an example, let's use a typical situation in which a 6 x 6 floor joist is joined to a 9 x 12 summer beam. Both timbers are white pine. First we need to determine the shrinkage of the joist, then we can determine the resulting visible gap in the housing after aging is complete. In this case, a 6 x 6 pine timber would shrink .219" or about 7/32" (refer to shrinkage formula earlier in this chapter). This shrinkage would be divided equally between both side faces of the joist, resulting in a gap slightly under an eighth inch on each side. The bottom may shrink away the whole amount, resulting in a 7/32 inch gap. In this case, the shrinkage of the housing in the summer beam will be minimal, however there will be some slight change. After complete aging and drying, we would be left with about an eighth of an inch gap around the whole timber.

If these same timbers were joined without housing, the result would be a gap between the end of the joist and the summer beam of .219 inches again (half of the shrinkage of summer beam) or a little more than 3/16". By tightly wedging the dovetails, we may reduce some of the effect of the pulling away, possibly by half, however we will never do away with all of it. In this case, it's a toss up. What do you prefer seeing, the gap around the housing, or space between the joist and summer beam? What you may do to minimize this is to size the joist and summer beam to complement and minimize shrinkage. In this case, the narrower the summer and narrower the joist, the less the adverse effects due to shrinkage.

If we analyzed the joint of the summer beam to the tie beam, using the same dimension of summer, we would find that the same summer beam would shrink .4392" or about 7/16". In this case, the summer, joining to the tie beam housing, would end up with almost a quarter of an inch gap around the beam. Quite a large gap. If the summer beam was not housed, but butted, to a seven inch wide timber, the resulting gap would be about 1/8 inch (half the timber shrinkage). In this case, the eighth inch gap may be much preferred over almost a quarter inch in a housed joint. When making decisions on whether to house a member or not, it is important to consider the location in the house, and where the dominant viewing angle will come from. Design the joint so that it will minimize the visible effects of shrinking.

This is just one example for determining appropriate joint and timber size in relation to shrinking. By taking the time to run calculations on a variety of joinery details throughout the frame, we can determine some basic guidelines that may be followed that may result in better frames. In doing so, we will gain a clearer understanding of what forces are at play, and begin to confidently design and produce joinery of higher quality.

Checking & Twisting

Anyone who has worked with wood, and especially timbers, knows that wood is lively stuff, to say the least. And, no matter what the conditions, no two timbers will ever react in the exact same way to the process of aging. With this in mind, all joinery should be designed so that even in the worst-case scenario, no problem will arise that could seriously affect the function of the joint.

As wood dries, it shrinks. In a timber, the drying process is extremely slow, about a half inch a year in hardwood, and an inch a year in softwood. We also know that as the wood shrinks at an uneven rate, checking occurs. The shrinking wood fibers, locked next to greener, wetter, wood fiber, begin to build up an enormous amount of tension within the timber. The theory of checking in timbers is much the same as that of an earthquake. Tension builds and builds until the amount of force built up becomes stronger that the bond or friction of the wood fibers, and all of a sudden... whamo! The quake erupts. Anyone living in a timber framed home will know the eerie sound of these 'timber quakes', waking you out of deep sleep, wondering if the house is falling down.

As in an earthquake, the timber's check will travel the path of least resistance. If the end of the timber has an open-ended mortise, it is very likely that the check will begin within, or travel through, the mortise. The width of an open-ended mortise may increase up to a half an inch, or even more depending on the wood species, after checking. Subsequently, what may have been a snug, tight fit of mortise and tenon, will now become loose and sloppy. On the other hand, a closed, or housed mortise (one at a mid point within a timber), may spread only up to an 1/8th of an inch, even under the most dramatic checking condition. This is because the wood fiber is working to resist the checking on both sides of the mortise, instead of only one.

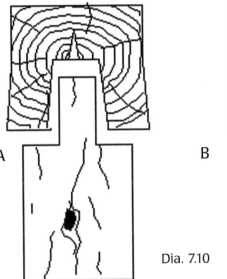

A

B

Dia. 7.10

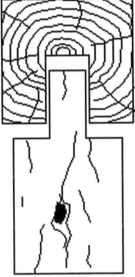

Open ended mortises will start out like diagram B above and will tend to splay open as in diagram A after aging. This will allow the timbers to twist with no resistance. It is best to make closed mortises (or housed tenons) whenever possible.

Now comes enemy number two—twisting. As a timber dries, it dries at an uneven rate, the exposed surfaces drying quicker than the heart of the timber. As this uneven drying occurs, twisting may be one of the negative effects. These negative effects are known as *defects due to aging*.

Just how much a particular timber may twist is based on a number of factors: the unique characteristics found within the individual tree from which it was cut, the particular species of wood, where it was grown, or how it was sawn. Some woods tend to twist more than others. White pine is fairly stable and not apt to twist dramatically, as say, spruce or oak. All timbers will check, but in most situations, it will not affect the strength of a timber or the effectiveness of the joinery. If heavy checking does occur—leaving a sloppy fit in the mortise and tenon—the twisting forces will find less resistance, and subsequently, the joint may open or roll. If this joint is subjected to a great amount of force, there may become a concern as to its strength.

The negative effects due to aging can be down played through proper surveying of timbers, coupled with an understanding of how to read the grain and overall quality of a timber, appropriate joinery design, and accurate layout and execution.

Ahhh, the joy of seeing the roof tree nailed to the eastern peak. To the builder a sign of a job done, and to the owner the beginning of a new life.

Chapter 8
Tips & Techniques

Preparing to pare the shoulder to the scored line.

Tips & Techniques

Setting up the Beamery

The most efficient setup for laying out and cutting timbers is to set all of the principal members up on cribbing in groups so that every timber can be surveyed and assessed at any given time during the layout and cutting process. Saw horses can be used, but they are limited in length, and allow only one or two timbers to be placed at any given time. Extra long horses are cumbersome and difficult to move around the shop, or on site. Blocks, or drops from timbers, can be used to set up cribbing, but if it's your first frame, there's none to be had until you've cut several timbers.

The best method I've found to create cribbing is by using what I call *ponies*. In the early 70's, there were plenty of times when we would cut timbers on site, and with a plethora of 2x10 or 2x12 cutoffs from the first floor joists it occurred to me that these could be used to make short cribbing stands, in lieu of timber drops, to make long rows of cribbing. The term pony was coined, as they were little horses, and they have become a standard in our shop ever since.

Pony's are light weight, easy to transport, and make great stools for sitting around a campfire after a raising. As I see it, they are indispensable to the life of a timber framer, and perhaps the next best thing to a good chisel for making a profitable living in this trade.

The cribbing wants to be set up so you have plenty of room to move around the ends and the sides. Setting up a crib for each set of principal framing members, posts, rafters, tie beams, etc., will make it easier to keep the frame organized in your mind. Orient the timbers on the crib in relation to how they will be in the frame. For a set of rafters for instance, start left to right in pairs with North I, South I; North II, South II, etc., and keep feet and peaks all in the same direction.

Laying out timbers requires careful attention to detail. Even slight discrepancies in measurements or angles can lead to problems during assembly, and or joints with gaps. This is especially true for joints with critical angles and multiple interfaces, like the rafter to haunched king post joint above.

Timbers should be set up on cribbing at the correct height and with sufficient space to work on both sides and to roll them. In this photo you can see the rafters, plates, and principal posts are all grouped together and oriented by their location in the frame.

Surveying Timbers

The first step in the layout process is to survey the load of timbers for the frame. Spread and organize all the principal framing members out on cribbing and take an initial survey for natural and milling defects, and the milling method. Place visual defects on exterior faces. Center-cut timber faces should be placed on the exterior surface of the frame. The center bents will be subjected to twice the loading as gable bents, so put the best timbers in these locations. They are also the most visible. Survey for knot clusters and grain run out to avoid putting them in the middle of a joint, or the middle of a carrying timber subjected to substantial loading. Grain slope, or run out, with a ratio less than 1 in 15 should be considered carefully. Grain run out of less than 1 in 10 should be avoided for any horizontal member, except sills resting on a foundation. Isolated grain slope around knots is less worrisome, and can be considered to reduce the beam strength the same as a knot, but you need to survey all four sides of the timber to see what percentage of the timber is affected by the defect. Isolated grain slope and knots larger than 25% of the face should be oriented to the compression side of the beam.

Don't assume the timbers were milled accurately, even if they came planed four sides. Take a random measure of all timber dimensions and check for square before you start laying out and making cuts. All of the timbers in the frame are connected, so to lay out a principal post you need the plates, ties, rafters all accessible to map and coordinate joinery. If all the timbers are spread out on cribbing, this is easy to do. If it is not possible to measure the actual timber that will be joined to the posts, tie beams, etc., take a survey and use the smallest timber to be the standard dimension. This allows for the initial layout of mortises and the rough out to begin, with the option to go back and make final scoring layout after the adjoining members have been worked and the final dimensions established. If the timbers do measure up to standard dimension, you can easily make adjustments to mortises after all of the initial layout and cutting is complete. I call this the finesse work. This approach will help to maintain tight fitting joints, and to achieve perfection & grace.

Mark timbers near the end with a builders crayon for preliminary labeling. If changes are made, use a different colored crayon. Orient the frame in your mind. Note the universal glazed look of someone visually orienting a frame member in their mind (or is that just confusion?).

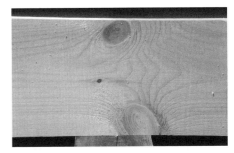

Isolated grain runout around knots in white pine. One of the first steps is to survey all timbers to understand the quality of the wood to determine where to best place them in the frame. This process will also help to build the frame in your mind, which is immeasurably valuable. Mistakes are best made before you cut—they are easier to fix.

All of the principal timbers in this photo are set up on cribbing at the appropriate height and spacing, and in proper order. Ponies and the purlins for the project made up the cribbing. Timber should be spaced on cribs about 30" apart, and overhang the crib timber by 3 feet. Iowa workshop yard, 2004.

Paring white oak rafter feet shoulders with cribbing at the right height in the Kansas City Workshop, Summer 1996.

Fine joinery requires sharp tools.

All of the principal framing members should be set up on cribbing at the start of the project. Using ponies to set up cribbing is fast and flexible. Keep all like members—posts, rafters, tie beams, etc.—grouped together. A separate crib setup for each different group of members is best. Timbers should be spaced between 30-36 inches apart so they can be rolled without hitting each other, and overhang the crib timber about 3 to 4 feet to allow adequate room to work, but not enough to make the timber springy. Proper setup will speed up layout and cutting time, and allow a thorough and comprehensive survey of the timbers—preventing mistakes due to orientation.

Squaring & Preliminary Layout

Check timbers for square in all locations where other timbers will join. This will help to get an overall sense of the milling regularity, and allow you to start building the frame in your mind. If the timbers vary in dimension significantly, you may adjust your layout technique to compensate, and you will need to decide this at the outset. If a timber is out of square it will need to be adjusted before you can begin the layout process. Choose one face as a reference face and plane the others to bring them into square in the areas where joinery will fall. The basic rule is to take the least amount of material away as possible.

The surveying process is one of the most important aspects of cutting a frame. Spend the necessary time and don't get ahead of yourself. Make preliminary labeling on the faces near the end of timbers with a blue, red or black builders crayon. Choose a color and stick with it in this initial surveying phase. If changes need to be made (and they most likely will), use a different color to mark the changes. If the initial labeling was red, make any changes in blue, or black. From there on out, blue takes precedence over red, etc. By creating this standard up front, it is easily understood by everyone working on the frame that there is a hierarchy to the color scheme. Fewer questions will arise, and therefore, fewer mistakes.

Begin by first designating the crown side with a small X, or other standard marking. This becomes a reference for all of the other surveying decisions. Always mark on the outside faces, or the presumed outside faces, of the timbers. Designate the foot, or top, or peak of the timber. During this process, begin building the frame in your mind.

Determining the crown face and the milling method are the two most important aspects to determine in the initial surveying stage. These two aspects will give the most information and clues about how the timber might age, and insight as to how and where it may be best placed in the frame. The crown will always be oriented up (as in floor joists and rafters), or better stated, opposed to the direction of the force load. The way the timber was milled will give you clues as to which faces may be more likely to check, or the direction of a likely sweep, etc. With these clues you will begin to have sufficient information to begin designating timber location and orientation.

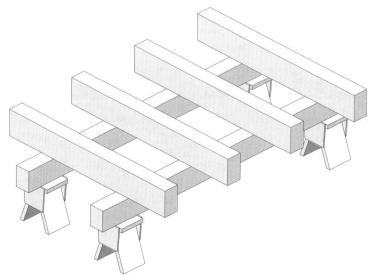

Once the final labeling in the surveying stage is complete, make bright, clear markings on both ends and the middle of the timbers (avoiding joinery locations that may be cut away) so that there is no question where the timber is placed in the frame. Never mark or label on the interior faces of the timber. Aside from the fact that they must be planed or sanded off, it will help in maintaining orientation by everyone during the layout and cutting process. A labeled face means it is an exterior face, an unlabeled face means it is an interior face—which is a label too.

Creating Standards

Establishing standards is important to ease the mind of unnecessary thought processes. In a frame with 300 timbers, there is plenty to think about, so don't make it more complicated than necessary. For example, lay out all mortises 2" from outside faces of timbers, or a consistent number based on the frame and joinery design and timber dimensions. Designate a reference face for all interior bent framing members, based on one of the cardinal points—all west faces, for instance. Make all dovetail tenons identical, or cut all post tenons the same. This procedure will assure uniformity and allow fewer opportunities for individual measurement or orientation errors. A far cleaner, more accurate frame will be the result. Cultivate a strong visual image of where every piece of timber will be oriented and placed in the frame. Don't start cutting until you know what you are cutting and where it is going. Mentally place each timber in the frame (as it lays flat on a crib), visualizing its orientation and the the way it will be in the frame before you begin the layout or cutting. Remember, the cut man is ultimately responsible for all joints cut in the wrong location—the cut man needs to know what he is cutting.

Make a sample layout on timbers to know how knots and defects will affect joinery locations. Locate all joinery areas on the timber before committing to final layout so as to make the best use of the timber.

Above: Timbers cribbed to proper working height and spaced to allow easy rolling and working room between each other.

Left: Surveying timbers set up on cribbing. The cribbing allows a thorough survey by being able to easily roll all timbers to analyze quality of timbers on all faces. The first check is to find the crown, then the milling method, knots, knot clusters and grain run out. From this you can gauge where best to place the timbers in the frame.

A 2 inch framing chisel can be used for both paring or chopping to the shoulder score line, and as a slick to flatten tenon faces. Sharp tools are required to do fine work.

Plunging the end of the timber with a 13" saw to expose the tenon.

Final layout should be made with a knife to score absolutely accurate, clean and clear lines. Saw cuts should be made shy of the score line anywhere from a 32nd to a fat 16th inch, depending on the type of wood. Harder and brittle woods like oak and fir (or when knots cannot be avoided) need to be cut closer to the line than pine or softwoods. Brittle and dry woods may need a splash of linseed and turpentine painted on the ends to make paring easier. Final cutting to line will be made with a chisel.

Layout of Mortises & Tenons

Use a scoring knife to mark all layout lines. Pencils should be used only for reference, preliminary layout, or for highlighting scored lines (or leaving notes to the cut man).

The tongue, or blade, of the square should always be placed over the wood remaining, scoring on the side toward the drop or waste. This not only protects the visible surface, but as importantly makes a sharp knife-edged score line on the shoulder side of the joint. The side of the line away from the square is always rolled a bit, and will not produce a sharp, clean cut.

When cutting tenon shoulders, make the rough cuts with the circular saw slightly away from the score line—into the waste wood. In pine and softwoods cut shy of the score line a strong 16th of an inch. In hardwoods this should be a strong 32nd to a 16th. This may vary from timber to timber, so get a feel for the wood you are working with. Cutting too far away will create too much force on the chisel making it want to dive, and also risks crushing the scored shoulder line, especially in softwoods. Cutting too closely will not allow the chisel to bite into the wood.

Make deep score lines with a sharp utility knife for the final layout. Score lines make an absolute, knife edged, incision and will make it easier to chop fine joinery by creating a positive and definite location to put the edge of the chisel. Using a pencil the question is always, "do you want me to take the line, leave it or split it?". Using a knife, the score line *IS* the mark, no questions. Extremely accurate knife edged shoulder cuts will result.

Normally the sides of mortises going with the grain are not visible, and because it is difficult to see a scoreline *with* the grain, a sharp pencil can be used. However, when the edge of a mortise will be visible, as in a brace pocket, it is important to score the line and pare up to it cleanly with a chisel, the same as a tenon shoulder. It is important to make snug fits of tenons. If the mortise is to be 2 inches, make the mortise 2 inches. You need to always remember that; *two inches is two inches, and 90 degrees is 90 degrees.* Use the body or blade of the square as a gauge to check the width of mortises, and a combo square to check that mortise sides are all 90 degrees (or 45 degrees if that be the case).

Never leave a joint unfinished prior to a lunch break, or at the end of the day, unless you leave your chisel in it. Never partially finish a series of joints and plan to go back later to clean them up. The one you didn't clean up will be the one that shuts down a raising with a $120 per hour crane, and 12 people standing idle. This can be costly and frustrating. I call it the 12 people watching one guy work syndrome.

Accurate layout, and careful paring with a sharp chisel, will ensure clean, well-fitted joints. Pay attention to the small details, they have a way of becoming major if you take them for granted.

Set the chisel snuggly in the score line and drive it with the mallet with confidence. Feel it, and allow it to be perfect with the first chop. You want to make clean flat cuts in one stroke. Don't nibble the wood away. Get the feel of making a perfect 90° cut so you know what it feels like. Once you know what it feels like, you can then repeat it. You have to learn to Jean-Claude the cut. Perfection and grace most definitely puts a smile on your face. Vive Jean-Claude!

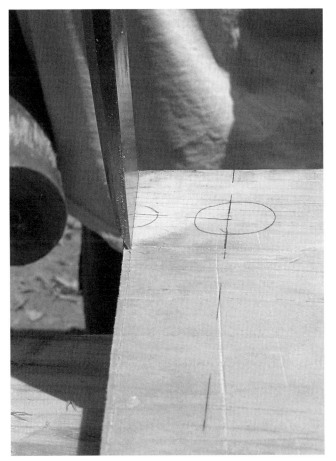

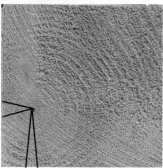

The way in which a timber is milled will have a big effect on how the timber ages. Top photo shows a perfectly boxed heart timber. Any face could be interior. The lower will have greater checking where designated by the lines projecting from the heart. These two faces should be oriented as exterior faces.

Point all pegs before driving them to avoid blowing out the back side, but not too much. The peg needs to fill the hole as it exits. Pegging is an art form.

Organizing Crews

When working with two or more people, it is best to designate one person as the lead layout person. This will maintain uniformity, reduce the possibility of mistakes and make the process more efficient by allowing the other workers to concentrate only on the cutting and chiseling. It is easy for things to become confused if too many people are laying out joints. If more than one layout person is necessary, divide the duties by designating one lead layout person for the roof system, and one for the post or wall system. In most cases, one person laying out can stay ahead of two or three people cutting, but they need a half day head start. Speed is important, but not at the expense of accuracy and uniformity.

It is the duty of the cut man to understand the layout and to double check it before cutting. Don't blame the layout man if you cut a joint that is laid out wrong. Recognize it before you cut, and then gloat over it.

Everyone working on the frame must be able to visualize the completed structure as if it were standing in front of the shop. All these visions must be the same. To assure this, get the group together and determine how you will be viewing it as if it were standing in front of the shop, or cutting yard. Designate the cardinal points, north, south, west, east. See it, standing there. Build it in your mind. Quiz the group. Have each person orient the north rafter in bent 2, or the south post in bent 3, etc., before the job begins.

Strive to do the best work. Make a competition out of who can cut the best joinery—not who can cut the fastest joint (of course, that will come later, when you can cut really nice joints fast). This is not only fun, but it will tend to make the crew bond and become more cohesive, and care more about the quality of the final project.

A good cut man is like a good linebacker. They may not make any touchdowns, but they can win the game.

Pegging

When driving pegs, be sure they are not too large for the hole. If they split the timbers, you are reducing the effectiveness of the joint. Make a sample drill hole in a drop of timber from the frame. Check out the fit with a peg. If the peg slides freely in and out, make an adjustment on the bit by filing the outer side of the spur, or use another bit. Sometimes it is necessary to use a bit 1/16 inch smaller and shave the pegs. To prevent splitting, shave the pegs slightly narrower on the sides, making them slightly oblong or octagonal. They can be fairly tight and slightly oversized on the side opposing the end grain. This will not split. If, however, the sides are oversized, they act as a wedge and can easily split the side grain of the hole. When driving a peg through oak, the peg size must be extremely accurate. Oak will not "give" and absorb the peg as readily as pine or softwoods will. Tapered pegs work well, but it is important to make sure they don't taper too rapidly. Complete contact with the peg hole is necessary. When draw boring, a sharp point is necessary, but it must flare back out to the full dimension so that full contact is made as it exits the hole.

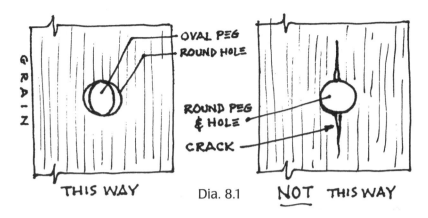

Dia. 8.1

Pegs should be fine-tuned to fit the peg holes. Fat pegs may split the face, so they may need to be shaved on the sides to slightly oval or octagonal. Octagonal pegs will drive easier than round, but oiling the tips, or using paraffin end sealer, will make them all drive easier.

Measure Twenty Seven Times - Cut Once

The old adage is "measure twice, cut once." This may not be enough. I now say, "measure 27 times, cut once." It is imperative to double and triple check all measurements before cutting. For the time it takes, it can prevent costly and time-consuming mistakes. Lay out and cut all similar timbers at one time—rafters, posts, tie beams, etc. If one person cannot lay out the whole frame, have one person lay out the roof system and another the posts and plates, or sets of principal framing members—rafters, posts, tie beams, etc.

Timbers should be spread out on a cribbing in the eventual order of use, with all ends pointing in the same direction. Survey all the timbers as you lay them out, allowing defects such as waney edges, gouges, checks, etc., to be on unexposed surfaces if possible. A little time spent doing this will make for a better job. With all posts or rafters lying in the same direction, next to each other, you can visually check to see if all joinery is lined up and marked accurately and uniformly. A common mistake is to lay out in the wrong direction from the reference point. This often happens after a lunch break, or at the end of the day. It's best to complete a process before leaving the work, no matter how long it may take, but never begin a new process that you can't complete before days end. Don't start laying out rafters at 4 o'clock in the afternoon. Start fresh in the morning to avoid stupid mistakes. After completing the layout for a set, check measurements by letting someone else read the smart end of the tape, and the layout person hold the dumb end.

Never trust the end clip on the tape to make accurate measurements. Most carpenters will use the 1 inch mark as the reference, or starting point, but this is why 1 inch mistakes are the most common. It is difficult to see a difference of 1 inch in a 16 foot timber. If you are accustomed to laying out in inches (which is what I prefer) use the 10 inch mark as the zero point on the tape. It is easy to add 10 to any number, and easy to see a variance of 10 inches, rather than 1 inch, if a layout mistake is made. If you prefer working in feet and inches, use the one foot mark as the zero point. By doing this, fewer inadvertent mistakes will result. Take nothing for granted, and always have someone else check the measurement. Perfection and grace is no accident.

Fit all braces and easily handled timbers prior to assembly to assure all fits are fully engaged and seat perfectly. For larger timbers, check all critical dimensions and criteria once positioned and ready to assemble. It will be the one tenon you don't check that will be fat or long, leading to the 12 guys watching one guy work syndrome come raising day.

Cribbing Ponies

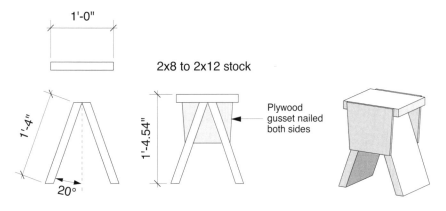

1'-0"

2x8 to 2x12 stock

1'-4"

20°

1'-4.54"

Plywood gusset nailed both sides

Cribbing ponies are quick and easy to make from scrap 2 by stock, compact, lightweight and easy to transport. Heights can be adjusted to fit the workers, but I find that 16 inch legs are the most flexible (additional blocks can be placed on top to raise the total cribbing height). Two by 10s works best, but 2x8s or 2x12s will also work. Cut pairs of 16 inch legs at a 20° angle on both ends. Nail or screw the top to the legs, then nail plywood gussets to both sides to stabilize. The top piece should be 12 to 16 inches.

Making ponies the first day of the workshop.

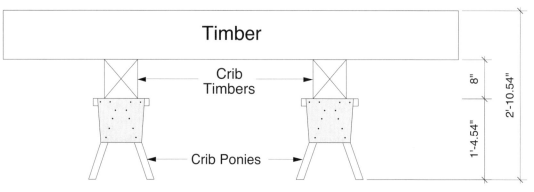

Timber

Crib Timbers

Crib Ponies

8"

1'-4.54"

2'-10.54"

With 4 ponies and a pair of crib timbers, cribbing setup is quick and easy. The crib timbers can be any extra timbers, or timbers from the frame being cut. There's no need to buy extra timbers. I often use the purlin stock, because they are generally the last timbers to be cut in the frame. The working height can be adjusted by the size of the crib timbers, or additional blocks. To determine a comfortable working height, stand with your palm bent parallel to the ground. The top of the working timbers should be about this height. Space cribbing so that 3 to 4 feet of the working timbers are overhanging the crib timbers.

Chapter 9

Joinery Details

In this frame a double tenon was used to join the hammer beam to the hammer post.

King post joinery.

Joinery Details

Pegging scissor arches joining to principal rafters in an arch braced truss. Rafters have dovetail pockets.

King post with lowered ridge beam to support tongue and closed fork commons.

Cantilevered English tying joint.

Top plate for English tying joint with a concealed offset cheek scarf on the post.

Traditional timber framing is based upon systems of mortise and tenon joinery that have evolved primarily through trial and error over many centuries of practice and experimentation. The examples left for us to study and to admire from centuries past were the ones that proved to be worthy—both structurally as well as aesthetically. Perhaps as importantly, the joined structures that have stood the test of time were also the ones deemed to be the most practical and efficient—in both execution and in use—by the carpenters fashioning them. The poor examples failed long ago and now serve only as compost in some ancient garden, propagating flowers and nectar and honey... and indeed, sustaining life itself even in failure. Not a bad fate even in the worst of circumstances.

The broad variety of joinery details used to construct dwellings in the colonial timber framing era of America (say from 1600 to 1900) evolved from methods and systems that began to emerge in western Europe dating back to the early 13th century. The overall structural forms and joinery designs were largely dictated by geographical region coupled with the species and relative dimension of timber available. As an example, prior to the 17th century the timber frames built throughout most of Europe used massive timbers, hewn mostly to square, hefty dimensions and straight. By the end of the 18th century the frames had transformed into what may be considered light-framed structures for the day, using small dimension curved and often waney timbers. This was due directly to the depletion of the native forests throughout most of Europe through overuse and bad management, firewood being a main culprit. However, the essential joinery details used to construct the frames changed only slightly in design and function. The greatest changes had more to do with the proportions of the joinery than with the essential design.

While there is seemingly a broad and varied assortment of joinery details that make up the vocabulary of traditional timber framing, the truth is that there is actually a relatively small number of essential joints that make up the basic lexicon. And even within this essential vocabulary, there is a thread of commonality that links all traditional joinery.

Joinery is less a rigid science than it is a malleable, flowing art form that allows flexibility and freedom to create within a structured framework similar in many ways to that of the musical scale. It is a science of proportion, scale and balance. Just as there is an infinite number of arrangements that may be derived from a very finite number of full notes from A to G on the musical scale, so are there an equally infinite number of possible configurations in the structural scale of joinery. The success of each, be it song or structure, is based in large part on the intrinsic harmonic balance. Bad harmonics in structure end up with examples such as the Tacoma Narrows Bridge. Good examples end up with the Taj Mahal, or the

Three of the essential joints in the vocabulary of timber frame joinery as described in this book.

Stave Church at Borgund, Norway, just as good harmonics in music ends up with a Mozart or the Beatles, and not Tiny Tim. And just as music evolves in mode and melody to reflect the social expression of each new generation, so has joinery evolved in equal measure and tempo to express the technological expressions of the day.

The slow process of natural evolution may have allowed a carpenter in any age of the golden era of timber framing to never have noticed the subtle changes taking place. But then, as in all forms of art and science, a real provocateur comes along occasionally who stretches the limits of the known geometry and physics of structure. One might argue that Isaac Newton was one of these figures. Newton was not a timber framer, but he set down for the first time in history hard and concrete scientific rules for the laws of statics and motion. He gave proof to the mechanics of the ancient systems of joinery, which allowed timber framing to flourish directly for another 200 years after his death. Even now, post revival, it is because of our ability to express timber framing in the language of science that we are able to engage in this craft in the age of steel, concrete and bureaucratic building inspectors. Though in equal measure, I believe it is the inherent jazz-like rhythm of timber framing that makes it so appealing to both the builder *and* the client. Both are essential elements necessary to propagate timber framing into the 21st century.

The historic similarities of timber frame joinery may be found in the layout approach and the basic techniques used to cut them. Specific joinery designs are very often determined by the tools at hand, the planned raising sequence, along with the manpower or mechanical advantage available, as much as by the overall frame design. It may be argued that it was these most fundamental human factors—those that seek the most efficient and practical approach to solve a problem—that have driven the design process through the millennia. In the end, timber framing is based on the human scale. It may be considered the perfect union of the Pythagorean concepts of a universal monad—harmonic scale or interval—merging music with geometry and perfect proportion, melded with the bright light of Newtonian science. Truly, perfection and grace in action.

The hammerbeam bent with upper scissor truss above uses only the basic joinery as described in this chapter. The variety of design concepts using these joints are as unlimited as the number of songs one can create using only the chords of C, D & G. The valley system is merely a simple jazz twist in the C-maj 7th scale.

A collar tie joining to rafter with the upper hammer-arch joining to the collar with a sleeved mortise. A simple chord pattern with a slight improvisational twist.

Joinery Details

The detail above is a truly modified English tying joint. The cantilevered upper tie was designed to create an overhang for straw bales. A bearing plate supported the double tenoned lower tie so that the entry could be in the center of the 3 bent white oak frame. Oskaloosa, Kansas Workshop 2002.

The truth is that timber joinery is an improvisational art form. So long as the carpenter knows the underlying modal patterns, and the key progressions, they can create a nearly infinite variety of different frame designs with relatively few chord (or joinery) patterns. There is indeed a natural harmonic rhythm intrinsic to timber framing that makes it so very uplifting to use *only* joinery, fashioned from the timbers alone to make such large structures that do indeed resonate harmonically with tones and melodies and rhythms in every aspect—from the crafting to assembling and in the living. This is why I consider timber framing the jazz of building.

Timber frames truly are alive. In the end, timber frame joinery is one of the great examples of mankind working harmoniously with nature to alter the present by creating a new built environment in such a direct, satisfying and fulfilling way. And if longevity is a measure of sustainability, then what better example than a joined timber frame.

Many of the joinery options available, and the criteria for their proper design, have been covered in earlier chapters. In the following chapter we will review some of the common joints used in traditional frames and discuss the layout procedures and specific criteria. The diagrams on the following pages should be used for visual reference only. Timber dimensions will vary in any given frame plan from the dimensions given here, but most often, the proportions and essential design requirements will remain the same.

The frame above is essentially a modified hammerbeam design, with aisle posts in lieu of hammer arches and upper hammer struts. Appleton, WI, 1992.

Bent Framing Members & Joints

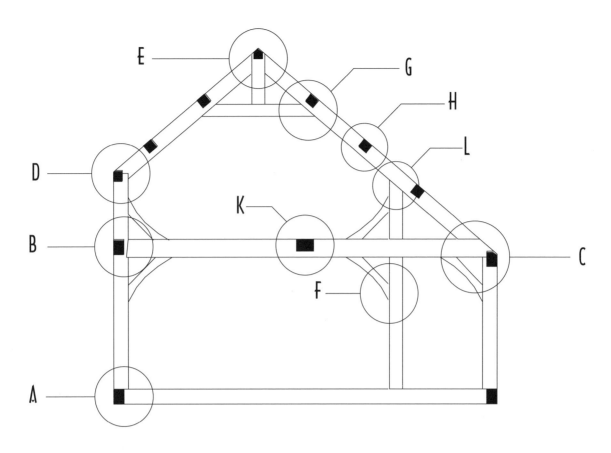

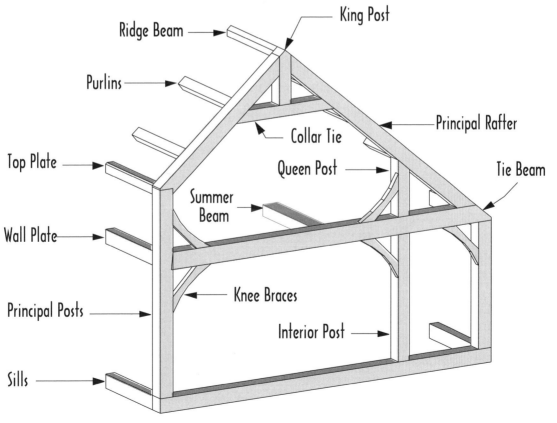

Posts with square tenons that will be joined through the tongue and fork joints of the sill plates.

Assembling tongue & fork rafter peak. Note the side pocket for ridge purlin.

The tongue and fork is the likely joint to join rafter peaks when there is no king post. For roof pitches other than 45°, the purlin tenon and face should be parallel to the forked rafter and a bevel must to be ripped its length to plane into the opposing roof plane. The frame above is a 10/12 pitch, the frame to the right is a 15/12 pitch. Note the side mortise to accept the ridge purlin in each is parallel to the top of the rafter. To determine the rip angle double the roof pitch degree and subtract 90. This will give the angle off a line perpendicular to the top of the rafter.

A) Tongue & Fork Joint
Post to Sill Joint & Rafter Peaks

The tongue and fork is an ideal joint for both rafter peaks and for joining sills at the corners and intermediate joint locations on the foundation sills. It has become increasingly popular in modern frames to use the tongue and fork joint to join principal rafter feet to the top of the post. This is less appealing to me for two reasons.

The first being that the tongue and fork is an open ended mortise. Open-ended mortises have a tendency to splay open as they age. The splaying fork is a likely place for a natural check to occur running along the center line of the face of the timber, creating a great avenue for the internal stresses to further accentuate the check. This may potentially cause splitting in the timber over long-term loading, and even if it is in no danger of failure, it can look like it is failing to the unwary eye—which can be equally disturbing. The forces acting on the joint due to horizontal thrust (producing torsion) are much greater at the post/rafter interface (which in theory is carrying half of the total roof load) than at the peak. The peak is subject only to compressive forces due to the resultant loading, and actually zero vertical loading at the apex (the ridge beam).

The second is that in this joint the end grain of the post is exposed to the roof plane. In the likelihood that the roof will ever leak in the next few hundred years, the water will be absorbed directly into the heart of the wood, which in time and repeated dampness, will cause rot. Couple a damp, rotting timber with horizontal and rotational loading and it is a prime candidate for failure. In my years of repairing old barns in the western foothills of Maine and New Hampshire, I found the number one cause of death to be a leaking roof that allowed water to run down a

rafter and into the principal post. It was always the odd dimension post, the one that was wider than the tie beam or rafter that had exposed end grain that was the one to rot. Once the water is allowed to repeatedly enter the end grain of the post, it takes just a few short years to rot the timber.

The true character of a joint is not measured in years or tens of years, but in hundreds of years. I have yet to see an example of a fork joint used to join a post to a rafter foot in any frame built prior to 1985, which leads me to believe that if they were once common in some long ago age, they have all long ago returned to compost. I prefer to cultivate compost from garden greens and table scraps.

The post to sill connection is not subjected to any critical forces, so it's best to keep it simple. Gravity is its greatest asset. In most cases a simple tenon on the post, mortised into the sill timber 3" to 8" deep, is sufficient to resist any lateral movement of the post. The tenons on the corner posts should extend through the full depth of the sill—locking the tongue and fork joint together. No pegs are necessary, however I usually put one peg on the inside corner.

Corner post tenons should be square in section, from 2 to 3 inches, though 2-1/2 inches is most common. The interior post tenons may be 2 inches by the full width of the timber—if they do not land on top of a floor girt or other member joining into the sill. If a floor girt or connecting member falls directly below the post, it should be treated like a corner post, with a square tenon extended through the tenon of the connecting member, creating a self locking joint.

The tongue & fork joint can be used whenever two members are joined to create a corner. It is ideally suited for joining sills plates as shown to the left, and in the photo below, and also for joining rafter peaks, as shown in the photos on the opposite page. It is best used when there is little or no force tending to create torsion, thrust or tension. In modern frames it is sometimes used to join rafter feet to post tops, as in the photo above, but it is most appropriately used for joining sill joints and rafter peaks.

A) Post/Sill Joint

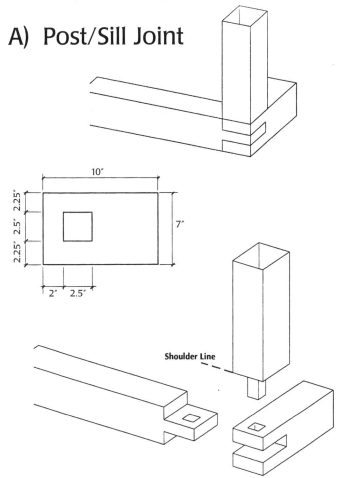

B) Tie Beam to Post
Wedged Half-Dovetailed Through Tenon

The wedged half-dovetail joint is one of the best pure tension joints used traditionally in timber framing.

This is one of the most interesting and effective tension joints in timber framing. The wedged half-dovetail allows the tenon to resist tensile forces directly, reducing its reliance on the pegs. Care should be taken when laying out the half dovetail on the tenon and the mortise so that they make full contact when wedged. It is best to make the mortised dovetail first, then transfer the exact angle to the tenon. This can be done with a protractor or bevel square and a framing square. Two to three 1" pegs are required and they should be placed 1-1/2 times the peg diameter from the top and bottom edges of the tenon, and 5 times the peg diameter from the end of the tenon.

This joint can also be used in many other areas in the frame where tensile forces are acting to pull the joint apart. One example is when joining the foot of a king post to a continuous tie beam. This is especially important if the tie beam will be subjected to floor loading. It can also be used when joining tie beams to a king post that passes through the ties with the ties joining to the side of the king post (a two piece tie, as shown in the photo on the opposite page bottom right). I also use it many times when joining struts to a king post in polygonal structures to serve as tension struts (see page 110).

The haunch should always be oriented to the side of the timber that is resisting the force loads.

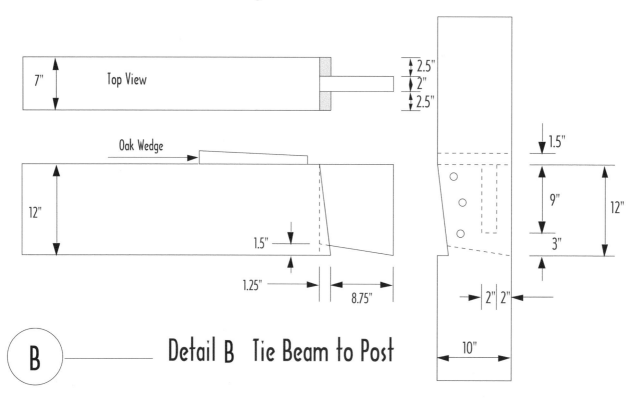

Detail B Tie Beam to Post

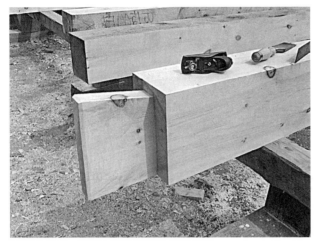

Half dovetailed through tenon. Both tenon and mortise dovetail surfaces need to be carefully cut to the same angle so complete surface contact is made when wedged.

Transferring the angle from the half-dovetailed mortise (below) to the tenon above. The mortise should be cut first and the actual angle transferred to the tenon using a framing square and a protractor square as shown.

The wedged half-dovetail tenon can be used to join other tension members. Above it is used to join tie beams to a king post. The drawing to the right shows the detail for joining the king post to a continuous tie beam. Note the tenon stops short of the bottom side of tie beam by 2 inches.

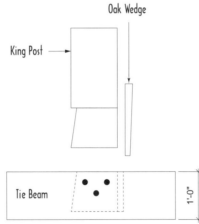

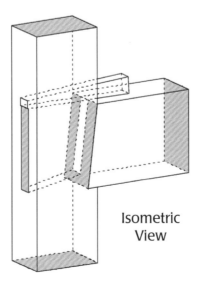

Isometric View

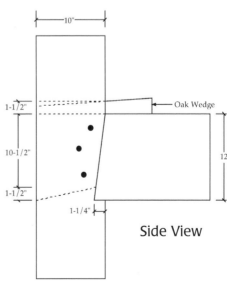

Side View

C) English Tying Joint

The English tying joint could very well be the perfect timber frame joint. It has been in use extensively in Europe since the middle ages. It is common to virtually every barn frame built in New England since barns were first built, and is found in house frames—Colonials, Saltboxes, and Capes—from Maine to the Carolinas. It is a self-locking, compression joint, and does not rely on pegs for its immediate strength. The exploded drawing shows the details of each member. As you can see, each member opposes the other, creating the optimum factors for a strong timber joint. This is a true compression joint.

During the civil war era the tall post cape became in vogue throughout New England—perhaps as a way to build an almost-two-story house in those economically depressed times. Many of these houses with tall posts extending 3 to 4 feet above the tie beam have collapsed under heavy snow loads, or if still standing, show severe bowing of the top plates. While this design gives additional headroom upstairs, it must be designed correctly (as described earlier). The English tying joint is the most effective traditional method to redirect thrust at the eaves to a vertical loading on the posts, and is perhaps the reason why so many of these traditional Cape houses dot the landscape from Maine to the Carolinas. These frames are as true and straight today as the day they were built from 150 to 300 years ago.

In a continuous top plate version, cutting the top of the post requires extra care. The width of the top plate must be accurately measured so that it fits snugly between the sleeved post face wrapping around the plate and the spar tenon extending through the plate. The front face of the post has an extended tenon, 4" or 5" long, called a teasel tenon. This enters a mortise in the bottom of the tie beam, effectively locking the two together.

Dovetail shoulders on the bottom face of the tie beam fit into a corresponding dovetail slot on the top of the plate, preventing any possibility of spreading or rolling of the plate. This is optional if a purlin roof system is used as there is no force tending to roll the plate, as there is in a common rafter system.

The rafter foot is joined to the tie beam with a 2" wide tenon that is set back 3 inches from the end to increase the relish on the tie beam. This is pegged through with 2 or 3 pegs being sufficient.

The tie beam is cut to the angle of the roof pitch at each end starting at 2" from the bottom of the timber (leaving a 2" vertical nose on the tie beam). This is designed to increase the cross section of the tie beam at the vertical plane on the inside face of the post. This can, and should be increased as the roof pitch shallows.

The top plate is raised up 1 inch from the eaves line and bevelled on the outside edge corresponding to the roof pitch, allowing roof boards to be nailed to a flat surface. 1 inch pegs are required through the rafter foot/tie beam joint, and through the spar and teasel tenons.

Assembling modified English tying joint using intermediate plates. Note the joinery on the rafter foot above, with set back tenon, that will join to the tie beam.

Teasel Tenon

Spar Tenon

English Tying Joint with Continuous Top Plate

Top left and above show the continuous top plate to post detail. The plate has a dovetail slot for the tie beam to sit and the plate is locked in by the sleeved post face and the spar tenon. The teasel tenon projects from the post sleeve.

English Tying Joint

Above shows the intermediate plates joining to the post in a modified English tying joint with a dovetail slot cut into the plates. Below shows the assembly of post, tie & rafter in a modified version without the dovetail slot.

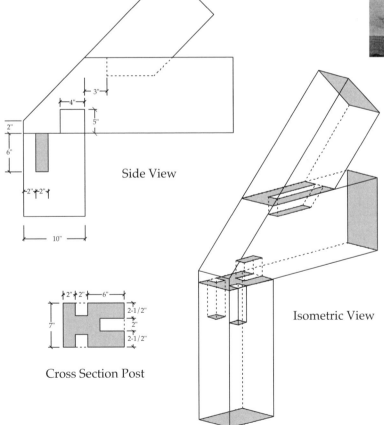

Side View

Cross Section Post

Isometric View

English Tying Joint with Intermediate Top Plate

Rafter Foot without shoulder.

D) Rafter Foot/Post Joint

This is a common joint used when the rafter is joined directly to the top of the post—as in a high posted cape. It also allows the rafter truss to be placed after lower bents are raised, which is especially helpful if a hand raising is anticipated. It can also be used in full bent raising's, but strong-backs should be secured across the joint from post to rafter during raising. The joint does not resist thrust or torsion very well, so it should be used in designs that adequately redirect roof loads through additional intermediate members within the bent (see the High Post Cape in the Plans chapter) so that the forces imposed on the post remain vertical in nature.

Rafter to post joint without shoulder.

The 1 inch vertical cut at the eaves line creates greater horizontal shear resistance on the rafter by lowering the shear line at the inside corner of the bird's-mouth below the neutral plane of the rafter. The joint can be made with or without a 1 inch shouldered bird's-mouth. The shoulder effectively reduces the shearing stresses at the inside corner of the bird's-mouth. The structural significance of the shoulder increases proportionately as the roof pitch lowers, and therefore should be used on roof pitches less than 10/12. The shoulder effectively reduces the net vertical depth of the tenon as well. The minimum vertical tenon depth should be no less than 3 inches (this being dictated mathematically by the timber depth and roof pitch). For roof pitches of 12/12 and greater, the shouldered version is less likely to be used, as the tenon depth diminishes rapidly.

Shouldered Rafter Foot.

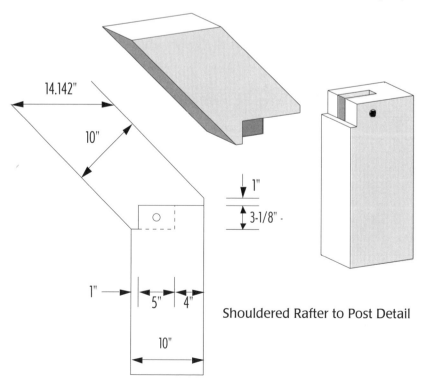

Shouldered Rafter to Post Detail

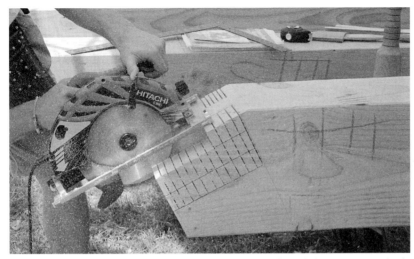

The photo above shows a rafter foot with a vertical rise of 3 inches, which was necessary due to the shallow roof pitch. A student is cutting the side of the reverse teasel tenon. Above right; my son Asher is setting the same shouldered rafter into the post in a two phase raising. Asturias, Spain 2008.

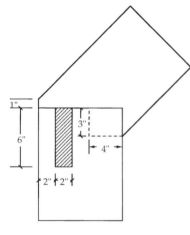

Side View

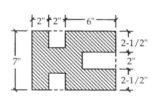

Cross Section Post

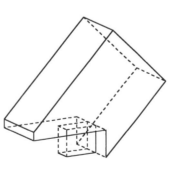

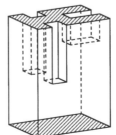

Isometric View

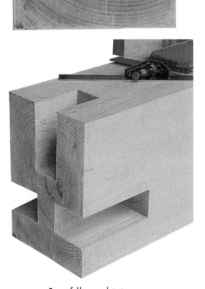

Top of the post joinery.

The king post joinery above uses a ridge beam beveled to the roof pitch and fitting flush to the roof plane, as depicted below. This design is commonly used in a purlin system.

E) Rafter Peak/King Post Joint

The peak of the rafters may be joined directly by using the tongue and fork, or they may join to a king post. The tongue and fork is a simple and effective joint suitable in designs that do not rely on the ridge beam to transfer intermediate loads, such as common rafters to the principal bent frame. When common rafters are used, or when long clear spans are required, the King Post Truss has many advantages.

If the Ridge Beam is intended to support secondary rafters (common rafters), a greater portion of the roof load will be directed to the principal rafter peak. The king post provides more material and greater resistance to vertical forces to support the ridge beam, and also allows the placement of struts from the king post to the ridge beam. This not only stiffens the ridge beam, but also provides more lateral resistance to wind and horizontal forces imposed on the roof. From a structural standpoint, the dynamics of a rafter joined to a king post is virtually identical to a rafter foot joining to a tie beam joint in an English tying joint—only on a different plane. Both are compression joints, and as we have seen throughout this book, compression is good.

The King Post is a key element in truss design and in timber framing. When clear spans are desired, or when bent spans begin to exceed 24 feet, the interjection of a king post is one of the most effective design options, and one of the better ways to join rafter peaks.

As the photos and drawings show, the tenon needs to be stepped back 3 inches (just like the foot of a rafter in an English tying joint) to increase the relish behind the king post mortise. This increases the resistance to shear by increasing the area resisting shear behind the mortise.

Ridge beam with bevel cut to match roof pitch and a vertical tenon designed to join to the king post as in the photo above.

Haunched king post ready for assembly. In this design, the ridge beam is dropped so that common rafters can pass over.

The beveled, or haunched shoulder on the King post is designed to increase resistance to upward thrust by adding additional frictional area to the interface. This increases resistance to compressive forces and reduces shearing stress on the tenon. Structurally, it may be likened to the key stone of an arch. Two 1" pegs are normally required.

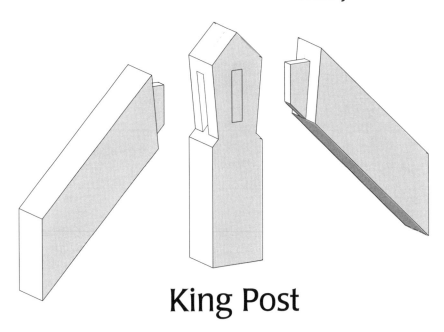

King Post

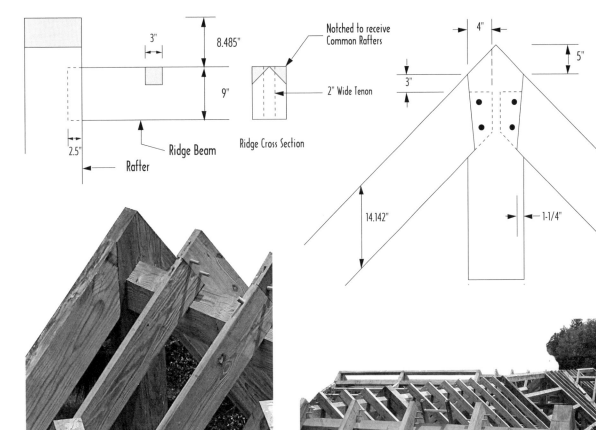

3"

8.485"

9"

2.5"

Ridge Beam

Rafter

Notched to receive Common Rafters

2" Wide Tenon

Ridge Cross Section

4"

5"

3"

14.142"

1-1/4"

10"

The ridge beam can be joined flush to the peak or dropped to allow common rafters to pass over the top. When dropping the ridge beam it can either be fully beveled with the commons pegged to the ridge, as in the photos above and right, or set into notches cut to match the width of the commons as depicted in the drawing above.

F) Braces

The forces of wind, snow and settling all tend to rack a building (making it out of square). Braces are necessary to resist these forces and maintain the timber frame in a rigid and square state. Modern conventional framing methods rely on the exterior sheathing for rigidity, with plywood or diagonal sheathing boards commonly used. Do not rely on structural stress skin panels or applied sheathing to hold a timber frame square! Build a proper frame by using braces in appropriate number and location.

A joined timber frame relies on all frame members as integral and necessary parts of the whole. In theory, all parts must be present to create a structurally sound frame. Bracing, consequently, is a very important element in a timber frame and should not be thought of as an afterthought, or a mere nuisance.

Braces are most effective in resisting forces when in compression—when the forces are pushing on each end of the brace. Braces in compression utilize the full cross-section of the brace to resist the force, resulting in maximum strength. Braces in tension—when the forces are pulling—must rely only on the pegs and the reduced cross section of the tenon to resist the force. In order to properly compensate for this disparity in strength, every brace must have an opposing brace in equal number in the same wall plane. In this way, regardless of the direction of the wind or lateral force, there will be an equal number of braces in compression resisting the force, relieving the opposing braces from undue tensile strain under loading.

For such a minor member in the frame, the layout and execution of braces are one of the most difficult to achieve perfection—so pay attention. It is extremely important to measure accurately when laying out both the length of braces and the location of brace pockets. Start by laying out and cutting one end of the brace, then measure from the finished shoulder cut to layout the other end. A measurement off by only scant 1/32" in a mortise placement, or in the brace length, can make a huge difference in the brace fit, making it potentially impossible to square up the frame.

If you are using rough cut timbers, compensate for the actual post width and beam depth by measuring at the actual location that the brace will enter the adjoining member, not just on the ends of the beam. It may be necessary to compensate for any variation in beam thickness by slightly adjusting the location of the brace pockets plus or minus the specified measurement. Or, square-rule layout may be used. Square-rule layout is when a faceted surface is made at joint locations on each member at a specified distance from, and parallel to, a reference line located along the length of the timber.

Braces can be one of the most difficult frame members to fit accurately. This is compounded because there are so many of them. Their orientation in the frame also needs to be clearly thought out and visualized during the lay out process, which must be carried out carefully and methodically—and double checked before cutting.

All braces, except interior braces, should be cut to fit flush with the exterior faces of timbers. Knee braces should be made from 3 or 4 inch thick stock by

Braces on interior bents can be cut with the tenons centered, or as in the photos above and below, with an offset tenon. For knee braces the offset tenon is the best approach. In this case, the mortises are laid out offset to one side of the center line of the mortised timber. This way the brace will fall in the center of the beam. This has advantages in that all of the braces can be cut the same and will be interchangeable anywhere in the frame. Struts that will be transferring loads, such as hammer arches, are best with centered tenons.

5 to 8 inches deep. My preference is to us 3"x 8" oak. This allows for an attractive arch to be cut from 2 to 3 inches deep at its midpoint, leaving 5 to 6 inches of net brace depth. A minimum of two thirds of the stock depth should be remaining at the narrowest point of the arch.

The brace tenons should be half the thickness of the brace stock used. The tenon length should 3 to 4 inches. For 4 inch stock use a 2 thick inch tenon, for 3 inch stock, us a 1-1/2 inch tenon. Exterior braces (those on exterior walls) should all be cut as a half-lap tenon with the shouldered side flush to the outside of the post. When laying out the brace mortises, always measure from the outside face of the timber to the inside face of the pocket, then back the width of the tenon toward the outside face of the timber (pull 3" then back 1-1/2, or 4" and back 2).

The rule of thumb is that knee braces should join at the upper third point of the post. For a nominal 8 foot wall, this makes 32 inches the ideal run for braces, and is actually the most common in use for wall heights in the range of 8 feet. A 10 foot tall post would require a 40" or 42" run. This makes a brace length of 42.25" for a 32 in run and 56.569 for a 40" brace run.

All knee braces are cut at a 45° angle. Brace lengths can easily be calculated using trigonometry for any brace run by using the following equation:

$$\text{Brace run} \div \cos 45 = \text{brace length}$$
$$32 \div .7071 = 42.25$$

You can also find the brace length by multiplying the brace run or rise (both the rise and run are equal for a 45 degree angle) by the square root of 2.
$$\sqrt{2} = 1.414 \qquad 32 \times 1.414 = 42.25$$

The brace pocket being chopped above is for a brace using 3 inch stock with a 1-1/2 wide lap type tenon. The tenon is offset to the inside face of the brace and the pocket cut in the post above is laid out 3" to the inside face and back 1-1/2", making for a housed tenon.

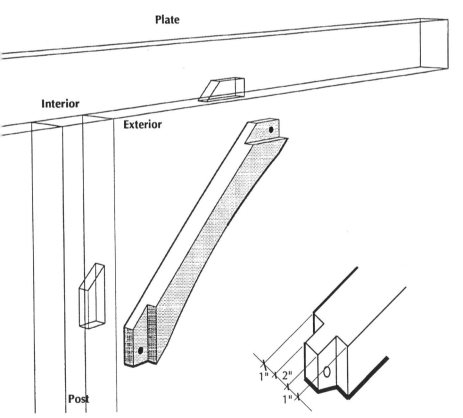

Brace tenons on interior bents can be cut with offset, or centered tenons. Centered tenons should be half the width of the brace, or 2 inches, whichever is greater.

Fitting an exterior brace with offset tenon to wall plate prior to assembly. While it is not necessary to pre-fit joinery as a whole, it is best to actually pre-fit braces prior to assembly so as assure that all brace shoulders set fully into the mortise. It is the braces that will square and plumb the frame, so it is important to make sure they are laid out and cut to the precise criteria. Perfection and grace is no accident.

G & L) Collar Tie/Queen Post

The Collar Tie is a compression member joined between Common or Principal rafters. The requirement for its placement in the frame is based on the span of the rafters. In its purest form, it is designed strictly to resist the bending forces of the rafters and is purely a compression member. As such, it is best located at the mid point of the rafter. As spans increase the collar tie can migrate up to the upper third point of the rafters. In this case, a Queen Post usually becomes necessary and should join from the mid point down to the lower third point of the rafters. A very common design would place the Collar at the upper third point and the Queen Post at the lower third point. It is the basic proportion that allows a basic tie beam bent evolve into a hammerbeam bent.

The Queen Post is the likely addition when spans begin to exceed 20 feet. They can effectively transfer a portion of the roof load to the lower tie beam (which must then be sized sufficiently to support the added load, or supported by another post), thereby reducing the outward thrust at the rafter feet, and serves to stiffen the rafter as well. This is necessary especially when the principal posts are cantilevered above the tie beam, as in a high posted cape frame. In this design the additional load transferred to the tie beam must be considered carefully, as additional support posts directly in line with the Queen Posts may be required. When bents span 28 feet or more, additional members or trussing systems may be necessary to sufficiently transfer loading safely.

As a general rule, the length of the tenons for both the collar ties and queen posts should be equal to one half the depth of the timber to which they are being joined. This would be a 5 inch tenon (as measured perpendicular to the shoulder cut) for a rafter 10 inches deep. The tenon width is normally 2 inches wide. In an English tying joint truss the queen post can be designed as a tension member to stiffen the tie beam to support secondary floor loads. In this case the tenons may be increased in thickness to 2-1/2 inches, and in length to increase the resistance to the increased force load in tension.

Above: Laying out and chopping the collar tie tenon. This is a common joinery detail, and is essentially a simple tenon cut at an angle other than 90°. The blunt nose of the tenon is cut perpendicular to the shoulder, corresponding to a mortise cut 90° to the face of the rafter. This provides a square surface to resist compression at a right angle to the load force. The collar tie and queen posts in the photo to the right join directly to the rafter and are essentially identical in layout and execution. For pitches other than 45°, the angles between queens and collars would be complimentary. When joining queens and collars as in the photo, the space between mortises should be 4 inches at minimum.

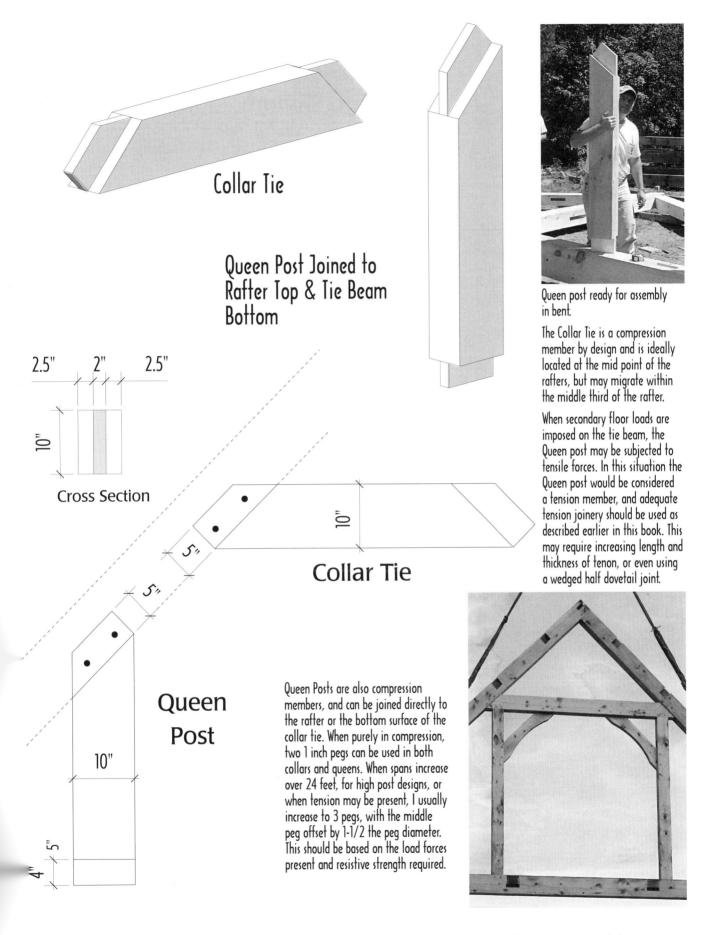

Collar Tie

Queen Post Joined to Rafter Top & Tie Beam Bottom

2.5" 2" 2.5"

10"

Cross Section

10"

5"

5"

Collar Tie

10"

Queen Post

10"

5"

4"

Queen post ready for assembly in bent.

The Collar Tie is a compression member by design and is ideally located at the mid point of the rafters, but may migrate within the middle third of the rafter.

When secondary floor loads are imposed on the tie beam, the Queen post may be subjected to tensile forces. In this situation the Queen post would be considered a tension member, and adequate tension joinery should be used as described earlier in this book. This may require increasing length and thickness of tenon, or even using a wedged half dovetail joint.

Queen Posts are also compression members, and can be joined directly to the rafter or the bottom surface of the collar tie. When purely in compression, two 1 inch pegs can be used in both collars and queens. When spans increase over 24 feet, for high post designs, or when tension may be present, I usually increase to 3 pegs, with the middle peg offset by 1-1/2 the peg diameter. This should be based on the load forces present and resistive strength required.

Purlin mortises cut in principal rafters above. Chopping dovetail mortise that was kerfed with a circular saw below.

Mother and daughter team cutting purlin dovetails in the Grand Junction, Iowa Workshop 2004.

H) Dovetail Purlin to Rafter, Joist to Summer Beam Joint

Purlins, as well as joists, are ideal timbers to be joined using dovetail tenons. Dovetails are actually very rare in Colonial frames as they usually made just a simple lap joint, sometimes pegged, but often not, that sat into a simple slot mortise. The beauty of dovetails is that when wedged they are extremely strong tension joint that can help to make the frame more rigid. They are also quite easy to lay out and to execute. It is actually possible to tune the frame to the pitch of a perfect A (the natural frequency of wood) by judicious wedging of purlins and floor joists. It is actually quite amazing, not only the tone, but also the rigidity that is obtained in the frame through a proper dovetail wedging process. It is hard to explain, so one really has to experience it on their own, but once the dovetails are wedged, the frame feels just so harmonically complete.

Dovetail tenons should be cut slightly narrower than the mortise so they will enter easily. Wedges are then driven down the sides of the dovetails to tighten the joint. The end of the tenon should be cut 1/8" shallower than the back of the mortise, so that there is clearance for the joint to be snugged tightly with wedges. To accomplish this, lay out all mortises and tenons at 2" (or the designated depth) and cut the tenon off to the inside of the line. On the mortise, chop or plunge the saw right on the line. This will allow a blades width space which is the perfect amount of clearance. The same procedure should be used for the side dovetail cuts—saw to the inside of the line, allowing a saw blades-width space for the wedge.

It is important that the 3/4 and 5/8 rules (as described earlier in this book) are followed if appropriate joinery design is to be obtained.

Soffit or tusk tenons may also be used to join floor joists and purlins, especially when the design loads approach the design limits of a beam.

In theory, the integrity of a beam is compromised when mortises are cut on the top edge surfaces of a beam (as in a dovetail pocket) because the continuous resistance to compressive forces are interrupted. Increasingly building codes frown upon this, as they frown upon making any holes in structural timbers. There is great validity to this, and in general practice one does not want carpenters in the field to be making random holes in their structural timbers. In a properly wedged dovetail, however, the compressive resistive forces can be compensated for completely because the mortise is solidly filled, and in many cases may even exceed the resistive forces of a solid beam.

While there are real structural benefits to the soffit or tusk tenon, there are also real questions as to their practical use in such a redundant system as floor joists and purlins in a joined timber frame structure. This is primarily because they are extremely difficult to place in the frame, requiring many hands, or a large crane to fly in major roof or floor sections. This can be an extremely costly and dangerous undertaking. It is my opinion that if the design loads approach the critical design limits on a timber strictly because it has dovetail mortises, there are likely other much more serious design problems in the frame design to evaluate.

Properly fitted dovetails require a space of up to 1/8 inch on the sides and back of mortise to allow easy entry of sturdy red oak wedges, and sufficient end space to allow draw when tightly wedged.

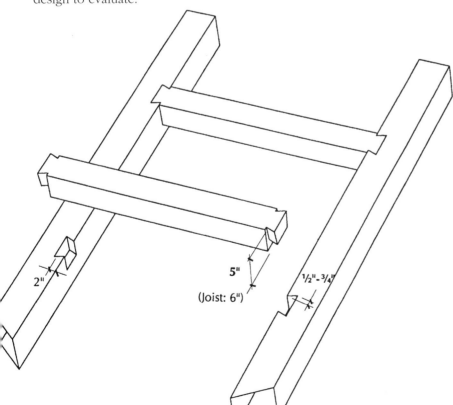

2"

5"
(Joist: 6")

1/2"-3/4"

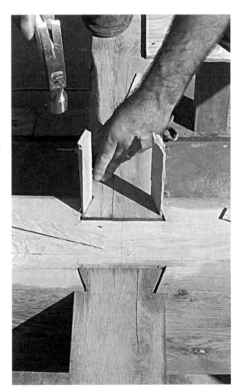

Wedging dovetails with red oak wedges. Red oak and locust are ideal, white oak and most other hardwoods don't have the right properties. Use a steel hammer to drive wedges home.

The Tusk tenon on the summer beam above is directly above a lower post to support the tie beam. This allows the lower shoulder to be lower than 5/8 the beam depth. The beveled shoulder above the tenon is designed to increase the cross section of the tenon and shearing strength. The tenon is pegged, which are relied upon to prevent pull-out only.

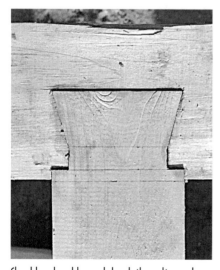

Shouldered and housed dovetail mortise and tenon seated into its mortise above. Dovetail mortise to the right.

K) Summer Beam

The summer beam is one of the primary carrying timbers in the second floor framing. As such, it carries a considerable portion of the second floor load and must be sized and joined accurately to be effective.

According to one version of traditional lore the name *summer beam* comes from the Latin word, *summa*, which means, 'sum of'. Being the major load bearing timber in a floor system, and due to the fact that the summer beam does in fact carry the sum of the floor load, this seems quite logical. Another theory arises from the fact that in colonial houses of Massachusetts Bay, a large beam was often the primary timber supporting the floor above what was called the *summer kitchen* (a kitchen built off the back of the house that was used during the summer to keep the heat generated from the wood stove out of the main house). Therefore, the name 'summer beam' was coined for this beam. Each theory can provide a suitable argument. However, the divergent stories may actually have occurred due more to the accent of the Massachusetts Bay residents, who's colloquial dialect say the word *summer* quite emphatically as '*summa*'.

There are two types of joints traditionally used to join the summer beam to tie beam. In the earliest examples of frames built in the Massachusetts Bay area of New England, the tusk, or soffit, tenon was used extensively. As settlements moved northward and eastward into Maine and interior New England, the tusk tenon was replaced with the shouldered dovetail. Dovetails are actually a rare joint in New England timber frames built after 1700 (giving way to a simple lap tenon), but the one place it survived was in joining summer beams to tie beams. The shouldered dovetail has most of the structural attributes of a tusk tenon, but has a significant advantage—it is easier to place in the frame. This is an appealing trait to those doing hand raising's. It is designed to maximize the cross sectional area of the tenoned member, while removing minimal material on the mortised member. When two summer beams join to the tie beam or connecting member at the same location, a post directly below the joint is a definite requirement.

It is very important to lay out and pare all surfaces accurately so that complete contact of each horizontal bearing surface is made in both the dovetail and tusk tenon versions. The joint relies on this total contact of both surfaces for maximum strength and to reduce horizontal shear stress on the beam. It is also important to follow the 3/4 & 5/8 rules when designing either the shouldered dovetail or tusk tenon versions of this joint.

Shouldered Dovetail

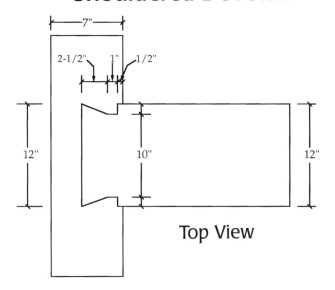

Top View

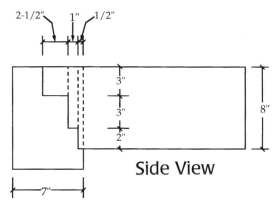

Side View

Shouldered dovetail header joining to tie beam. This example is not housed.

The diagrams above show a shouldered and housed dovetail mortise and tenon seated into its mortise. Housing the summer beam is done strictly for aesthetics, and may not be the best approach due to long-term drying and shrinking of Timbers. The critical aspect of the joint is that the bearing shoulder is sufficient to carry the load. This would normally range from 1 to 1-1/4 inch.

Shouldered dovetail summer beam above and a shouldered tusk tenon summer beam below. Both are upside down, just so you know.

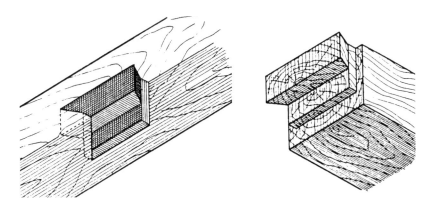

Isometric View

Topping the frame at the frame raising in the Spring 2004 workshop at Fox Maple.

Chapter 10
Timber Frame Plans

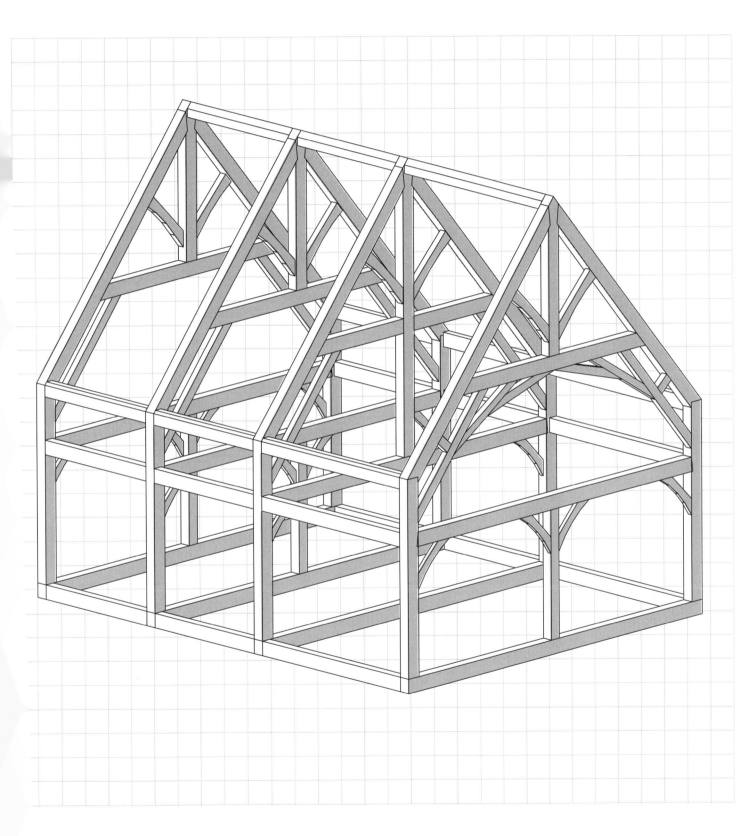

The Library frame at Fox Maple was cut in the Fall 1996 Timber Framing Workshop. This was followed up with a straw bale enclosure workshop led by Athena and Bill Steen, to enclose the frame with straw bales. In following workshops students harvested phragmites (common reeds) on the coast of Maine and thatched the roof under the instruction of British master thatcher Jason Morley, who thatched the Globe Theater, and in following workshops with Scottish master thatcher, Colin McGhee. German clay builder, Frank Andresen, led students in workshops in the art of clay plastering. The frame sits on a rubble trench foundation. The objective was to build the library completely with materials that came within 50 miles from the site. The design evolved directly from this objective, and the result wound up being an uncanny replica of a medieval Japanese Minka.

The Fox Maple School Site

The dining hall at Fox Maple was also a result of student input. Like the library, the objective was to use only natural material that came within the same 50 mile radius, but in this case our design vision was modeled after a medieval English cottage. In this project we wanted to explore the full panoply of natural building systems. Thatch for the roof, wattle & daub, straw light clay, wood chip light clay, cob, cellulose fiber compressed blocks (using sawdust, peanut shells, hemp fiber, straw and wood chips), and clay plaster interior and exterior finish. The overriding goal was to understand these systems in order to determine which ones were the most effective and practical for the region in which we lived. Viability must factor in both cost and efficiency (in both construction system processes and long term maintenance and energy use), but it also must include the aspect of human input, as in, "is this something that people will be willing to actually undertake on an ongoing and professional level?" If it's not viable on a professional level, no matter how wonderful the concept may seem, it will never make it in the real world as viable building option.

Building systems must be adaptable to all aspects of the building environment and processes if they are to prove viable. An instrumental ingredient to this adaptability must include the people who will be working with the material. It must be easy to assimilate for the average professional building crew of 3 to 5 people, and they must be able to earn a reasonable income. Lacking this, all may be folly. Our efforts at Fox Maple are geared to understand and promote those systems that prove to be viable in all aspects of the building process.

Frame Plans

Our first workshop in the spring of 1983. On the bottom floor were my crew and instructors, from left; Don Morrison, Me, Joe Hanley and Ken Wilson.

Raising the bents in the Waldoboro, Maine, workshop, 1994. Queen post, King post and Hammerbeam bents.

The primary objectives of this book is to provide the information, insight and understanding that will allow anybody willing to commit the time energy to go out and cut their own timber frame with confidence. I have stressed the point throughout that aside from all the seeming variations in frame designs and joinery details, there is a thread of similarity that is intrinsic to every variation. In this section, the frame designs should be considered as templates, from which a countless number of frames can be designed and built. I strongly urge you to apply the principles provided throughout this book—and feel free to be creative. Though a given design may be a three bent frame with bays spaced at 10 feet, the same design can be extended to bays of 16 feet and additional bents may be added, or the bents can be shortened or lengthened to fit your needs. However, I do caution that before you begin redesigning the frame plans that follow, do so only after thoroughly reading the book from front to back, and back again.

Timber framing is a wonderful and fluid structural system. I think of it as the jazz of building because of the freedom to be creative. Once the essential design elements are understood there is nothing to hold one's creative instincts back. If it still seems difficult to grasp all of the information contained within this book merely by reading, and you are really intent on engaging with this thing we call timber framing, attending a workshop will certainly round out your knowledge, and greater confidence and creativity will result.

I have tried to use photos of projects cut by students for the most part in this book. Photos of some of our professional work has been used only when no other workshop examples were available to demonstrate a system or design approach. As I said, my hopes in writing this book is to instill the confidence to build your own timber frame. It is about much more than just building a house. Timber framing, by its nature, is more about building community.

Frame built in the Spring 1984 workshop at Fox Maple. This was our third workshop class. This workshop set the mode to design workshop frames to contain the broadest variety of joinery details possible. The saltbox did the trick. New crew member, Mike Sandman (bottom left), joined the crew and instructed for this workshop. Don Morrison is sitting to the left of Mike.

Roof tree placed atop the frame cut in the 1995, Stow, MA workshop.

The culmination of any frame raising is highlighted by the roof tree ceremony. It may be even more so wonderful in a workshop because it all happens in just six days, through any torment that may come along, and with people who have usually just met for the first time. The Oskaloosa, Kansas, workshop in 2004, above, was filled with days at 100 plus degrees, chopping white oak, with no trees or shade in sight. One day we had 4 generations in one family chopping joints in this workshop. The sense of community in instills is priceless. Those memories will remain a part of the house for generations to come.

16'x22' Saltbox Frame

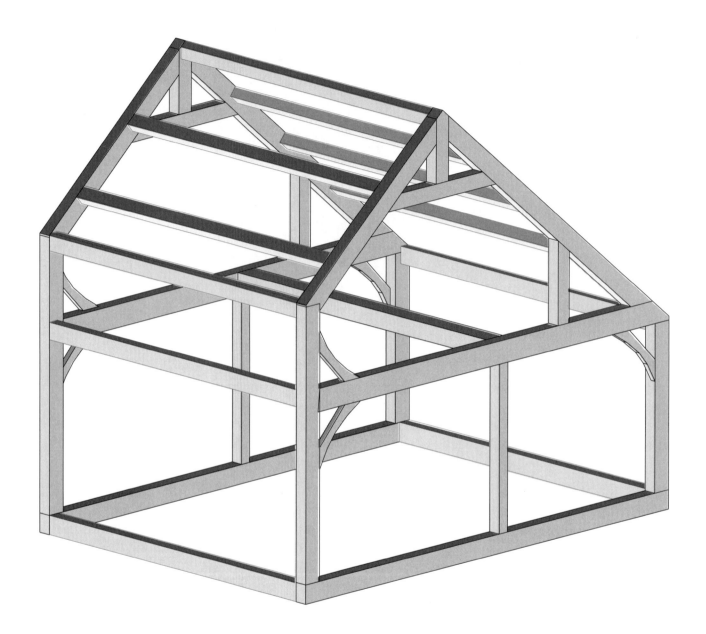

Isometric View

We have built this frame design, with minor variations, in a number of timber framing workshops over the years. It is the perfect design for learning because it contains the essential traditional joinery details. With these few joinery details I believe one could build for a lifetime and never build the same frame twice. The choices are unlimited. But first practice on a small frame such as this to hone your joinery and design skills.

16'x22' Saltbox Frame

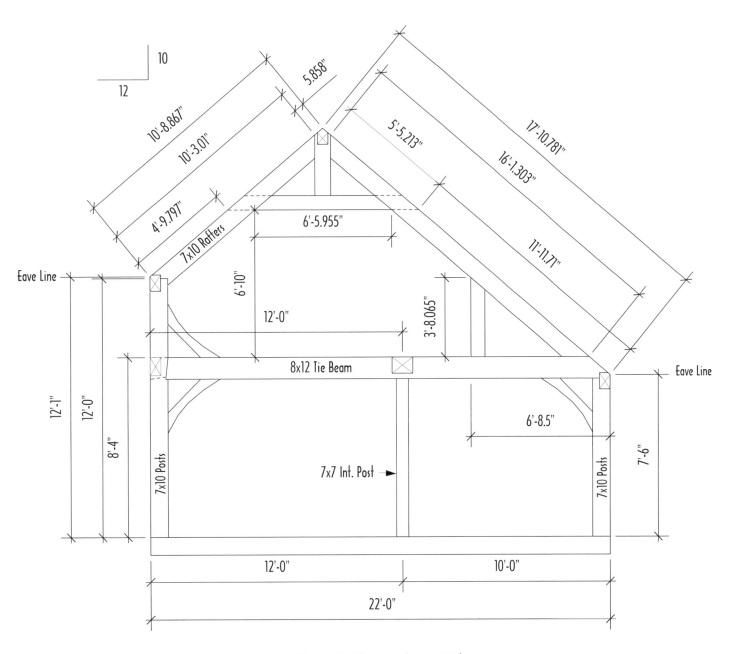

Bent Framing Plan

This bent plan can be adapted easily by changing the roof pitch or by making the tie beam shorter. However, this is the maximum span for a bent plan with this configuration. To create a saltbox bent with a longer span the cantilevered post would need to be raised to a full story height. The tension brace is limited in scope beyond instruction purposes. This plan is ideal for instruction and learning, or building a small cottage, but limited to this scale or smaller. However, with these joinery details one could build an unlimited number of new and different timber frame designs without replication.

16'x22' Saltbox Frame

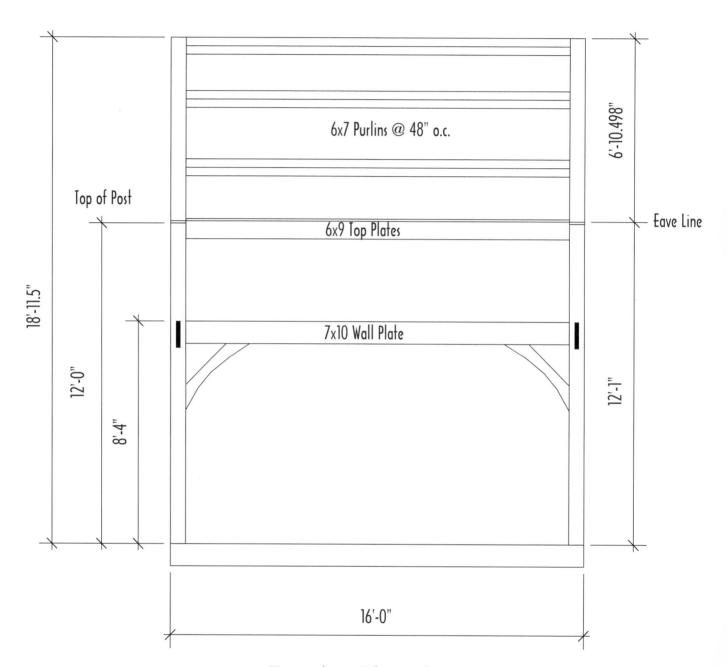

6x7 Purlins @ 48" o.c.

Top of Post

6x9 Top Plates

Eave Line

7x10 Wall Plate

18'-11.5"

6'-10.498"

12'-0"

12'-1"

8'-4"

16'-0"

Framing Elevation

This frame can be built with a continuous or intermediate top plate. The drawing above depicts an intermediate top plate. Additional bents could be added. One extra bent would make a two bay, 32 foot frame.

Timber Schedule

	Width (inches)	Depth (inches)	Length (feet)	Quant.	Bd. Ft.
EXT POSTS FRONT	7	10	12	2	140
EXT POSTS REAR	7	10	8	2	93
INTERIOR POSTS	7	7	8	2	65
TOP PLATES	6	9	16	2	144
WALL PLATES	7	10	16	1	93
TIE BEAMS	7	12	22	2	308
PRINCIPAL RAFTERS REAR	7	10	16	2	187
PRINCIPAL RAFTERS FRONT	7	10	12	2	140
KING POSTS	7	10	6	2	70
QUEEN POSTS	7	8	6	2	56
COLLAR TIES	7	10	8	2	93
PURLINS	6	7	16	6	336
JOISTS	6	7	12	5	210
SUMMER BEAMS	9	13	16	1	156
BRACES (OAK)	3	8	4	10	80
TOTAL MATERIAL				43	2,172

CUT ALL TIMBERS 6 TO 8 INCHES LONGER THAN SPECIFIED LENGTHS.
WHITE PINE TIMBERS SPECIFIED. MAY BE SUBSTITUED WITH ANY SUITABLE SPECIES.

The office at Fox Maple School combines this saltbox design, with the high post cape frame on the following page. The saltbox was cut in the spring 1995 workshop, and the high posted cape in the spring of 1996. The frames were enclosed with Stramit, wheat straw panels. The library is in the background in this photo.

24'x24' High Post Cape Frame

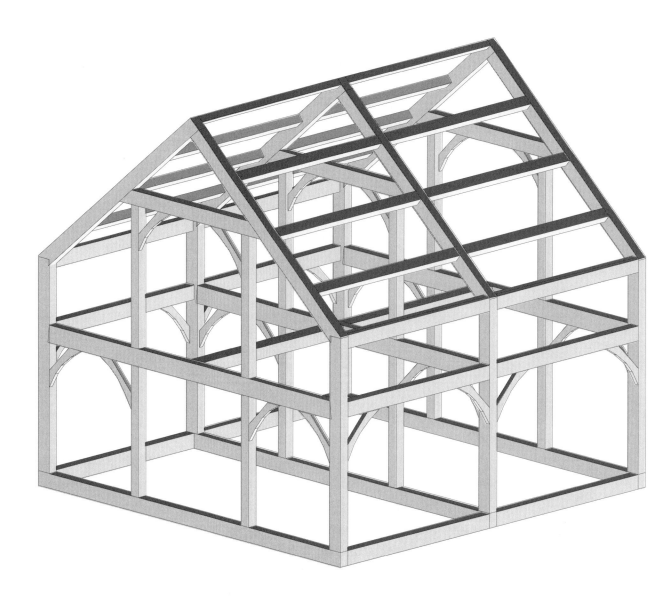

Isometric View

This is another common workshop plan that provides a variety of joinery details. It is an economical design, in that the amount of timber required, and the labor input, provides a generous amount of space. This frame plan was used to build a wing of our offices at Fox Maple.

24'x24' High Post Cape Frame

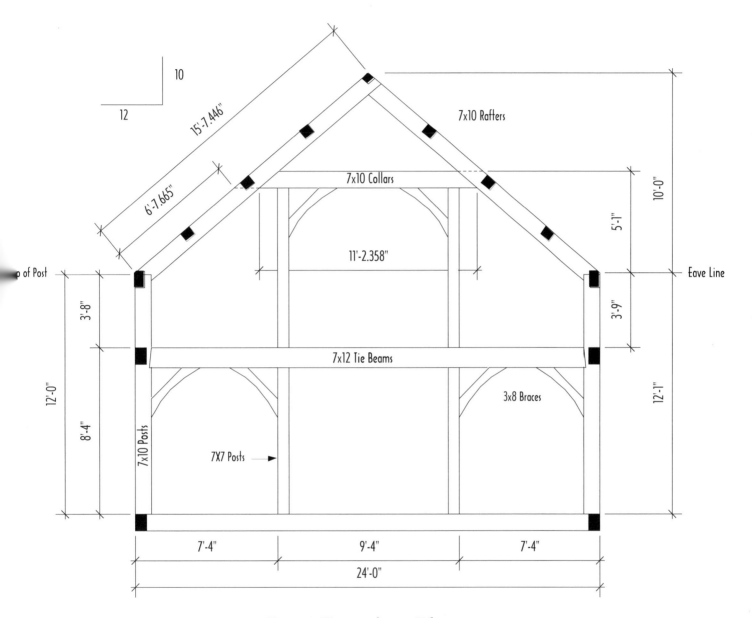

10

12

15'-7.446"

6'-7.665"

7x10 Rafters

7x10 Collars

11'-2.358"

10'-0"

5'-1"

Top of Post

Eave Line

3'-8"

3'-9"

12'-0"

7x12 Tie Beams

12'-1"

8'-4"

7x10 Posts

3x8 Braces

7X7 Posts

7'-4"

9'-4"

7'-4"

24'-0"

Bent Framing Plan

In this bent plan, the first floor interior posts can be arranged to fit the floor plan. One post in the middle of the bent is all that is really required, though this would require two opposing brace struts to the tie beam. Post placement should fit with the intended use and the floor plan. This plan can be expanded to 48 feet with the addition of only a king post. In this case the collar would join at the upper third point of the rafter and the queen posts at the lower third points. Timber dimensions would not necessarily need to be increased.

24'x24' High Post Cape Frame

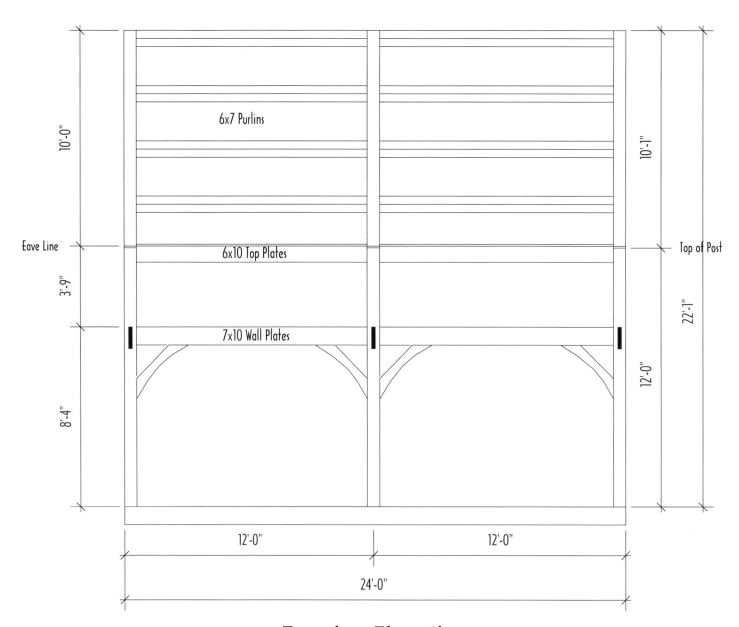

6x7 Purlins

10'-0"

10'-1"

Eave Line

6x10 Top Plates

Top of Post

3'-9"

22'-1"

7x10 Wall Plates

12'-0"

8'-4"

12'-0"

12'-0"

24'-0"

Framing Elevation

The bay spacing in this frame can be increased to 16 feet. Adding another bent would make a four bent frame. In this case the outer bays could be 12 to 16 feet, with a middle chimney bay of 8 to 12 feet. This would make a wonderful layout for a 2 to 3 bedroom house.

The photo to the right shows the installation of the top plate connecting the bents. With one bent braced or fixed, straps and come-alongs are used for safeties (and to pull it all together once fitted) and the free bent is leaned out to fit the plate. Braces must enter all at the same time. It is good to have a few hands on deck for this. Note the notched tenon that wraps around the tie beam.

Timber Schedule

	Width (inches)	Depth (inches)	Length (feet)	Quant.	Bd. Ft.
EXT POSTS	7	10	12	6	420
1ST FLOOR INT POSTS	7	7	8	6	196
2ND FLOOR INT POSTS	7	7	8	6	196
TOP PLATES	6	10	12	4	240
WALL PLATES	7	10	12	4	280
TIE BEAMS	7	12	24	3	504
PRINCIPAL RAFTERS	7	10	16	6	560
COLLAR TIES	7	10	12	3	210
PURLINS	6	7	12	14	588
JOISTS	6	6	8	12	288
SUMMER BEAMS	8	12	12	2	192
BRACES (OAK)	3	8	4	20	160
TOTAL MATERIAL				83	3,834

CUT ALL TIMBERS 6 TO 8 INCHES LONGER THAN SPECIFIED LENGTHS.
WHITE PINE TIMBERS SPECIFIED. MAY BE SUBSTITUTED WITH ANY SUITABLE SPECIES.

Installing the compressed wheat straw panels on the office frames at Fox Maple. The frames were cut in the spring 1995 and 1996 workshops using the two previous framing plans.

24' x 36' Hammerbeam Cape

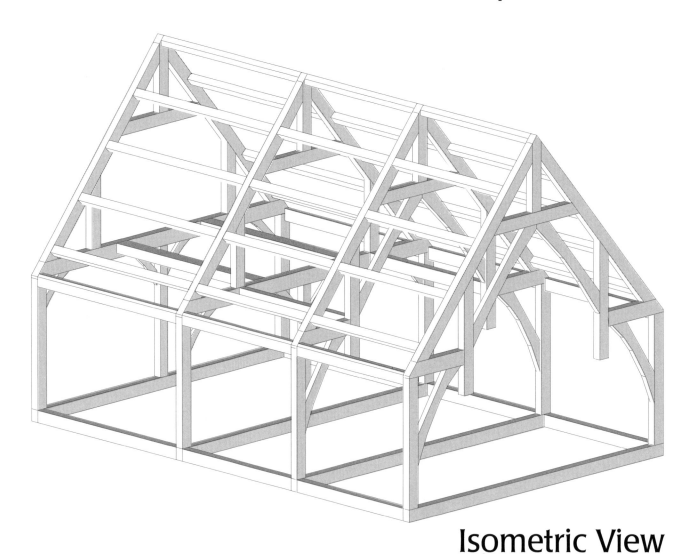

Isometric View

Bent spans in a hammerbeam truss must be based on proper proportion and design, but there is no span that cannot be accomplished if all of the mechanical and structural principals are followed. Bay spacing can range from 8 to 16 feet. It is best to let the bay spacing be dictated by the intended use of the living area.

There may be no other design in timber framing that has as much allure as does the hammerbeam bent. From a joinery standpoint, a hammerbeam bent offers no difficulties beyond that of a simple queen post bent. But, in its nature and ability to offer free and clear open spaces, its beauty is magnified to the point that it almost seems to defy our sense of structure.

In this frame plan, the hammerbeam bents create the Great Room—the space in which one wants to sit and revel, read, entertain and just enjoy structure and space. I have often felt that the better elements of design are those that seem to elevate the space enclosed, but that do not take elevated talent to achieve. This is the case with a hammerbeam. There are definite concrete structural guidelines to follow in designing and building a hammerbeam that will actually work, but once these elements are understood, the cutting and the execution offer very little difficulty.

This frame was built in the Spring 1998 Workshop in High Rolls, New Mexico.

24' x 36' Hammerbeam Cape

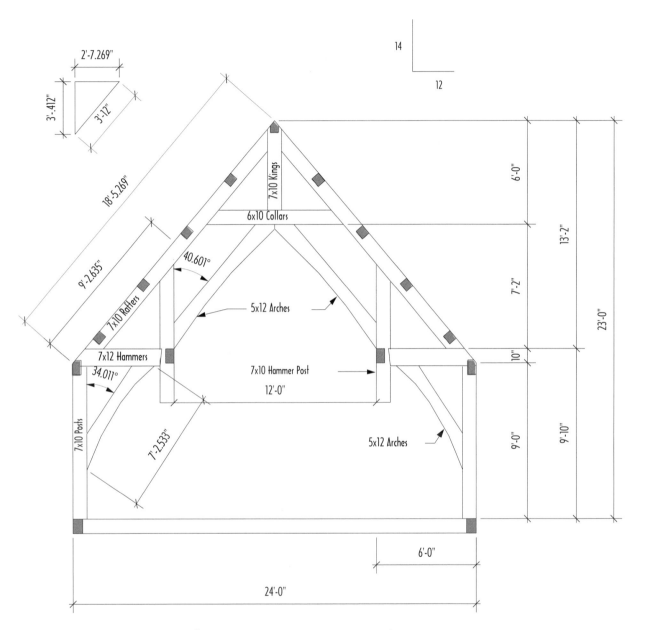

Bents #1-#2 Framing Plan

If you tackle this frame, you're going to need to brush up on the trigonometry. The upper arched braces can project from the hammer post level with the top of the hammer beam, or up to 6 inches above it. The joinery is straightforward, but it is a great lesson for anyone willing to extend their math talents. This design uses a 14/12 pitch, but this could be changed. A 9/12 pitch is the lowest pitch one would consider for a hammerbeam bent. Eaves dropper floor joists would need to be used in the second floor loft system.

24' x 36' Hammerbeam Cape

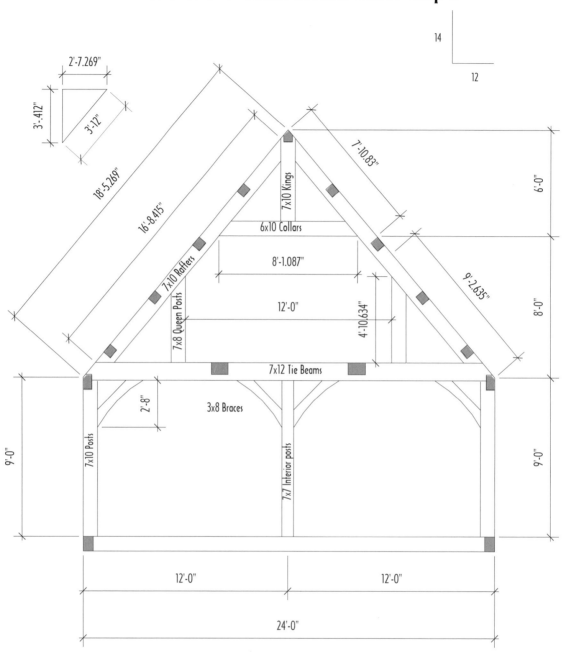

14

12

2'-7.269"

3'-.412"

3'-12"

18'-5.269"

16'-8.415"

7'-10.83"

7x10 Kings

6x10 Collars

8'-1.087"

12'-0"

4'-10.634"

9'-2.635"

6'-0"

8'-0"

7x10 Rafters

7x8 Queen Posts

7x12 Tie Beams

2'-8"

3x8 Braces

7x10 Posts

7x7 Interior posts

9'-0"

9'-0"

12'-0"

12'-0"

24'-0"

Bents #3-#4 Framing Plan

Eaves dropper joists would be used to join the floor joists in the loft to the plates in this frame.

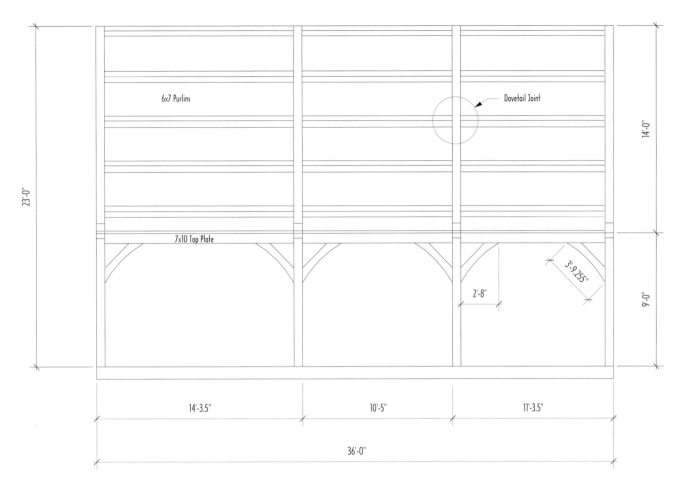

6x7 Purlins

Dovetail Joint

7x10 Top Plate

3'-9.255"

2'-8"

23'-0"

14'-0"

9'-0"

14'-3.5"

10'-5"

11'-3.5"

36'-0"

East Framing Elevation

There are countless variations in the design of joinery that can be used in a given frame. In this frame design, utilizing an English tying joint, the plates can be intermediate, or continuous. In the photo to the left, the post of an English tying joint is designed to accept a continuous top plate. The plate is scarfed over the middle post with an offset cheek scarf. This conceals the vertical butt cuts behind the post face, and to all appearances, the top plate looks as one continuous timber after assembled. The dovetail cuts in the top plate and tie beam form an interlocking connection that prevents outward rolling of the plate, helping to secure the complete connection.

This frame plan is designed to use intermediate top plates, but continuous plates can be used.

24' x 36' Hammerbeam Cape

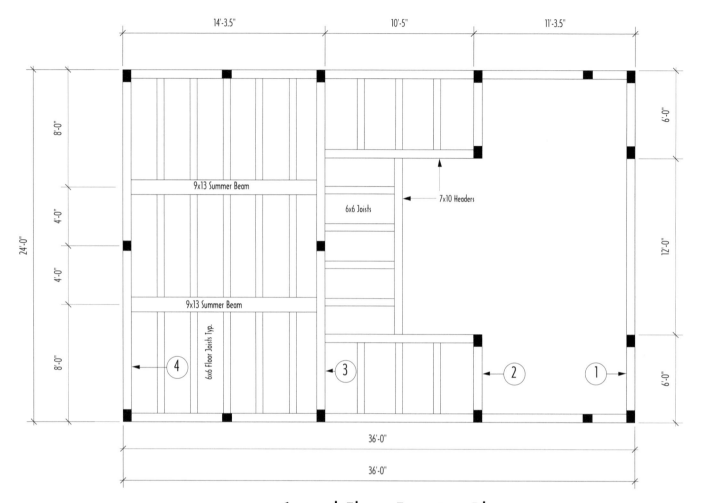

14'-3.5"   10'-5"   11'-3.5"

8'-0"

9x13 Summer Beam

4'-0"

7x10 Headers

6x6 Joists

4'-0"

24'-0"

9x13 Summer Beam

6x6 Floor Joists Typ.

8'-0"

④   ③   ②   ①

6'-0"

12'-0"

6'-0"

36'-0"

36'-0"

Second Floor Framing Plan

Top plates connecting to post in a modified English tying joint similar to that used in this frame.

Timber Schedule

	Width (inches)	Depth (inches)	Length (feet)	Quant.	Bd. Ft.
EXT POSTS/MAIN	7	10	10	8	467
1ST FLR INT POSTS	7	8	10	2	93
TOP PLATES	6	10	14	2	140
TOP PLATES	6	10	12	4	240
COLLAR TIES	7	10	10	4	233
TIE BEAMS	7	12	24	2	336
PRINCIPAL RAFTERS	7	10	18	8	840
KING POSTS	7	10	8	4	187
HAMMER BEAMS	7	12	8	4	224
HAMMER POSTS	7	10	8	4	187
ARCHES	5	12	8	4	160
ARCHES	5	12	12	4	240
QUEEN POSTS	7	8	6	4	112
PURLINS	6	7	14	9	441
PURLINS	6	7	12	18	756
JOISTS	6	6	8	25	600
SUMMER BEAMS	9	12	14	2	252
HEADERS	7	10	12	3	210
BRACES	3	8	4	25	200
TOTAL MATERIAL				**136**	**5,918**

CUT ALL TIMBERS 6 TO 8 INCHES LONGER THAN SPECIFIED LENGTHS.
WHITE PINE TIMBERS SPECIFIED. MAY BE SUBSTITUTED WITH ANY SUITABLE SPECIES.

Workshop frame cut in the summer 1998 High Rolls, New Mexico, workshop, using this framing plan. The gable bent was cut and erected by the workshop sponsor and a few of the local students after the workshops.

Scissor trusses and lower hammer struts were used to allow clear-span and open living areas on both the first and second floors in this house frame built in Sag Harbor, NY in 1989. Understanding trigonometry not only allows one to determine the distribution of forces in the framework, but also the precise member lengths, location, layout and design of the joinery. The frames to the right and below required just a little insight to math.

The bath house frame at Fox Maple was cut in the Fall 2004 Advanced timber framing workshop. The four valley roof system marries curved round maple timbers with square timbers in the Japanese tradition. The posts are scribed to fit to the stones. Dragon beams and natural cherry upper struts resist thrust of the valley rafters. The frame was a lesson in trigonometry and engineering. Advanced workshops can get pretty wild.

Chapter 11
Builders Math & Engineering

Builders Math

The wonderful thing about math, and especially trigonometry, is that you can determine any angle, at any rotation, with absolute accuracy. Then use this to lay out and cut the frame, put it on a truck and travel across the country, and when you arrive it will all fit together. There is no guesswork involved. It is absolute. They say math is the language of God. If it is true, then I have had some very interesting conversations with him over the years.

In any building project it is essential that the builder have a working understanding of geometry. Webster's defines geometry as: *a branch of mathematics that deals with the measurement, properties and relationships of points, lines, angles, surfaces and solids.* To apply geometric principles in building, a rudimentary understanding of algebra is necessary for determining and solving equations, but the greatest tool that a builder can own is a thorough understanding of Trigonometry. Trigonometry is the branch of mathematics that deals specifically with right triangles. Gaining a strong working understanding of trigonometry will open the doorway to unlimited freedom and creativity in designing, building and engineering structures.

Roof framing, in its myriad variations, is nothing more than a combination of right triangles. In every building we start out with a set of givens. The footprint gives us the building's width and length. The elevation gives us the height and roof pitch. A common gabled roof lies on one plane, or two dimensions—width and height. The width gives us the span of the rafters and subsequently the overall rafter run. The roof pitch, given as rise per foot of run, allows us to determine the overall rafter rise. With this information we can then determine the rafter length by using the Pythagorean Theorem or Trigonometry.

Pythagorean Theorem

I would venture to say that most builders have a working understanding of the Pythagorean theorem which states: *"in any right triangle the square of the hypotenuse is equal to the sum of the squares of the legs."* The common formula being: $a^2 + b^2 = c^2$. If we know the length of the two legs of any right triangle we can calculate the third side (hypotenuse) by using this formula.

11.1) Rafter Span, Run & Rise

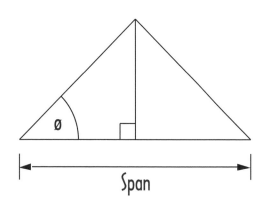

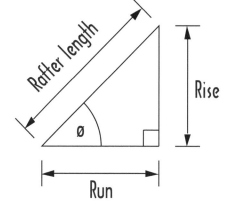

The span of the rafters is equal to the width of the building. In a simple truss with equal pitches, the run is 1/2 the span. The roof pitch is the angle of inclination off the level plane (ø). The pitch is given as the rise in inches per foot of run. In our example: 10/12

By determining the rafter run and rise, the rafter length (hypotenuse) can be determined using the Pythagorean theorem: $a^2 + b^2 = c^2$, in which: a = run, b = rise, c = hypotenuse. The degree of angle ø is not required when using this formula.

This formula can be used to determine any diagonal between the two legs of a right triangle. Builders commonly use it to determine the diagonal measure of a foundation or deck in order to check for square.

As illustrated in Diagram 1 the hypotenuse, *c*, is equal to the rafter length; *a*, is equal to the rafter run (span÷2); and *b*, is equal to the vertical rafter rise. Thanks to the pocket calculator with square root function, the results of the formula can easily be determined in just a few seconds.

Using the example of a cape with a rafter span of 28 feet, and a roof pitch of 10 inches of rise for every foot of run (10/12), we can use the Pythagorean theorem to determine the rafter length (see diagram 11.2).

The run of the rafter, *a*, is half of the span, or width of the building. In this example, 14 feet. The rise, *b*, is the distance from the horizontal plane at the eaves level of the building to the peak. We now know that *a* equals 14' and that angle *ab* equals 90°. To find the rise, we simply multiply the run, *a*, by the rise of rafter per foot of run, and divide by the run, 12. The equation for our example would read: (14 x 10) /12 = 11.666'

If we happened to know the rise of the roof and needed to determine the run, the formula would be: (11.666 x 12) /10 = 14

In these equations the run of 12 is a constant (roof pitches are referred to as the inches of rise per foot of run); the rise is given by the designer.

In most buildings, the actual run is an exact given, so we usually start with this. We can find the rise in another way by simply multiplying the run (in feet) by the rise per foot of run (in inches). The result is the rise in inches:

14 x 10 = 140 inches. To transfer to feet, divide by 12: 140 ÷ 12 = 11.666'. I prefer to work in inches, so I would transpose the run to inches by multiplying by 12, giving a run of 168 inches and a rise of 140 inches.

Upon determining the rise and the run of the building, use the equation below to determine the rafter length.

Equations to find Rise & Run

$$Run = Span \div 2$$

To find rise in feet:
$$Rise = (a \times R) \div 12$$
in which:
a = run, in feet
R = rise, inches per ft. run

To find rise in inches:
$$Rise = a \times R$$
in which:
a = run, in feet
R = rise, inches per ft. run

To find run if rise is known:
$$run = (b \times 12) \div R$$
in which:
b = actual rise in feet
R = rise, inches per ft. run

11.2) Pythagorean Theorem

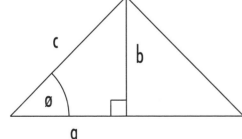

Simply stated, the hypotenuse is equal to the square root of the sum of the squares of the legs of a right triangle. In our example *a* = 168 inches, *b* = 140 inches. To solve for *c* use the following formula:

$$c = \sqrt{a^2 + b^2}$$

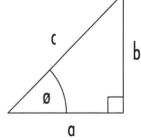

a = 168; b = 140

$$c = \sqrt{168^2 + 140^2}$$

$$c^2 = (168 \times 168) + (140 \times 140) = 47,824$$

$$\sqrt{47,824} = 218.686$$

The rafter length is 218.686 inches.

Setting the hammerbeam dormer gable bent cut in the Spring 2004 timber framing workshop at Fox Maple. The frame, which was a four bent, high posted cape included a 4 valley system that was cut in the Advanced workshop. Trigonometry was an essential aspect of designing and laying out the all aspects of the frame. This, of course, was carried out by students who for the most part had never had any building experience prior to the workshop.

Trigonometric Ratios

While the Pythagorean theorem is unfailing in determining rafter lengths, it is useless when it comes to finding angles, and limited in its reliance on two specific known factors. Many times, only the angle and one leg of a triangle is known, or two sides are known, and the angle needs to be determined. This is often the case in remodeling, or when designing strut placement within a truss, and especially when working with compound roof frames. *Trigonometry* opens the doorway to greater flexibility and creativity, and is the direct path to unfold the mystery of intersecting planes and the right triangle. While this subject may seem to be quite complex, it is really fairly easy to understand and master. By focusing on the functions as they relate directly to roof framing, a working knowledge can be gained rather quickly.

It was found by Thales (the Greek mathematician) sometime around 600 BC, that the ratios of the length of the sides of a right triangle remained constant between all similar triangles. Once these ratios were determined, the length of the sides of any similar triangle could be determined by multiplying or dividing by these constant ratios. The understanding of these trigonometric ratios were revolutionary to ancient builders, and guarded as mystical knowledge for centuries by building brotherhoods such as the Masons. It was this knowledge that allowed the ancient Greeks, Romans, and the Mediaeval Cathedral builders to build such magnificent structures.

Thanks to Thales, for providing the insight, and the folks at Texas Instruments, who invented the pocket calculator, we are able to apply some rather complex trigonometric calculations in a matter of seconds with only a basic understanding of the underlying principles. *(If you do not own one you should go immediately and purchase a calculator with trigonometric functions. The Texas Instruments TI-30XA is inexpensive and easy to use, however, Casio, Hewlett Packard and Sharp all make similar models. If you are new to this buy the lowest cost model).*

Trigonometry is based on the ratio of the sides of a right triangle to each other. These ratios are called the *sine, cosine* and *tangent* (see Dia. 11.3). The *sine* is the ratio of the side opposite to the hypotenuse, and is determined by dividing the side opposite by the hypotenuse. The *cosine* is the ratio of the side adjacent to the hypotenuse, and found by dividing the side adjacent by the hypotenuse. The *tangent* is the ratio of the side opposite to the side adjacent, and is determined by dividing the side opposite by the side adjacent. Knowing and understanding these ratios allows you to find the run, rise and rafter lengths with fewer known factors. With the use of the scientific calculator, any angle, in any given triangle, may be found if the length of any two sides are known.

Once an angle in the overall roof frame is determined, and the *sine, cosine* and *tangent* noted, the layout of joinery, determining the exact location of all struts, collar ties and queen posts joining to the rafters will become a simple matter. When the concept is fully grasped, no frame design or joinery detail will ever cause any problems. Understanding trigonometry, if not mandatory, certainly will help maintain sanity, and go a long way in extending your talents as a builder.

11.3) Determining Trigonometric Ratios

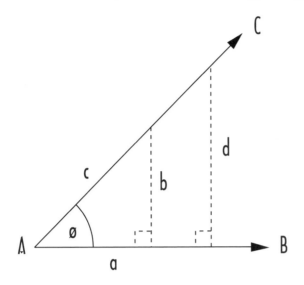

$$\frac{\text{Opposite}}{\text{Adjacent}} = \text{Tangent}$$

$$\frac{\text{Adjacent}}{\text{Hypotenuse}} = \text{Cosine}$$

$$\frac{\text{Opposite}}{\text{Hypotenuse}} = \text{Sine}$$

In the diagram above, two lines radiate from point A; AB and AC, creating angle ø. If at any point along line AB a perpendicular line is drawn that intersects with line AC, a right triangle is formed. Line AB (side *a* of the new triangle) is said to be Adjacent to angle ø. The two dotted lines, *b* & *d*, are said to be Opposite angle ø, and create one leg of triangles *abc*, and *adc*. Side *c*, of these new triangles is called the *hypotenuse*. The three sides of the triangle are called the side Adjacent, side Opposite and the Hypotenuse, all being in reference to angle ø.

The relationship of the sides of the triangle, in reference to the angle ø, remain constant and are known as the **Sine**, **Cosine** and **Tangent**. The equation to determine their ratios is as follows:

Side Opposite ÷ Hypotenuse = Sine
Side Adjacent ÷ Hypotenuse = Cosine
Side Opposite ÷ Side Adjacent = Tangent

To determine values for the *sine, cosine* and *tangent*. Two factors, or givens, must be known: 1) the degree of angle ø and length of one side; or 2) the length of two sides. As the ratios are constant in all similar triangles, we can use the given rafter pitch (rise÷run) to find the angle, sine, cosine and tangent, and then apply the actual run and rise to the building.

The sides of the right triangle above are designated in relation to the angle. By giving values to two of the sides, or one side and specifying the degree of angle ø, we can determine the sine, cosine, and tangent.

In our example, we have specified a roof pitch of 10/12. We can directly find the angle by applying the 10 to the side opposite and 12 to the side adjacent. The result will be the tangent of angle ø: 10÷12=.83333.

To find the degree of angle ø, we need to find the arctangent, which is the inverse of the tangent. Without the scientific calculator this can be quite a complex equation. With the calculator, it is easily found by any novice as follows.

Reading .83333 on the calculator, press 2nd function (often marked INV), then the TAN key. The result is 39.80557. This is the angle in degrees. Make a note of this, and also of the tangent. To find the *sine* and *cosine* proceed as follows:

Reading 39.80557 on the calculator, press SIN. It should read .64018. This is the *sine*, make a note. Push 2nd, then SIN, this gives the degree again. Now push COS, it should read .76822, the *cosine*. Make a note.

Do this again, but instead of using 10/12, use the actual rise and run in our example (140/168). The results should be the same.

The easiest way to understand this is by way of example. Using the same example as before, a 28' wide cape, let's use a scientific pocket calculator using the trig functions to determine the rafter length. In the example below, I refer to the INV key on the calculator. This key is programed to provide a variety of second functions on the calculator (it is labeled 2nd on many calculators). Using trig functions, the INV or 2nd key will translate the tangent, sine or cosine into the *arctangent*, *arcsine*, or *arccosine* in degrees, by displaying any one of these known values, then pushing INV or 2nd function, then the TAN, SIN or COS. Likewise, it works in reverse, and will give the sin, cosine or tangent if you display the degree of the angle, then press the TAN, COS or SIN key.

Mastering trigonometry allows one to fluently design and layout joinery as in this four valley frame with multiple valley dormers, scissor trusses, king posts and struts. This layout was all accomplished with a calculator, a two dimensional plan, a pencil, and a strong knowledge of trigonometry. As an aspiring jazz guitarist I learned that if you wanted to play wild improvisational riffs, you first needed to learn and practice the scales until your fingers executed without any mental thought processes telling them where to go. Trigonometry is the musical scale of timber framing, and the first prerequisite if you want to express your own jazz. Indianapolis, IN, 1991.

In the diagrams to the right, the development of a triangle is illustrated. By drawing a line perpendicular to the base and intersecting the apex (dividing the triangle into equal parts), two similar right triangles are created. A span of 28 feet is the given. A roof pitch of 10 over 12 is also given. By applying the known values to the triangles, we can begin to solve all of the unknown values using trigonometry. For the following operation, key in all functions using full decimal readouts. Rounding off can be done later.

Step 1) **Determine run or side adjacent:**
   Run = span ÷ 2. In our example: 28' ÷ 2 = 14'
   side adjacent equals 14 feet.

Step 2) **Determine the degree of angle Ø:**
   Ø = Arctangent (opposite ÷ adjacent)
   10 ÷ 12 = .83333333 then push INV then TAN = 39.80557109°
   angle Ø = 39.80557109°

Step 3) **Determine Sine, Cosine & Tangent:**
   Reading 39.80557109° on the calculator push SIN = .6401844
   Make a note: sine = .6401844. Then push INV then SIN; the degree
   is displayed again (39.80557109).
   Next push the COS key. This will read .76822128, make a note, this
   is the cosine. Next push INV then COS, to read the degree, then push
   TAN. This will read .83333333. Make a note, this is the tangent.

Make a note of the results by rounding the degree to 3 decimal places, and the sine, cosine, and tangent to five decimal places as follows:

Angle Ø = 39.805; Sine = .64018; Cosine = .76822; Tangent = .83333

Once these ratios have been determined, you want to keep them noted on the plan or on your clipboard—you will use them over and over again. The results above were determined by simply using the given roof pitch rise and run (10/12). Once the ratios and angle are determined, we will use these ratios to determine all members within the roof framing—rafters, collar ties and strut lengths and locations on the rafter for layout—by plugging in the actual known measurements of the frame. Create a triangle diagram for each situation, plug in the givens for the specific situation, and run through the same equations. A few examples will be provided at the end of this section.

The following diagrams illustrate the trigonometric relationships of the sides of a right triangle to the angle. Angle ø is created when two lines radiate from any given point. A right triangle is created when a line is drawn perpendicular to one line and intersects the other. Always identify the angle, then the relationships of the sides. In a roof system, we can easily relate the sides of the triangle—in both horizontal and vertical planes—to the members in the roof. However, when we begin designing joinery, the triangle is often flipped in space. Get into the habit of identifying the sides in relation to the angle of origin. Angles are created when two lines radiate from a single point in space. A triangle is created when a third line, opposite the angle, encloses the space. The sum of all the angles in a triangle equal 180°.

Formula to determine Sine, Cosine & Tangent of a right triangle	
$\dfrac{\text{Opposite}}{\text{Adjacent}}$	= Tangent
$\dfrac{\text{Adjacent}}{\text{Hypotenuse}}$	= Cosine
$\dfrac{\text{Opposite}}{\text{Hypotenuse}}$	= Sine

Dia. 11.4a

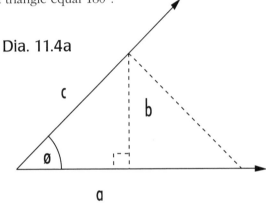

Angle ø is created when two lines radiate from a given point. A right triangle is created by drawing a third line perpendicular to one, and intersecting the other (dotted lines).

Dia. 11.4b

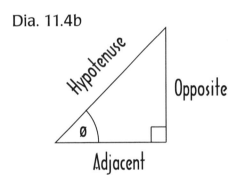

The diagram above illustrates the trigonometric relationships of sides of a right triangle to the angle. This relationship remains constant, regardless of where the triangle is in space.

Dia. 11.4c

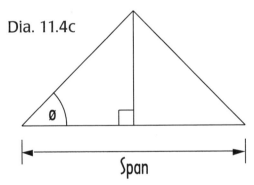

In a simple roof frame, the angle of the roof pitch is usually a given, as is the width of the building, or the span of the rafters. In the drawing above, a line drawn from the apex to the base creates two similar right triangles. By applying the known factors of length to any two sides, or the length of one side and the degree of the angle, all other unknown values can be determined by using trigonometry. Assume that the span above is 28 feet, and the pitch is 10 over 12. Applying our known values, the unknown values can be determined using the scientific calculator. See the example to the right.

Dia. 11.4d

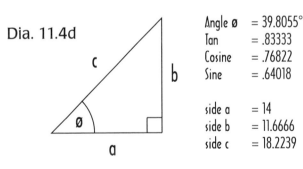

Angle ø	= 39.8055°
Tan	= .83333
Cosine	= .76822
Sine	= .64018
side a	= 14
side b	= 11.6666
side c	= 18.2239

Span ÷ 2 = 14'; a = 14'.
Angle ø = 10 ÷ 12 = .83333; INV TAN = 39.8055°
Tan ø = .83333; b = a x TAN ø = 14 x .83333 = 11.6666
To find c; c = a ÷ Cosine ø; To find Cosine ø; reading 39.8055 on the calculator push COS = .76822; Cosine ø = .76822;
c = a ÷ Cosine = 14 ÷ .76822 = 18.2239
Check by using sine function:
Sine ø = b ÷ c = 11.6666 ÷ 18.2239 = .64018;
to confirm angle ø push INV then SIN = 39.8055
Check again: b ÷ SIN ø = c;
11.6666 ÷ .64018 = 18.2239

Any angle can be applied to the framing square by using the tangent of the angle to determine the numbers on the opposite legs as described below. By extending it to numbers near the end of the square and clamping the square into a jig, the square can cover the full face of the timbers, as depicted above. This method allows for repetitive angles to be laid out quickly and accurately.

Before the invention of the calculator, it was common to use a reference chart listing numerous angles and trig ratios. Angles not shown would be determined by extrapolating the next higher and lower angles listed. The chart on the following page can be used to determine angles if you do not have a scientific calculator.

Referring to the chart we find that a 10/12 pitch is a 39.8055 degree angle. The chart also tells us that the tangent is .8333. This is also the answer we get if we were to divide 10 by 12 (*tangent* = side opposite / side adjacent). Using the previous example for the run (side adjacent) as 14 feet, we can find the rise by multiplying 14 by the *tangent*: 14 x .83333 = 11.6666

If we should happen to know the rise only, then we would divide the rise by the *tangent* (11.6666 ÷ .8333 = 14). If we know only the run (side adjacent) is 14', we can find the hypotenuse (rafter length) by dividing the run by the *cosine*. The chart tells us the cosine is .7682, so: 14 / .7682 = 18.224'

This same method and logic may be carried out from any direction, dictated by the known factors. For instance, if only the rise was known and you needed to know the hypotenuse you would simply divide the rise by the *sine*:
11.6666 / .6402 = 18.224'

The importance of these trigonometric functions will become more and more evident as you begin to work with roof systems to design joinery, locate strut and brace placement within a truss, and especially, when you begin to work with compound joinery. If you begin using trig when determining relatively simple applications, soon, even the most complicated frameworks will begin to appear straightforward.

Using Trig to Facilitate Layout

When laying out joinery, you'll want to use the framing square to make the layout. When a pitch is given as 10/12 or 14/12, etc., it's a simple matter to use these whole numbers on the square to replicate the angle. In many cases you will not be working with whole numbers, or even roof pitches, or you may want to extend the points on the square so that it will cover the whole timber. Any angle can be transferred to the square quite simply by choosing a random number on the square, let's say 20 on the body of the square, and using the tangent to find the corresponding number on the tongue. In this case, the body is the side adjacent, the tongue is the side opposite (run and rise) of the angle.

Example: we have a 34.25° angle and want to set the square to this angle using 20 on the body. Find the tongue location as follows:

Tangent 34.25° = .68087

20 x .68087 = 13.617. Set the square to 20/13.617 for a 34.25° angle. Convert the decimal .617 into 16ths by multiplying by 16: .617 x 16 = 9.872/16ths

You can sample a few numbers, 21, 20.5, 18, etc., to find a number easily located on the square:

18 x .68087 = 12.255. Close enough to round to a 1/4 inch, so I would use this, and set the square to 18/12.25.

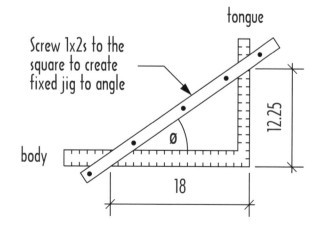

Screw 1x2s to the square to create fixed jig to angle

tongue

body

12.25

18

Ø

Table 5) TRIGONOMETRIC RATIOS

RISE inches per ft.run	RAFTER length per ft. run	DEGREE	SINE	COSINE	TANGENT
1	12.0416	4.76	0.0830	0.9965	0.0833
1.5	12.0934	7.125	0.1240	0.9923	0.1250
2	12.1655	9.4641	0.1644	0.9864	0.1667
2.5	12.2577	11.7664	0.2040	0.9790	0.2083
3	12.3693	14.0362	0.2425	0.9701	0.2500
3.5	12.5000	16.2619	0.2800	0.9600	0.2917
4	12.6491	18.4332	0.3162	0.9487	0.3333
4.5	12.8160	20.556	0.3511	0.9363	0.3750
5	13.0000	22.6214	0.3846	0.9231	0.4167
5.5	13.2004	24.6219	0.4167	0.9091	0.4583
6	13.4164	26.565	0.4472	0.8944	0.5000
6.5	13.6473	28.444	0.4763	0.8793	0.5417
7	13.8924	30.255	0.5039	0.8638	0.5833
7.5	14.1510	32.0053	0.5300	0.8480	0.6250
8	14.4222	33.69139	0.5547	0.8321	0.6667
8.5	14.7054	35.3099	0.5780	0.8160	0.7083
9	15.0000	36.8698	0.6000	0.8000	0.7500
9.5	15.3052	38.3686	0.6207	0.7840	0.7917
10	15.6205	39.8055	0.6402	0.7682	0.8333
10.5	15.9452	41.18592	0.6585	0.7526	0.8750
11	16.2788	42.5114	0.6757	0.7372	0.9167
11.5	16.6208	43.7801	0.6919	0.7220	0.9583
12	16.9706	45	0.7071	0.7071	1.0000
12.5	17.3277	46.17	0.7214	0.6925	1.0417
13	17.6918	47.2897	0.7348	0.6783	1.0833
13.5	18.0624	48.3664	0.7474	0.6644	1.1250
14	18.4391	49.3995	0.7593	0.6508	1.1667
14.5	18.8215	50.3885	0.7704	0.6376	1.2083
15	19.2094	51.3401	0.7809	0.6247	1.2500

In the chart above, <u>Rise</u> is in inches per foot of run. <u>Rafter length</u> is the length of the rafter, or hypotenuse, per foot of run. This number can also be used as a factor to determine overall rafter length by multiplying it by the total run, in feet. The result is the rafter length in inches. Example: Rise = 8; Total run = 16 feet: 16 x 14.4222 = 230.755 inches.

The roof system of the Bathhouse at Fox Maple was designed and cut by students using the basic trigonometry as described here. Compound joinery can be quite complex, as there are seven basic rotations off the level plane, resulting in seven planes of intersection. Each rotation can be unfolded using trigonometry. So, get used to using trig for all your general layout, and when the time comes to cut your first compound roof system you'll be prepared.

Using a square jig allows the square body to go beyond the end of the timber, allowing accurate layout right to the end as illustrated in these photos. The jig also stabilizes the square allowing firm and accurate layout with a knife.

Math Quiz

Solve the following problems using trigonometry. The essentials are given for a few examples, but make up your own problems, and get in the habit of using trig whenever you need to work with right triangles. The answers to the following problems can be found on page 229.

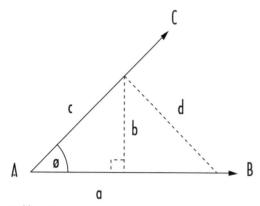

Problem #1

Givens: The roof pitch is a 7/12, and d = 120

Find: angle Ø; run a, rise b, and hypotenuse c

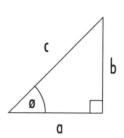

Problem #2

Givens: a = 17'3", b = 12'4"

Find: angle Ø; Hypotenuse c (in inches), and
roof pitch (in inches of rise per foot of run)

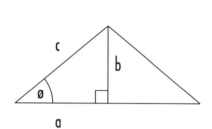

Problem #3

Givens: c = 196; b = 73

Find: angle Ø; run a, roof pitch (inches of rise per foot of run)

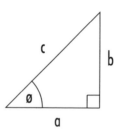

Problem #4

Givens: angle Ø = 73.75°; a = 179

Find: rise b, hypotenuse c, and roof pitch (inches of rise per foot of run)

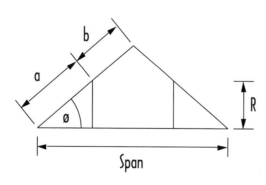

Problem #5

Givens: roof pitch = 11/12, span = 336, a = 107

Find: angle Ø, R, and b

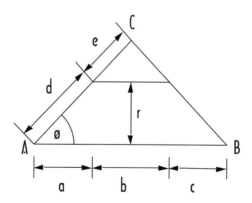

Problem #6

Givens: roof pitch = 9/12, r = 96, b = 100

Find: angle Ø, d, e, a, CB, and span AB

Engineering

Mike Sandman pulling together the last diagonal hammer truss into place on the new dance floor at the Eastern Slope Inn, in North Conway, New Hampshire, 1985. The clear span hipped roof structure spanned 65 feet diagonally. Trigonometry was an essential tool, as this was way before computers and CAD programs were available. Both the rafter peaks and the lower ties joined to the king post with wedged half dovetail joints. The timbers were douglas fir. The king post was carved from a 16" x 16" inch timber and the hip rafters were 10" x 16" x 40' long.

Engineering

Structural engineering is the science of analyzing the forces that are acting, or assumed to be acting, on a structural form. The objective is to isolate each structural component in a methodical and systematic way to identify the weakest link. Each component in a frame has a structural relationship to each other. The process begins with a set of givens, or assumed givens, of predetermined loads based on empirical evidence of what a building may be subjected to in its life, and how a specific material may respond. Roof loads, floor loads, wind and seismic loads are assumed to be present, and reasonable factors have been determined and published that can provide this information for most building situations. The handbook of the International Building Code (IBC) provides a comprehensive listing of minimum and safe design requirements pertaining to universally accepted engineering standards, with specific design criteria for all manner of building conditions. In using the following design formulae, the most updated information, as set by the IBC should be used. This can be obtained from your local building inspector.

A half octagon with a king post truss utilizing half dovetailed and wedged tension joints to join the tie beams to the king post.

The process begins by dissecting the structure into individual components and identifying the stresses that are acting on each particular timber, or member section, based on the reasonable expectation of what forces may be acting upon it. Identifying the type of stress, the magnitude and the direction of the load is important in determining the appropriate calculation for a particular member.

The principal stresses that are acting on any member is as follows:

Tension and Compression: which are considered the working stresses for timbers.
Shearing Stress: either as single or double shear with or across the grain.
Transverse or Bending Stress: the stress commonly placed on rafters, joists and tie beams.

It is not the intent of this manual to provide the complete engineering criteria for the structural design of timber frame structures. The structural analysis of timbers and timber structures under specific loading conditions is quite complex, requiring consideration of a multitude of factors which may be present in any given situation. Any error or oversight may result in serious errors in calculation. Do not take the engineering of a timber framed structure lightly. Simple beam design may be reasonably straight forward, but determining how loads are transferred in a truss or framework requires a thorough understanding of quite complex mathematical theory of force and motion. Don't take this lightly, but do explore the possibilities.

The following beam design formulas, data on the mechanical and scientific properties of a variety of wood species, load calculations for specific beam analysis, as well as a **Bibliography** of sources for further study, is included for the true enthusiast.

Strength of Beams

The following formulas are intended to be used in conjunction with data supplied in Table 7, page 236, titled **Mechanical Properties of Wood.** Additional information on the mechanical and scientific properties of wood are available, and the sources have been supplied in the appendices.

Modulus of Rupture — The breaking strength of a beam is found using the following formulas. When using these formulas, the results can be matched with the Modulus of Rupture of a given wood species in the Table 7, on mechanical properties of wood. For the beam to be acceptable, the results must be from 6 to 8 times less than those given in the table.

For a simple beam, rectangular in cross section, supported at the ends with a concentrated load at the center, the equation is:

$$R = \frac{1.5PL}{bd^2}$$

in which:

R = Modulus of Rupture, lb. per sq. inch
P = The maximum Load, Pounds
L = Distance between supports, inches
b = Width of Beam, inches
d = Depth of Beam, inches

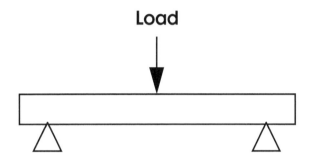

Pentagon frame cut in the 2002 advanced workshop at Fox Maple.

For a variety of other loading conditions use the following formulas. For a Small Simple Beam, uniformly loaded:

$$R = \frac{.75PL}{bd^2}$$

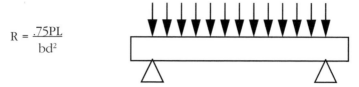

For a Small Simple Beam loaded at third points:

$$R = \frac{PL}{bd^2}$$

For large beams loaded at third points, considering weight of beam:

$$R = \frac{(0.75W + P)L}{bd^2}$$

W = Weight of Beam in Pounds
(The weight of the timber can be assumed to be 5% of the total load.)

The same rectangular beam uniformly loaded is equal to:

$$R = \frac{1.5PL \times 2}{bd^2}$$

The same rectangular beam, fixed at ends, loaded in middle is equal to:

$$R = \frac{1.5PL \times 2}{bd^2}$$

Two of my sons, Finn left and Jonah right, learning to make a "fine curve without faltering" from student, Michael Langford, in the spring 1990 Advanced TF workshop at Fox Maple.

A rectangular beam, fixed at ends, uniformly loaded is equal to:

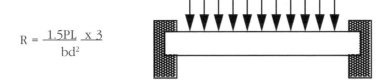

$$R = \frac{1.5PL}{bd^2} \times 3$$

A rectangular beam, cantilevered, loaded at end is equal to:

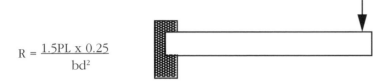

$$R = \frac{1.5PL \times 0.25}{bd^2}$$

A rectangular beam, cantilevered, uniformly loaded is equal to:

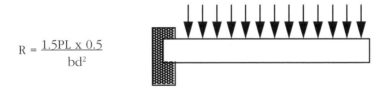

$$R = \frac{1.5PL \times 0.5}{bd^2}$$

The beam team grows up. Three of my sons and a helper at the end of a hot day of frame raising in Lithia, Florida in 2005. To my left are my sons, Finn, (Olivier), Asher and Tait. In 2008 my grandson (Tait's son) took part in a workshop in Asturias, Spain. He chopped a joint with the help of his dad, so now we officially have four generations of timber framers in the family. Hooray!

Determining the Strength of Pegged Connections

Testing of pegged joinery connections have recently been undertaken by the Timber Framing Engineering Council (TFEC), that for the first time can address the actual reactions to pegged joinery under loading. The following is an abstract prepared by John Wolbeck. (see also page 239 for TFEC excerpt).

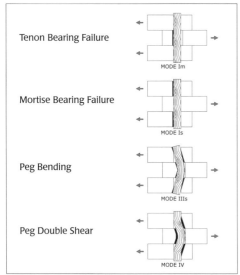

Tenon Bearing Failure

MODE Im

Mortise Bearing Failure

MODE Is

Peg Bending

MODE IIIs

Peg Double Shear

MODE IV

11.5) Four failure modes of pegged joinery as defined in the TFEC's Technical Bulletin 2009-01, Capacity of Pegged Connections.

Wooden pegged connections in tension can fail in a number of complex ways. Mortise splitting of the main post (cleavage) can be avoided by proper peg setbacks and spacing and the likelihood of tenon shear (block or relish failure) can be reduced by adequate tenon length. What we must then address is the failure of the pegs themselves. Engineering design standards such as the *National Design Specifications for Wood Construction* (NDS) and the *Timber Frame Engineering Council* (TFEC) identify four common failure modes for wooden pegged connections which are shown in Figure 11.5. In the world of engineering a connection does not need to fall apart to be failing. A connection which has permanently deformed or pulled out by more than 5% of the peg diameter is considered failing. For a one inch peg this is about 1/16th of an inch. While this may not seem like much, any deformation beyond this will likely cause extreme damage to the connection. If the load were applied repetitively (wind loads for example) the damage could add up over time, possibly leading to a catastrophic failure of the connection.

If you take a hammer and strike the side of a post as hard as you can it will make a deep round impression in the wood. This is called a *Bearing Stress* failure in that the wood fibers could not "bear" the compressive force applied by the hammer and permanent deformation occurred. If you had hit the end of the post instead the resulting dimple would not have been nearly as deep. This is because wood is much stronger along the grain of the fibers than it is perpendicular to them. As such we must be aware of two types of Bearing Stress; the weaker Compressive Stress perpendicular to the grain (S_L) and the relatively stronger Compressive Stress parallel to the grain (S_p). Safe values of S_L and S_p are listed for some common wood framing species in Table 8, page 238.

Tenon Bearing Failure

A pegged tenon under tension is a good example where S_L and S_p interact in an interesting way. Here the oak peg is being compressed perpendicular to its grain by the tenon. Meanwhile the pine tenon finds itself in compression parallel to its grain as the peg pushes against the back of the hole. Checking Table 8 we see that the S_p for white pine is more than five times larger than the S_L of the oak. This means that the oak peg will crush well before the pine tenon does. Although this is called a Tenon Bearing Failure it is actually the peg that is failing.

The resulting Bearing stress can be calculated as: $S_L = Z/A$, where a force (Z) is applied to a bearing area (A). In this case the bearing Area is the projected area of the peg where it pushes against the back of the hole in the tenon. For simplicity this area is approximated as a rectangle that is a peg diameter high (D) and the width of the tenon wide (L1) see diagram 5.

For a 1 inch oak peg in a 2 inch wide pine tenon:

S_L = 500 psi (oak peg)

A = D x L1 = 1" x 2" = 2 in².

Z = S_L x L1 = 500 x 2 = 1000 lbs per peg.

Mortise Bearing Failure

Alternatively the pegged connection may experience a Mortise Bearing Failure, where the cheeks or sides of the mortise retaining the peg begin to fail. Here both the peg and the mortise are in compression perpendicular to the grain so both members are of concern. In our example the mortise is made from a softer material than the peg so we will consider the mortise to be the weak link. This would not be true if the timber frame were made from hardwood.

For a 1 inch oak peg running through a 7" x 7" pine beam that houses a two inch wide tenon:

S_L = 250 psi (pine cheeks)
A = D x L2 x 2 = (1" x 2.5") x two cheeks = a net mortise bearing area of 5 in².
Z = S_L x A = 250 x 5 = 1250 lbs per peg.

Peg Bending

Peg Bending is one of the most complex modes of failure. As the peg bends both the tenon and the mortise cheeks begin to deform at the same time. As such the tenon the mortise and the peg all play a role in determining the ultimate bending strength of the peg. For now let us approximate the solution by using the beam bending formula for a distributed load found on page 222: **R = 0.75ZL/bd².** Here R is the extreme bending stress or Rupture modulus for the oak peg as listed in Table 1 (pg 98). In using this formula we are considering the peg to be a small beam that is loaded uniformly by the tenon. Since our peg 'beam' is round rather than rectangular the value of (bd²) or bd x d can roughly be approximated as peg area (D²/4) times peg height (D), where D is the peg diameter.

For a 1 inch oak peg in a 2 inch wide tenon:

R = 2050 psi (oak)
L = the tenon width = 2"
bd² ~ $\pi D^3/4$ = π x 1³/4 = 0.785 in³
Z = R(bd²)/ (0.75L) = 2050 x 0.785/(0.75 X 2) = 1073 lbs per peg.

We can be a little more creative by making a double tenon, as shown in the photo below. This would effectively increase the shearing resistance by a factor of two, however, the tenons in the detail shown are 1-1/2 inches wide. In this case the increase in strength would be 50%, as the net width of the tenons equals 3 inches. Jackson Square frame, 1985.

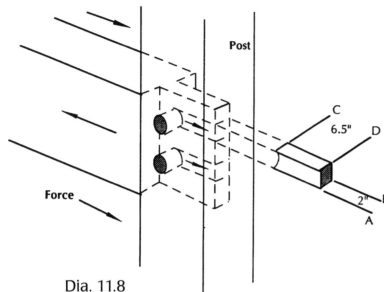

Post

6.5"

2"

Dia. 11.8

The diagram above depicts a tenon in double horizontal shear.

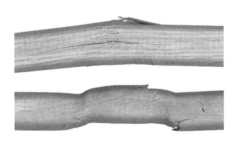

Two of the peg failure modes are exemplified in the above photos. Top) Mode III bending failure in a peg; Bottom) Mode V yielding with secondary bending failure. Photos from the Journal of Structural Engineering, October 2010. This issue of JSE has a very interesting article titled, 'New Yield Model for Wood Dowel Connections', relating to recent pegged joinery testing.

In actuality the length and strength of the mortise cheek plays an important role in determining the maximum bending load, see page 239 in the appendix for a more detailed calculation.

Peg Failure in Double Vertical Shear

If instead the peg begins to deform where it exits the tenon it is experiencing a Double Vertical Shear failure. Vertical shear stress (H_L) cuts across or perpendicular to the grain while horizontal shear stress (H_P) acts along or parallel to the grain. The safe values for vertical shear stress (H_L) are usually not given in tables but can be conservatively estimated as between 2 to 5 times the horizontal H_P values listed in Table 1 (pg. 98). Earlier we used the value of 500 psi, or 2.7 time the value of H_P in Table 1. Vertical Shear stress is defined as force per unit Area being sheared or: $H_L = Z/A$. In the case of a peg in double shear the shear area is that of two circles.

For our 1 inch oak peg in a pine frame:
$H_L = 2 \times H_P = 2.7 \times 185psi = 500$ psi
$A = 2 \times \pi D^2/4 = 2 \times \pi (1^2)/4 = 1.57$ in^2
$Z = H_L \times A = 500 \times 1.57 = 785$ lbs per peg.

From these calculations we find the capacity for each mode of failure to be: 1000 lb; 1250lb, 1073lb; and 785lb. Therefore the limiting failure mode for the connection is the pegs in double vertical shear and the maximum safe tensile force that can be applied is 785 pounds per peg. If the connection has two pegs the nominal force that can safely be retained is 785lbs x 2 = 1570 pounds. If more force is expected, more pegs may be used (assuming that there is adequate beam depth to maintain proper peg spacing), the diameter of the pegs may be increased to 1.25 inches, or a wedged half dovetailed mortise and tenon can be utilized. ∎

Pegs and Mortar

A brief not as a follow up. I have never felt it wise to rely too heavily on the pegs to resist and sustain major structural loads in a frame. I look at pegs in the same way a stone mason looks at mortar. The mason must lay up the stones so that the stones themselves form the structural basis, not the mortar. Mortar is simply a chinking between the stones, something to prevent air or water from passing through. A good stone mason attempts to use the least amount of mortar necessary, achieving strength by letting stone lie upon stone—allowing their compressive weight to create the strength. So it is in timber framing; that the compressive forces are best utilized wherever possible, the pegs being relied upon only as a binding agent. The structural form of timbers should be relied upon as much as possible as the primary element of strength.

There are times however, when tension joinery cannot be avoided, or is even desired. In this case, one must design wisely to utilize the compressive elements in the frame to greatest advantage to alleviate the tensile forces on the joinery and pegs as much as possible. And in this, make the beam itself resist the tension directly, such as by using the half-dovetailed wedged tenon. We saw earlier that the wedged half dovetail alone can resist tension forces nearly equal to three 1 inch pegs.

The first thing to do when designing joinery is to determine the amount of force and subsequent stress that is acting on a given joint, and then design the joint accordingly. The previous equations can be used to determine the load capacities, and with that you can add members, pegs or increase dimensions as necessary.

Single Shear

In the application below, the tie beam is said to be in single shear.

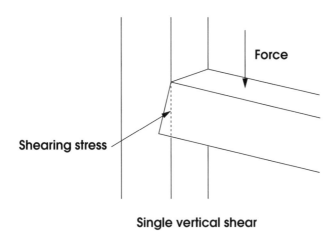

Single vertical shear   Dia. 11.6

Double Shear

In the case where a force is pushing against a post, with the tenon in resistance to the peg, the tenon is said to be in double horizontal shear because two surfaces must shear in order to fail.

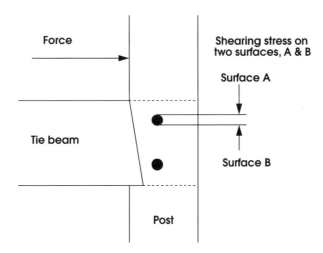

Dia. 11.7

Shear Formula = A x S = Safe Shearing Load in which:
A = sectional shearing area, inches²
S = safe shearing stress, lbs. per sq. inch

Member Notched at Bottom

In the equation below, the shear strength of a tenon can be determined. Determining the shear strength of a tenon is important because it may be the weakest link. The tenon shear strength is determined by the ratio of actual beam depth, **h**, to tenon depth, **d**. A beam notched 1/2 its depth has only 1/4 the shear strength of an unnotched beam. If, however, the end is notched with gradual change in cross section, so that the notch is not square-cornered, the shearing strength approaches that calculated for the net depth above the notch, **d,** therefore, the d/h factor does not apply in the equation below.

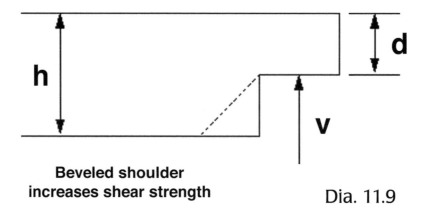

**Beveled shoulder
increases shear strength**

Dia. 11.9

$$V = \frac{2Hbd(d/h)}{3}$$

or, different equation, same result:

$$V = \frac{2/3[b(d)^2H]}{h}$$

V = vertical shear force, pounds
b = width of beam
d = depth of tenon
h = depth of beam
H = Working stress in horizontal shear, shear parallel to grain.
   (safe horizontal shear strength)

Member Notched at Top

Beams notched on the upper side suffer less from stress concentration effects than beams notched or beveled on the lower side. Shear stress should be checked with the following formula:

Dia. 11.10

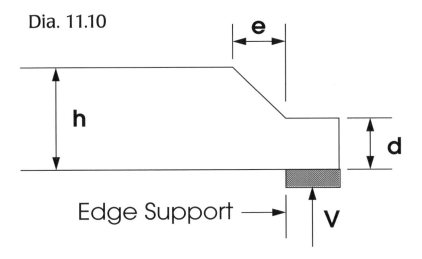

$$V = \frac{2\ Hb\ [h-(h-d/d)e]}{3}$$

V = vertical or external shear force, pounds

H = working stress in horizontal shear, shear parallel to grain

b = width of beam

h = total depth of beam

d = the depth below the notch

e = the distance notch extends inside inner edge of support

The depth of a notch on the upper side of the beam should not exceed 40% of the beam depth **"h"**. If **e** exceeds **h, do not** use this formula. In this case, the shear strength is evaluated on the basis of the depth of the beam below the notch, **d.** If the upper side of notch is beveled instead of a square notch, **d** would be taken as the height of the beam at the inner edge of support, and **e** as the distance from the support to start of bevel.

Answers to Problems on Pages 218

Problem #1) Ø = 30.256°, a = 103.653, b = 60.464, c = 120

Problem #2) Ø = 35.563°, c = 254.466, roof pitch = 8.57/12

Problem #3) Ø= 21.866°, a = 181.898, roof pitch = 4.815/12

Problem #4) b = 614.121, c = 639.676, roof pitch = 41.17/12

Problem #5) Ø = 42.51°, R = 72.30, b = 120.90

Problem #6) Ø = 36.869°, d = 160, e = 62.5, a = 128, CB = 222.5, AB = 356

Top: group photo after nailing the green tea leaves (the Hawaiian version of a roof tree) to the yagura. Bottom: Rodney Haraguchi, the grandson and director of the Haraguchi Rice Mill, after the calm of raising day.

Beams, Joists & Girders

The procedure to determine the structural design requirements of a given beam are generally based on three factors: 1) *Extreme fiber stress in bending*; 2) *Horizontal shear stress*; and 3) *Deflection*. A beam must be sufficient in all three to be considered safe.

Design for Bending

The design for strength in bending is usually the first calculation in determining beam design. The following equation, known as the flexural formula, results in the required Section Modulus (S) for a given timber under a given load. The Bending Moment (M) is determined based on the type and magnitude of loading. Formulas to find M for a few common conditions are given below.

$$S = \frac{M}{F_b}$$

M = Bending moment, in inch-pounds
F$_b$ = allowable extreme fiber stress in bending
S = required Section Modulus

To find the section modulus of a beam use the equation:
$$bd^2/6$$
Example for a 6x6 beam:

$$S = 6 \times 6 \times 6 = 216 / 6 = \mathbf{36}$$

The actual dimension of beam should be used.

Bending Moment

Bending moments are determined by multiplying forces by distance. For simple beams under standard loading conditions, the following formulas can be used.

For a simple beam uniformly loaded:
$$M = \frac{WL}{8}$$
W = total distributed load
L = length in feet
To use in the flexural formula multiply M x 12, to convert from ft.lbs to in.lbs.

For a beam loaded at mid point: $\frac{PL}{4}$
P = total load, concentrated

For a beam loaded at third points: $\frac{PL}{3}$

For a cantilevered beam loaded at the end: PL

For a cantilevered beam uniformly loaded: $\frac{WL}{2}$

Shear in Beams

Horizontal shear is the most common type of beam failure. The following formula results in the amount of horizontal shearing stress per square inch of sectional area. The resulting figure must be less than the safe horizontal shearing stress for the given species. This can be found in Table 8, *Basic Stresses of Clear Wood Under Long Term Loading,* on page 238.

Formula for Horizontal Shear :

$$H = \frac{3V}{2bd}$$

H = Horizontal shearing stress, psi
V = Vertical shear, pounds
b = width of beam
d = depth of beam

For simple beams, V = P/2, in which P is the total load.

The Haraguchi brothers, 91 and 88 years old carving pegs for the 2004 Kauai Yagura Workshop. They just didn't cut pegs, but timbers as well. A yagura is a Japanese watch tower that was used in battles, but also in farming rice. When they were young they were the ones who had to man the watchtower in the rice fields, "running home from school" each day when the rice birds (nutmeg mannikens) would flock in the rice fields to eat the ripening fruit. The young children in the community would be relegated to manning the towers that had strings running from the tower across the rice field with bells and metal objects to make noise to scare the birds away. Kind of like a proactive musical scarecrow. In the workshop we rebuilt a traditional yagura, scribed to stone close the where it once stood in the rice field of their youth. The idea was prompted by Tom, left, who had a dream abut once again climbing to the top of the tower.

Table 6) SAFE SHEARING STRESSES FOR TIMBERS

(Lbs. per sq. inch of shearing surface)

	With Grain	Across Grain
Oak	200	1,000
Yellow Pine, long leaf	150	1,000
Yellow Pine, short leaf	150	1,000
NC Pine, Douglas Fir	100	1,000
White Pine, Spruce & Fir	100	500
Hemlock	100	600

Green or wet wood, in general, shears about one-third more easily than dry wood.
From Audels Carpenters and Builders Guide #2, Theo. Audel & Co. Publishers, ©1923, reprinted 1948.

Deflection

The stiffness of wood is measured in terms of **Modulus of Elasticity.** The following formula is used in determining the deflection of beams. The deflection of a beam is the final analysis to make in determining the appropriate beam size. There are several approaches that can be taken. The following are some of the most common methods.

To determine the amount of deflection that a beam of a given species will deflect under a given load, the following formula can be used.

A simple beam, loaded at center, resting on supports at both ends:

$$D = \frac{PL^3}{48EI}$$

in which:
D = Deflection under load, inches
P = Total load, pounds
E = Modulus of Elasticity, pounds per sq. inch
L = Length of span, inches
I = Moment of inertia of the section, inches ^{4}

The **moment of inertia** is determined by the formula:
$I = bd^3/1$

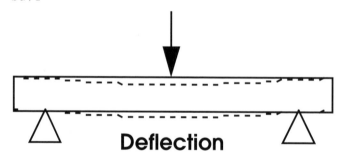

Deflection

For a simple beam uniformly loaded:

$$D = \frac{5PL^3}{384EI}$$

For a simple beam loaded at third points:

$$D = \frac{23PL^3}{684EI}$$

For a cantilevered beam loaded at the end:

$$D = \frac{PL^3}{3EI}$$

For a cantilevered beam uniformly loaded:

$$D = \frac{WL^3}{8EI}$$

A different approach can be used which will result in the Modulus of Elasticity required for a given species of wood under a given load. This is useful if you already have a predetermined timber which you want to make sure will be adequate in deflection. The results for **E** must be less than that for modulus of elasticity found in the table of mechanical properties for the given species.

The formula for a simple beam, loaded at center, resting on supports at both ends:

$$E = \frac{PL^3}{48yI}$$

In which:
E = modulus of elasticity, psi
L = length of span, inches
y = maximum deflection at mid span, inches (a given, see following page)
P = total load, pounds
I = moment of inertia, inches^4

For a beam of rectangular cross section the formula is:

$$E = \frac{PL^3}{4ybd^3}$$

In which: b & d are width and depth of beam, respectively, in inches.

Transposing this formula, it is evident that for a rectangular beam of the same material, support and loading, the deflection is affected as follows:

1) It is directly proportional to the cube of the length of span for beams of the same width and depth. In other words, to triple a span, allow 27 times the deflection.

2) It is inversely proportional to the width for beams of the same span and depth. If one width is tripled, the deflection is one third as great.

3) It is inversely proportional to the cube of the depth for beams of the same span and width. If the depth is tripled, the deflection is 1/27 as great. This is why timbers are placed with wider faces vertical.

Assembling arch braced truss.

To find the load in pounds, which will bend a timber one inch, the preceding equation may be used by substituting y = 1 inch and solving for P (load).

$$\text{Necessary Load (P)} = \frac{4Ebd^3}{L^3}$$

In the above formula, the value for E can be found in the Table 7, **Mechanical Properties of Wood** under *Modulus of Elasticity*, page 236. Modulus of elasticity is the ratio of stress per unit of area to the deformation per unit of length.

(E= stress per unit area/strain per unit length)

In the previous formula, we found the load in pounds that will bend a beam 1 inch under a concentrated load at the middle of span. If the maximum allowable deflection of a given beam is 1/4 inch, the maximum allowable load will be only 25% of this load. If 1/2 inch is the maximum allowable deflection, the maximum allowable load would be 50% and so on.

Most building codes restrict allowable deflection to 1/360 of beam length for plastered ceilings (commonly used for first floors also), and 1/240 for unplastered (commonly used for second floors). Therefore, for a timber 12 feet long, the allowable deflection for a first floor would be:

12' or 144" / 360 = 0.4"

These formulas are based on clear, dry timbers. Where knots are present, or timbers are green, allowances must be made.

Assembling a hammerbeam truss that was erected in two steps because continuous top plates were used in the English tying joint. The collar tie has a sleeved mortise to accept the upper arches. North Berwick, ME 1986.

Appendices

Band sawing the arch for an oak arched brace roof strut at the Boatbuilding Apprenticeshop, Bath, Maine, 1980.

Table 7) Mechanical Properties of Wood

	Common names of species	Specific Gravity[2]	Modulus of rupture	Modulus of elasticity[3]	Work to maximum load	Impact bending—height of drop causing complete failure[4]	Compression parallel to grain—maximum crushing strength	Compression perpendicular to grain—fiber stress at proportional limit	Shear parallel to grain—maximum shearing strength	Tension perpendicular to grain—maximum tensile strength	Side Hardness—load perpendicular to grain
Softwoods			Psi	Million Psi	In-lb per in³	Psi	Psi	Psi	Psi	Psi	Lb
Cedar	Atlantic white	.31 / .32	4,700 / 6,800	.75 / .93	5.9 / 4.1	18 / 13	2,390 / 4,700	240 / 410	690 / 800	180 / 220	290 / 350
	Northern white	.29 / .31	4,200 / 6,500	.64 / .80	5.7 / 4.8	15 / 12	1,990 / 3,960	230 / 310	620 / 850	240 / 240	230 / 320
	Port-Orford	.39 / .43	6,600 / 12,700	1.30 / 1.70	7.4 / 9.1	21 / 28	3,140 / 6,250	300 / 720	840 / 1,370	180 / 400	380 / 630
	Western redcedar	.31 / .32	5,200 / 7,500	.94 / 1.11	5.0 / 5.8	17 / 17	2,770 / 4,560	240 / 460	770 / 990	230 / 220	260 / 350
Douglas fir	Coast	.45 / .48	7,700 / 12,400	1.56 / 1.95	7.6 / 9.9	26 / 31	3,780 / 7,230	380 / 800	900 / 1,130	300 / 340	500 / 710
	Interior West	.46 / .50	7,700 / 12,600	1.51 / 1.83	7.2 / 10.6	26 / 32	3,870 / 7,430	420 / 760	940 / 1,290	290 / 350	510 / 660
	Interior North	.45 / .48	7,400 / 13,100	1.41 / 1.79	8.1 / 10.5	22 / 26	3,470 / 6,900	360 / 770	950 / 1,400	340 / 390	420 / 600
	Interior South	.43 / .46	6,800 / 11,900	1.16 / 1.49	8.0 / 9.0	15 / 20	3,110 / 6,230	340 / 740	950 / 1.510	250 / 330	360 / 510
Fir	Balsam	.33 / .35	5,500 / 9,200	1.25 / 1.45	4.7 / 5.1	16 / 20	2,630 / 5,280	190 / 404	662 / 944	180 / 180	290 / 400
	California red	.36 / .38	5,800 / 10,500	1.17 / 1.50	6.4 / 8.9	21 / 24	2,760 / 5,460	330 / 610	770 / 1,040	380 / 390	360 / 500
Hemlock	Eastern	.38 / .40	6,400 / 8,900	1.07 / 1.20	6.7 / 6.8	21 / 21	3,080 / 5,410	360 / 650	850 / 1,060	230 / —	400 / 500
	Mountain	.42 / .45	6,300 / 11,500	1.04 / 1.33	11.0 / 10.4	32 / 32	2,880 / 6,440	370 / 860	930 / 1,540	330 / —	470 / 680
	Western	.42 / .45	6,600 / 11,300	1.31 / 1.63	6.9 / 8.3	22 / 23	3,360 / 7,200	280 / 550	860 / 1,290	290 / 340	410 / 540
Larch	western	.48 / .52	7,700 / 13,000	1.46 / 1.87	10.3 / 12.6	29 / 35	3,760 / 7,620	400 / 930	870 / 1,360	330 / 430	510 / 830
Pine	Eastern white	.34 / .35	4,900 / 8,600	.99 / 1.24	5.2 / 6.8	17 / 18	2,440 / 4,800	220 / 440	680 / 900	250 / 310	290 / 380
	loblolly	.47 / .51	7,300 / 12,800	1.4 / 1.79	8.2 / 10.4	30 / 30	3,510 / 7,130	390 / 790	860 / 1,390	260 / 470	450 / 690
	longleaf	.54 / .59	8,500 / 14,500	1.59 / 1.98	8.9 / 11.8	35 / 34	4,320 / 8,470	480 / 960	1,040 / 1,510	330 / 470	590 / 870
	Ponderosa	.38 / .40	5,100 / 9,400	1.00 / 1.29	5.2 / 7.1	21 / 19	2,450 / 5,320	280 / 580	700 / 1,130	310 / 420	320 / 460
	Red	.41 / .46	5,800 / 11,000	1.28 / 1.63	6.1 / 9.9	26 / 26	2,730 / 6,070	260 / 600	690 / 1,210	300 / 460	340 / 560
	Shortleaf	.47 / .51	7,400 / 13,100	1.39 / 1.75	8.2 / 11.0	30 / 33	3,530 / 7,270	350 / 820	910 / 1,390	320 / 470	440 / 690
	Western white	.35 / .38	4,700 / 9,700	1.19 / 1.46	5.0 / 8.8	19 / 23	2,430 / 5,040	190 / 470	680 / 1,040	260 / —	260 / 420
Redwood	Old growth	.38 / .40	7,500 / 10,000	1.18 / 1.34	7.4 / 6.9	21 / 19	4,200 / 6,150	420 / 700	800 / 940	260 / 240	410 / 480
	Young growth	.34 / .35	5,900 / 7,900	.96 / 1.10	5.7 / 5.2	16 / 15	3,110 / 5,220	270 / 520	890 / 1,110	300 / 250	350 / 420
Spruce	Black	.38 / .42	6,100 / 10,800	1.38 / 1.61	7.4 / 10.5	24 / 23	2,840 / 5,960	240 / 550	739 / 1,230	100 / —	370 / 520
	Engelmann	.33 / .35	4,700 / 9,300	1.03 / 1.30	5.1 / 6.4	16 / 18	2,180 / 4,480	200 / 410	640 / 1,200	240 / 350	260 / 390
	Red	.37 / .40	6,000 / 10,800	1.33 / 1.61	6.9 / 8.4	18 / 25	2,720 / 5,540	260 / 550	750 / 1,290	220 / 350	350 / 490
	Sitka	.37 / .40	5,700 / 10,200	1.23 / 1.57	6.3 / 9.4	24 / 25	2,670 / 5,610	280 / 580	760 / 1,150	250 / 370	350 / 510
	White	.33 / .36	5,000 / 9,400	1.14 / 1.43	6.0 / 7.7	22 / 20	2,350 / 5,180	210 / 430	640 / 970	220 / 360	320 / 480
Tamarack		.49 / .53	7,200 / 11,600	1.24 / 1.64	7.2 / 7.1	28 / 23	3,480 / 7,160	390 / 800	860 / 1,280	260 / 400	380 / 590

Common names of species	Specific Gravity[2]	Modulus of rupture	Modulus of elasticity[3]	Work to maximum load	Impact bending—height of drop causing complete failure[4]	Compression parallel to grain—maximum crushing strength	Compression perpendicular to grain—fiber stress at proportional limit	Shear parallel to grain—maximum shearing strength	Tension perpendicular to grain—maximum tensile strength	Side Hardness—load perpendicular to grain
Hardwoods		Psi	Million Psi	In-lb per in³	Psi	Psi	Psi	Psi	Psi	Lb
Ash Black	.45 / .49	6,000 / 12,600	1.04 / 1.60	12.1 / 14.9	33 / 35	2,300 / 5,970	350 / 760	860 / 1,570	490 / 700	520 / 850
White	.55 / .60	9,500 / 15,000	1.44 / 1.74	15.7 / 16.6	38 / 43	3,990 / 7,410	670 / 1,160	1,350 / 1,910	590 / 940	960 / 1320
Beech American	.56 / .64	8,600 / 14,900	1.38 / 1.72	11.9 / 15.1	43 / 41	3,550 / 7,300	540 / 1,010	1,290 / 2,010	720 / 1,010	850 / 1,300
Locust Honeylocust	.60 / —	10,200 / 14,700	1.29 / 1.63	12.6 / 13.6	47 / 47	4,420 / 7,500	1,150 / 1,840	1,660 / 2,250	930 / 900	1,390 / 1,580
Black locust	.66 / .69	13,800 / 19,400	1.85 / 2.05	15.4 / 18.4	44 / 57	6,800 / 10,180	1,160 / 1,830	1,760 / 2,480	770 / 640	1,570 / 1,700
Oak, red Black	.56 / .61	8,200 / 13,900	1.18 / 1.64	12.2 / 13.7	40 / 41	3,470 / 6,520	710 / 930	1,220 / 1,910	— / —	1,060 / 1,210
Northern Red	.56 / .63	8,300 / 14,300	1.35 / 1.82	13.2 / 14.5	44 / 43	3,440 / 6,760	610 / 1,010	1,210 / 1,780	750 / 800	1,000 / 1290
Southern Red	.52 / .59	6,900 / 10,900	1.4 / 1.49	8.0 / 9.4	29 / 26	3,030 / 6,090	550 / 870	930 / 1,390	480 / 510	860 / 1,060
Oak, white Bur	.58 / .64	7,200 / 10,300	.88 / 1.03	10.7 / 9.8	44 / 29	3,290 / 6,060	680 / 1,200	1,350 / 1,820	800 / 680	1,110 / 1,370
Chestnut	.57 / .66	8,000 / 13,300	1.37 / 1.59	9.4 / 11.0	35 / 40	3,520 / 6,830	530 / 840	1,210 / 1,490	690 / —	890 / 1,130
Post	.60 / .67	8,100 / 13,200	1.09 / 1.51	11.0 / 13.2	44 / 46	3,480 / 6,600	860 / 1,430	1,280 / 1,840	790 / 780	1,130 / 1,360
White	.60 / .68	8,300 / 15,200	1.25 / 1.78	11.6 / 14.8	42 / 37	3,560 / 7,440	670 / 1,070	1,250 / 2,000	770 / 800	1,060 / 1,360
Poplar Yellow	.40 / .42	6,000 / 10,100	1.22 / 1.58	7.5 / 8.8	26 / 24	2,660 / 5,540	270 / 500	790 / 1,190	510 / 540	440 / 540

[1] Results of tests on small, clear, straight grained specimens. Values in the first line for each species are from tests of green material; those in the second line are from tests of seasoned material adjusted to a moisture content of 12 percent.

[2] Specific gravity based on weight ovendry and volume at moisture content indicated.

[3] Modulus of elasticity measured from a simply supported, center-loaded beam, on a span-depth ratio of 14/1. The modulus can be corrected for the effect of shear deflection by increasing it 10 percent.

[4] 50-pound hammer.

[5] Coast Douglas-fir is defined as Douglas-fir growing in the States of Oregon and Washington west of the summit of the Cascade Mountains. Interior West includes the State of California and all counties in Oregon and Washington east of but adjacent to the Cascade summit. Interior North includes the remainder of Oregon and Washington and the States of Idaho, Montana, and Wyoming. Interior South is made up of Utah, Colorado, Arizona, and New Mexico.

The above values are taken from the Agricultural Handbook of the Forest Products Laboratory, Madison, Wisconsin. USDA Agricultural Handbook 72, revised 1987.

The above table is only a partial listing of the published *Mechanical properties of commercially important woods grown in the United States.* The species listed are the ones most pertinent to timber framing as described in this book. A complete list may be obtained from your local Building Department, or from the U.S. Government Printing Office, Washington, DC 20402.

Note: "*Most of the strength properties of wood improve as it dries... During drying, timbers of large size that contain defects [such as knots] do not increase in strength in the same proportion as small clear pieces, because these defects cause injurious effects that increase with drying, partially or wholly offsetting the increase in the strength of the fibers.*"* Therefore, the values for green material in this table should be used when designing for timbers.

*Excerpt from: Wood: A Manual for its use as a Shipbuilding Material, Vol. 1, Dept. Navy, Bureau of Ships, 1962, page 158. Reprinted by Teaparty Books, Kingston, MA 1983.

Table 8) Basic Stresses for Clear Wood under Long-Term Loading

Species	Extreme fiber in bending or Tension Parallel to Grain, psi (R)	Maximum Horizontal Shear, psi (H)	Compression Perpendicular to Grain, psi (S_L)	Compression Parallel to Grain, psi (S_P)	Modulus of Elasticity in Bending, 1000 psi (E)
Ash, black	1450	130	300	850	1100
Ash, commercial white	2050	185	500	1450	1500
Beech	2200	185	500	1600	1600
Birch, sweet and yellow	2200	185	500	1600	1600
Cedar, Alaska	1600	130	250	1050	1200
Cedar, northern and southern white	1100	100	180	750	800
Cedar, Port Orford	1600	130	250	1200	1500
Cedar, western red	1300	120	200	950	1000
Cottonwood, eastern	1100	90	150	800	1000
Cypress, southern	1900	150	300	1450	1200
Douglas fir, coast region	2200	130	320	1450	1600
Douglas fir, coast region, close-grained	2350	130	340	1550	1600
Douglas fir, Rocky Mt. region	1600	120	280	1050	1200
Douglas fir, dense, all regions	2550	150	380	1700	1600
Elm, American and slippery	1600	150	250	1050	1200
Elm, rock	2200	185	500	1600	1300
Fir, California red, grand, noble and white	1600	100	300	950	1100
Fir, balsam	1300	100	150	950	1000
Gum, black and red	1600	150	300	1050	1200
Hemlock, eastern	1600	100	300	950	1100
Hemlock, western	1900	110	300	1200	1400
Hickory, true and pecan	2800	205	600	2000	1800
Larch, western	2200	130	320	1450	1500
Maple, sugar and black	2200	185	500	1600	1600
Oak, commercial red and white	2050	185	500	1350	1500
Pine, western white, eastern white, ponderosa and sugar	1300	120	250	1000	1000
Pine, jack	1600	120	220	1050	1100
Pine, lodgepole	1300	90	220	950	1000
Pine, red (Norway)	1600	120	220	1050	1200
Pine, southern yellow	2200	160	320	1450	1600
Pine, southern yellow, dense	2550	190	380	1700	1600
Poplar, yellow	1300	120	220	950	1100
Redwood	1750	100	250	1350	1200
Redwood, close-grained	1900	100	270	1450	1200
Spruce, Engelmann	1100	100	180	800	800
Spruce, red, white, Sitka	1600	120	250	1050	1200
Tamarack	1750	140	300	1350	1300
Tupelo	1600	150	300	1050	1200

The above table provides the safe working stresses for a variety of species. Values are for dry timbers at a moisture content of 12%. From Recommendations for Basic Stresses, Forest Products Laboratory, Report R1715, Supplement 2 to U.S. Dept. of Agriculture Misc. Publications 185, 1948.

The Capacity of Pegged Connections: TFEC Technical Bulletin 2009-01

The Timber Frame Engineering Council (TFEC) has been carrying out research on the design and engineering of joined timber frames for the past several years. In 2009 they published a very informative bulletin titled *The Capacity of Pegged Connections,* concerning the results of testing pegged joinery. In this study they have defined 4 failure modes and determined appropriate design standards to follow. A brief synopsis follows, but it is highly recommended to solicit the complete bulletin.

Abstract

Timber frame structures often rely on pegged mortise and tenon connections to secure members together. Wood pegs, while large in diameter, are considerably more flexible than a steel dowel of the same size. Engineering design of these pegged tension connections is not addressed in the National Design Specification for Wood Construction (NDS) [1]. In an effort to standardize the design procedure used for timber frame structures, the TFEC has developed the Standard for Design of Timber Frame Structures TFEC 1-10 [2], which includes a straight-forward approach for analyzing the allowable capacity of pegged mortise and tenon tension connections. The design process included in TFEC 1-10, which is described in more detail in this article, is based on the NDS yield model equations and provides a similar level of performance to steel dowel connections. The TFEC approach is based on physical testing and numerical modeling of connections, coupled with corresponding reliability analyses. This bulletin provides a review and further explanation of the development of the design equations included in the TFEC approach, along with a numerical example of their application.

Tabulated Design Values

Most timber frame connections are fabricated using several predominant species of timber and peg, with standardized tenon thickness. In order to facilitate the design process, the design values for a single peg in a mortise and tenon connection have been tabulated in Table 2. The tabulated values may be used in lieu of the yield limit equations found in Table 1 (pg. 240), provided that:

- the tenon thickness is at least 1 ½" thick
- each mortise cheek is at least as thick as the tenon
- the tenoned member is loaded parallel to the grain
- the mortised member is loaded perpendicular to the grain

Table 2 – Tabulated peg capacities for various peg / timber species combinations.

Each cell lists the 3/4" Dia value (upper) and the 1" Dia value (lower) as "3/4" Dia / 1" Dia".

Peg Species	Eastern White Pine G=0.36	Lodgepole Pine G=0.38	Eastern Hemlock G=0.41	Ponderosa Pine / Yellow Poplar G=0.43	Baldcypress G=0.46	Douglas Fir-Larch G=0.50	Southern Pine G=0.55	Red Oak G=0.67	White Oak G=0.73
Red Maple G=0.58	330 / 587	344 / 611	364 / 647	377 / 670	397 / 705*	422 / 751*	454 / 806*	(shaded)	(shaded)
Birch G=0.63	358 / 637	373 / 664	395 / 703	410 / 728	431 / 766	459 / 815*	493 / 876*	(shaded)	(shaded)
White Ash G=0.64	364 / 647	379 / 674	401 / 714	416 / 740	438 / 778	466 / 828*	500 / 890*	(shaded)	(shaded)
Sugar Maple R. Oak G=0.68	387 / 688	403 / 716	427 / 758	442 / 786	465 / 827	495 / 880*	532 / 945*	617 / 1096*	(shaded)
Locust G=0.71	404 / 718	421 / 748	445 / 792	462 / 821	486 / 863	517 / 919*	555 / 987*	644 / 1144*	(shaded)
W. Oak G=0.73	415 / 738	433 / 769	458 / 814	475 / 844	499 / 888	531 / 945	571 / 1015*	662 / 1177*	706 / 1255*

1. Tabulated design values (Z) in lbs, may be multiplied by all applicable adjustment factors per NDS Table 10.3.1.
2. Proper detailing for end, edge, and spacing distances is required to achieve tabulated values. See TFEC 1-10 Section 3.4.8.
3. Tabulated values are based on 1½" thick tenons with 2" thick mortise cheeks except where designated by a *, signifying 2" thick tenons are required.

Table 1 - Yield Limit Equations for Pegged Double Shear Connections

Yield Mode	Capacity		
1) Tenon Bearing Failure I_m	$$Z = \frac{D l_m F_{em}}{R_d}$$	MODE Im	(1)
2) Mortise Bearing Failure I_s	$$Z = \frac{2 D l_s F_{es}}{R_d}$$	MODE Is	(2)
3) Peg Bending III_s	$$Z = \frac{2 k_3 D l_s F_{em}}{(2 + R_e) R_d}$$	MODE IIIs	(3)
4) Peg Double Shear V	$$Z = \frac{\pi D^2 F_{vy}}{2 R_d}$$	MODE IV	(4)

Lateral Design Procedure

The yield limit equations included in the NDS as well as TFEC 1-10 are used to design mortise and tenon connections where the applied load causes the tenon to withdraw from the mortise. Pegs in mortise and tenon connections are loaded in double shear, with the corresponding yield mode equations shown in Table 1. The NDS Mode IV cannot occur in normal configurations of mortise and tenon joints. This limitation occurs because the Mode IV dowel yield points occur well outside the mortise cheek bounds [4]. Thus, Mode IV does not need to be analyzed in pegged connections. This paper focuses on using the existing yield mode equations included in the NDS coupled with the new peg shear yield mode (Mode V) to determine a design capacity of pegged connections.

The nominal design capacity for a single peg in a connection is the minimum of the four yield modes shown in Table 1. The nominal design capacity must be multiplied by all applicable NDS adjustment factors to achieve an allowable design capacity. For a connection consisting of multiple pegs, is multiplied by the total number of pegs in the connection to arrive at the total joint design capacity. Use of yield mode equations in Table 1 will result in a similar level of reliability as steel-bolted timber connections [13], provided that the requirements of the TFEC 1-10 are maintained. Several of the more notable requirements of TFEC 1-10 are that:

- The mortise cheeks (side walls) must be at least as thick as the tenon.
- The peg specific gravity must be greater than or equal to the timber specific gravity, and be at least 0.57. The limits on specific gravity are a result of full-scale testing conducted on pegged joints. Due to limits in the test data, the upper bounds of peg specific gravity must not exceed 0.73. When denser pegs are used, a specific gravity of 0.73 may be assumed for analysis purposes.
- The yield mode equations were developed for pegs between 0.75 inches to 1.25 inches in diameter. As rigorous testing and modeling has not been conducted on peg diameters outside of this range, the equations may not be valid for smaller or larger pegs. The use of smaller or larger diameter pegs is not precluded by the TFEC 1-10, although no design guidance is provided.
- Mortise and tenon connections must be loaded such that the tenoned (main) member is loaded by the pegs parallel to the grain. Pegs may not be used to transfer load to a tenon at any other angle to the grain.

where:

D = peg diameter, (in)

F_{em} = tenon dowel bearing strength, (psi)

F_{es} = mortise dowel bearing strength, (psi)

$F_{e\parallel}$ = $4770G_p^{1.32}$, parallel to grain dowel bearing strength, (psi)

$F_{e\perp}$ = $4900G_p\sqrt{G_T}$, perpendicular to grain dowel bearing strength, (psi)

$F_{e\theta}$ = $\dfrac{F_{e\parallel}F_{e\perp}}{F_{e\parallel}\sin^2\theta + F_{e\perp}\cos^2\theta}$, angle to grain dowel bearing strength. (psi)

G_p = specific gravity of the peg material (from NDS Table 11.3.2A [1])

G_T = specific gravity of the timber material where $G_T < G_p$ (from NDS Table 11.3.2A [1])

F_{vy} = $4850G_pG_T^{0.75}$, effective dowel shear strength, (psi)

F_{yb} = bending yield strength of the peg, (psi)

   = $24850G_p^{1.13}$ (approximated from Wood Handbook [14])

k_3 = $-1+\sqrt{\dfrac{2(1+R_e)}{R_e}+\dfrac{2F_{yb}(2+R_e)D^2}{3F_{em}l_s^2}}$

K_θ = correction factor to account for loading at an angle to the grain

   = $1+\dfrac{\theta}{360}$ $(1\le K_\theta \le 1.25)$

l_m = tenon thickness, (in)

l_s = mortise cheek thickness, (in)

R_e = main to side member dowel bearing ratio

   = F_{em}/F_{es}

R_d = reduction term to calibrate yield capacity to allowable capacity, where

   = $4K_\theta$ (Modes I_m, I_s),

   = $3.2K_\theta$ (Mode III_s)

   = 3.5 (Mode V)

θ = maximum angle of load to any timber grain, (deg) $(0°\le\theta\le90°)$

From the Timber Frame Engineering Council (TFEC), Technical Bulletin No. 01.
The above notations to be used in conjunction with the formulas on the opposing page.

Miscellaneous Notes

Cleavage resistance is the term used to denote the resistance that wood offers to a splitting stress, in which the force acts like a wedge.

Maximum compression parallel to the grain, or endwise compression, involves columns, props, and posts, in which the load tends to crush or shorten the piece lengthwise. In long columns, where the length is great compared with their least cross-sectional dimension, greater than 1:11, bending occurs before full compressive strength is reached. This critical load is known as the **Euler load.** If the same stick is braced so that flexure is prevented, its supporting strength is enormously increased.

Maximum compression perpendicular to the grain, or sidewise compression, is the greatest stress that the material will take without acquiring a permanent set, used in calculating bearing areas for beams, joists, etc.

Fiber stress at proportional limit is the maximum load a beam will support for a short time without acquiring a permanent deformation; it is seldom used, preference being given to **maximum crushing strength**, which is less variable.

Horizontal shear is the stress along the longitudinal axis of a beam tending to move the fibers past each other in a longitudinal direction. Shear stresses are maximum at the neutral plane. In large members, failure by horizontal shear may occur above or below the neutral plane, owing to the presence of shakes or checks.

Modulus of elasticity is a measure of the stiffness of wood, used in calculating the ability of intermediate and long columns to resist deformation or bending.

Modulus of Rupture represents the maximum load-carrying capacity of a member, and is proportional to the maximum moment borne by a specimen. It is an accepted criterion for strength, although it is not a true stress value because the formula by which it is computed is valid only to the proportional limit.

Moment of Inertia may be defined as a measurement of the resistance which a cross-section of a beam offers to rotation about its neutral axis. For any rectangular section loaded normally, **$I = bd^3/12$**, in which
   b = width in inches
   d = depth in inches
   I = moment of inertia, inches^4

Section Modulus may be defined as the moment of inertia divided by the distance of the most remote fiber from the neutral axis. The section modulus for a rectangular beam can be found using the equation: **$S = bd^3/6$**

Shear parallel to the grain is the maximum load in pounds **(P)** required to shear off the surface parallel to the direction of load in square inches **(A)**. Shear =P/A

Shear perpendicular to the grain is closely related to **compression perpendicular to the grain**, which is defined as the stress at proportional limit, and to **hardness**, which is resistance to wear and marring.

Work to Maximum Load in Bending represents the ability to absorb shock with some permanent deformation. It is a measure of the combined strength and toughness of wood under bending stresses.

LOADS:

Concentrated load occurs when the load is applied at a single point or points. In material of structural sizes containing defects, it is usually applied at two points, one third of the span of the beam apart. This, known as **third-point loading**, is extremely important in studying the influence of defects on the strength of wood, since the resultant stresses are uniform throughout the center third of the beam.

Safe load is the load considered safe for a material to support in actual practice. It is always less than the load at proportional limit and is usually taken as a certain proportion of the ultimate or breaking load. The ratio of the breaking load to the safe load is termed the **reduction factor,** and is often as high as **4** to **8**, especially if the safety of human life depends on the structure. This means that only **one-fourth** to **one-eighth** of the average computed strength value is considered safe to use in structural timber.

Dead Load is the force of gravity acting on the weight of the structure itself.

Live Load is the sum of the forces acting on the frame as a result of its intended use, such as occupants and furnishings.

Snow Load is based on the maximum accumulation of snow that can be expected to fall on the roof and remain on the roof. It becomes an even greater factor when coupled with high wind loads.

Wind Load is the force exerted on walls and roof by wind. Wind load is accentuated by snow load, and they are often used in combination to determine resultant external loading. Wind load is often not accounted for in residential structures under 3 stories tall.

The Resultant Load is the combined effects of wind load and snow load.

Glossary

ADZE-an axe-like tool with a curved blade at right angles to the handle, used for dressing wood.

ARCH-a curved structure spanning an opening.

ARCHITECT-one who designs and supervises the construction of buildings.

ARCHITECTURE-the art and science of designing and erecting buildings.

ARCH BRACES-curved braces in a truss such as a hammerbeam or arched brace truss; braces beneath tie beams, frequently curved or arched.

ARRIS-the edge at which two surfaces meet.

ASHLAR-blocks of stone wrought to even faces and laid in horizontal courses with vertical joints.

AUGER-a tool for boring holes in wood.

BALCONY-a platform projecting from a wall.

BAREFACED-a timber joint with only one shoulder.

BASE CRUCKS-timbers placed as wall posts, curving inward with the natural bend of the tree, ending into a collar tie.

BAYS-the divisions between principal frame sections.

BASEMENT-the lowest story of a building, usually below or partly below ground level.

BEAM-a main horizontal timber.

BEETLE-a large mallet used to bring timber joints together.

BELFRY-the timber frame inside a church steeple to which bells are fastened.

BENT-a transverse structural truss-like framework that makes up the primary structural element of a timber frame.

BIRD'S MOUTH-a joint bearing a visual resemblance to an open bird's beak.

BLADE-the term applied to the timber in a cruck frame.

BLUE STAIN-a bluish, anaerobic fungus that grows on the sap wood of pine lumber.

BOUND WATER-the water bound within the cellular walls of wood fiber.

BOXED HEART-a timber sawn so that the pith is centered equally from all faces.

BRACE-any timber reinforcing an angle, usually subjected to compression.

BRESSUMMER-breast-summer, a timber extending for the length of a timber building, normally forming the sill of a jettied story.

BRIDGE-a built construction spanning a river or connecting two points.

BRIDLE-timber joints having open-ended mortises, and tenons resembling a horse's mouth with the bit of the bridle in place.

BUNGALOW-a single-story house.

BUTTRESS-a mass of masonry built against a wall to counteract the lateral thrust of a roof vault.

CAMBER-a horizontal timber in which the center is higher than the ends.

CANTILEVER-a horizontal projection supported by a downward force behind a fulcrum.

CAPE-a style of house derived from Cape Cod, originally two rooms wide, a room-and-a-half deep, with a roof of two equal pitches.

CARPENTER-a workman who engages in the construction and repair of wooden structures.

CARYATID- a sculptured female figure used as a column.

CASEMENT-a window with the sash hung vertically and opening outwards or inwards.

CASTLE-a fortified habitation.

CENTER CUT-a timber milled so that the pith is exposed on one face.

CENTERING-wooden framework used in arch or vault construction.

CHAIR RAIL-a moulding round a room to prevent chairs damaging the wall.

CHAMFER-the bevel created by removing a timber's corner.

CHASE-a long mortise into which a tenon may be inserted.

CHALET-a Swiss herdsman's hut or mountain cottage.

CHISEL-a cutting tool with a beveled edge, which is pushed with the hands or struck with a mallet.

CHIMNEY BAY-the narrower middle bay in a four bent frame in which the stairway, chimney and mechanical systems are located.

CLAPBOARD-thin, beveled planks applied horizontally as weatherboarding.

COLLAR BEAM or TIE-a horizontal roof timber uniting a rafter couple between the base and apex, holding either extension or compression load.

COLLAR PURLIN-the longitudinal beam supported by the crown posts that supports the common rafters in a crown-post roof.

COMMON-the majority member of either kind, joist, rafter, or purlin, as opposed to principal.

COMPASS TIMBER-timber of natural and grown curvature.

COMPOUND TRUSS-a truss made up of multiple simple trusses.

CORNER POST-the post standing at the intersection of two walls.

CONCRETE-mortar mixed with small stones, sand, and Portland cement.

CORBEL-a projection from the face of a stone wall, sometimes used to support timbers.

CORNICE-any projecting ornamental molding along the top of a building, finishing or crowning it. Sloping, it is called a raked cornice.

COTTAGE-ORNE'-an artfully rustic building, usually asymmetrical, often thatched, with rough-hewn wooden columns, late 18th, early 19th century English ornamental style.

COVE- large concave moulding, used at the wall-ceiling junction.

CRIB TIMBER-a timber used to make cribbing.

CRIBBING-low staging of beams used to support timbers being worked.

CRIBBING PONY-a low, stout and sturdy stool used to support a crib timber.

CROWN-the natural camber of a beam in the vertical direction.

CROWN POST—a vertical timber standing at the center of a tie beam and supporting a collar purlin.

CRUCKS-pairs of inclined, curved timbers used in timber framing. There are several types: base, full, jointed, raised, middle, and upper.

CRUCK BLADE-one half of a pair of crucks.

CRUCK SPUR-a short beam that joins the cruck blade to a stud post to stiffen the wall and support the wall plate.

CUPOLA-a small dome on a circular or polygonal base crowning a roof.

CURING-the initial stage of seasoning timbers in which the timbers relax and the free water evaporates from the wood fibers. Curing generally takes 6 to 12 weeks for timbers. Longer curing time adds no additional benefit to timbers.

CYMA-ogee complex curve formed by a concave and convex arc in a single linear association.

DENTIL-a small square block used in Greek architecture.

DOOR-a movable structure used to close off an entrance, consisting of a panel that swings on hinges, slides, or rotates.

DORMER-an upright window protruding from the pitch of a roof.

DOUBLE TENONS-two tenons cut from the same timber's end.

DOVETAIL-a self locking tension joint used in furniture and timber framing.

DRAGON BEAM-a timber bisecting the angle formed by two wall plates.

DRAGON POST-a jowled corner post supporting two intersecting jetties.

DRAWKNIFE-a hand tool with handles at either end of its blade, used with a drawing motion to shave a surface.

DUBBIN'-(Yankee slang) to work lazily and in an unworkmanlike manner.

DURNS-timbers with grown bends which form doorways in Gothic architecture, Harr has hinges, head is opposite.

EAVES-the underside of a roof's pitch that projects outside a wall.

EAVES DROPPER-a joist of deep cross section supported by a top plate that is sawn or hewn to a graduating diminished depth to match the common joist depth in a floor system.

EAVES LINE-the line created where the inclined roof plane intersects with the vertical wall plane.

ELL-a single story lean-to wing containing a kitchen.

ENGLISH TYING JOINT-a traditional joint used to join the rafter foot, tie beam and post.

FASCIA-a board forming a front, frequently used to cover a number of timbers' ends, as rafters at an eaves or joists at a jetty. From Latin, fasces, to bind together.

FETTLE-the act of adjusting a wooden plane.

FOLLY-a costly but useless structure built to satisfy the whim of some eccentric.

FREE TENON-a tenon used as a separate item, both ends being fitted into mortises cut into two timbers to be joined. Also known as a spline in modern timber framing.

FREE WATER-the unbound water in a trees fiber that is the first to evaporate after felling.

FROE-a cleaving tool for splitting cask staves or shingles from a block or bolt of wood.

FULCRUM-the supporting point of a cantilever.

GABLE-the triangular upper portion of a wall at the end of a pitched roof.

GAMBREL-a ridged roof with two slopes on each side, the lower slope having the steeper pitch.

GARGOYLE-a water spout projecting from a roof or parapet, carved into a grotesque figure.

GARRISON POST-the wall post in the upper story of a jettied wall.

GAZEBO-a small lookout tower or summerhouse with a view, usually in a garden or park.

GIRT-horizontal timbers in wall or floor frames.

GOLDEN PROPORTION-an irrational number known to ancient Greeks, defined as a line cut so that the proportion of the smaller section to the greater is as the greater is to the whole, 1:1.618.

GOTHIC ARCHITECTURE- the architecture of the pointed arch.

GREAT ROOM-the main open cathedral area in a timber frame house.

GROUNDSILL-the first horizontal timber laid for a timber building.

GUSSET-a bracket strengthening the angle of a structure, as in a gusset plate in a truss.

HALL and PARLOR-a two-room house.

HALVING-in jointing, removing half the thickness of two timbers, as in half-laps.

HAMMER BEAM-horizontal beam projecting at a wall-plate level on opposite sides of a wall like a tie-beam with the center cut away. A primary member of a hammerbeam truss.

HAMMER POST-a vertical timber set on the inner end of a hammer beam to support a rafter.

HAMMERBEAM TRUSS-a clear-span bent frame in which the rafters are supported by hammer beams and hammer posts.

HAUNCH-adjuncts of tenons, designed to resist winding.

HEMLOCK-poison associated with the death of Socrates.

HEWN-timber worked with an axe or adze.

HIGH POST CAPE-a traditional frame in which the principal posts cantilever above the principal tie beam to add a half story to the structure.

HIP RAFTER-a rafter pitched on the external angle of two intersecting roof lines.

HORIZONTAL SHEAR-the stress placed on a beam along its horizontal axis parallel to the grain and perpendicular to the load.

HOUSING or COGGING-a mortise large enough to hold an entire timber's end.

INGLENOOK-a recess for bench or seat built beside a fireplace.

IRISH WHISKEY-uisqebeatha, aqua vitae, water of life.

ISOMETRIC PROJECTION-a three-dimensional drawing in which parallel lines are of equal length, rather than diminishing as in a natural perspective.

JAMB-the side of a doorway, archway or window.

JEAN-CLAUDE KILLY- French Olympic alpine skier who won the downhill triple crown in the 1968 Winter Games in Grenoble, France, in miraculous fashion.

JEAN-CLAUDE KILLY EFFECT- The zone that one gets into when they understand their talent or craft so well that they stop thinking about what they are doing, but act without external or mental influence. Rooted in the Zen concept that before you can really excel you have to forget everything you know. A jazz musicians credo, and personified by Jean-Claude Killy's final run in the 1968 Grenoble Games that exhibited this effect across all talent, art, sports and craft boundaries, hence, the effect is associated with his name.

Glossary

JETTY-the projection of an upper story beyond its substructure, resulting in an increased floor area.

JOINER-a carpenter, especially a cabinetmaker.

JOINT-the intersection of two timbers.

JOINTING-straightening the edge with a plane.

JOIST-horizontal floor member.

JOWL-the thickening of a post beneath an entering beam, as on a story post or gunstock post.

KERF-the cut produced by a saw.

KEY-tapered piece of hardwood transfixing a scarf, drawing it tight.

KING POST-a timber placed in the center of a gable, reaching to the rafter peak.

KNEE BRACE-a common brace used to prevent racking.

LAP JOINT-any jointed timbers which overlap each other.

LINTEL-a horizontal beam bridging an opening.

LOAD-the total force acting on a member or truss.

LODGED-To put and cause to remain in place (OED). A term applied to floors retained in place by their weight alone.

LOG CONSTRUCTION-tree trunks laid horizontally, overlapping at the corners.

LOGGIA-a gallery open on one or more sides; it may be a separate structure, sometimes in a garden.

LOUVER-an opening partially closed by slanting boards to keep out rain.

LYCH GATE-a covered wooden gateway with open sides at the entrance to a churchyard, providing a resting-place for a coffin.

MAIN SPAN-in aisled buildings, this is the central and greatest distance spanned.

MANTELPIECE-the wood, brick, stone, or marble frame surrounding a fireplace, sometimes called chimney-piece.

MEMBER-a single stick which is part of a larger structure.

MID-STREY-the porch-like structure at the front of a barn.

MILL RUN-ungraded lumber or timbers milled from logs as they come from the mill.

MITER-a joint made by beveling the ends of two pieces, usually at a 45 degree angle to form a 90 degree angle.

MORTISE-a rectangular cavity in a piece of wood, to receive a tenon.

MULLION-a vertical post or upright dividing a window or other opening into two lights.

MUNTIN-the small members of a window which divide the individual panes of glass.

NAIL-a slender, pointed piece of metal hammered into wood as a fastener.

NUETRAL AXIS-the horizontal center axis of a beam that is neither subjected to compression or tension. Also known as the neutral plane.

NEWEL-the principal post at the end of a flight of stairs.

NEWTON, ISAAC-the father of modern engineering and classical mechanics as derived from his laws of motion.

NOGGING-the material used to infill a frame betwixt sill and top.

NOTCHED-LAP-a lap joint having a V-shaped indentation on plan-view to prevent lengthwise withdrawal.

OCTAGON-a geometric figure of eight equal sides, sometimes used as a ground plan for buildings.

ORIEL-a bay window in an upper story which does not extend to the ground.

OUTSHUT-an area of space added to a building's bays, normally at the sides; at the end they are called 'culatia', from the Latin.

PALLADIAN WINDOW- a tripartite window with a semicircular arch above the middle light, representing a Roman arch superimposed on a Greek rectangle.

PARAPET-a low wall, placed to protect any spot where there is a sudden drop, as at the edge of a roof.

PARGETTING-exterior plastering of a timber-framed building which has a masonry nogging.

PARQUET-flooring of thin hardwood laid in patterns over a subfloor and highly polished.

PENT-ROOF-a shed or sloping roof attached to the side of a building, without posts at the eaves.

PERGOLA-a covered walk in a garden usually formed by a double row of posts with beams above and covered with climbing plants.

PITH-the absolute center or heart of a tree.

PLAN-the arrangement of the parts of a building as viewed from above.

PLANE-a carpenter's tool with an adjustable blade for smoothing and leveling surfaces.

PLATE-a horizontal timber laid at the base of a timber frame. The term implies a structural footing, as distinct from a ground sill.

PLINTH-a projecting base, as on a column.

PONY-a small, stout saw horse used to support a crib timber.

PORCH-the covered entrance to a building.

POSTS-in timber-framed buildings, the main vertical timbers of the walls.

POST & LINTEL-a structural system in which a beam is supported by two posts.

PRINCIPAL RAFTER-a heavy rafter placed at bay intervals in a timber frame.

PURLIN-a longitudinal timber in a roof, spanning from rafter to rafter.

PYTHAGOREAN THEOREM-the equation relating to the sides of a right triangle which states that $a^2 + b^2 = c^2$

QUEEN POSTS-posts set in pairs between tie-beams and rafters or between tie-beams and collars and acting in compression.

RABBET-a rectangular recess made along an edge of a piece of wood.

RAIL-a horizontal member in the frame of a door, window, panel, etc.

RAKING STRUTS-inclined struts used in pairs between tie beams and principal rafters.

RELISH-the amount of wood, or meat, left on a tenon behind the pegs, or on a tension member, which resists shear.

REREDOS-a reflecting wall of masonry for an open hearth.

RIVE-to split timber lengthwise, as in riving shingles with a froe.

RIDGE BEAM-a horizontal, longitudinal timber at the apex of a roof.

ROOF-the exterior surface and its supporting structures on the top of a building.

ROVE-the washer placed over a rivet in clinker-type boat building.

SALTBOX-a house design with two roof pitches of un-equal length, traditionally developed by adding a shed, or salt-box, to the rear of a hall-and-parlor.

SAMSON POST-pillar erected in a ship's hold, between the lowerdeck and the keelson.

SCARF-a lengthwise joint in two timbers, with the four faces continuous.

SET-the divergence of the sides of a dovetail.

SHAKE-a defect in wood in which the annual growth rings separate after milling.

SHINGLES-wooden tiles for covering roofs and walls.

SHORE-an inclined timber supporting a vertical one, acting in compression. A temporary support under a structure.

SILL-the horizontal timber at the base of a timber framed structure into which the posts are tenoned.

SIMPLE TRUSS-a truss which is made up of 4 joints and 5 members all laying in one plane.

SLICK-a large chisel, usually 2-1/2 to 4 inches wide, with a long handle used for paring wide tenon faces and deep mortise sides.

SOFFIT-the underside of the eaves.

SOFFIT TENON-a horizontal tenon that protrudes from the bottom face of the beam, usually in joists and purlins.

SOLAR-an upper living room in a medieval house, a solarium.

SPAR TENON-a tenon on the post of a traditional English tying joint that passes through the top plate locking the plate between the sleeved face of the post, from which the teasel tenon projects into the tie beam.

SPUR TIE-a short tie such as connects a cruck blade and a wall plate, or a collar arch and a wall plate.

SPIRE MAST-central vertical timber of a framed spire.

SQUARE RULE-a system of layout in which every crooked or out of square timber is deemed to have a perfectly square timber within. Layout begins with a center line or a reference face, and all calculations are based on the 'perfectly square' timber within.

SQUINCH-an arch placed diagonally at the inner corners of a tower.

SQUINT-angle other than 90 degrees; an obliquely cut opening in a wall.

STEELY DAN-1970's rock band who became the first group to develop (or perhaps revive) 'timber framing' music in the early 70's, and who first coined the phrase, "perfection and grace... [puts] a smile on your face."

STORY POLE-a pole or stick used to make layout markings along its length that can then be transferred to multiple members rapidly and accurately.

STORY POST-a wall post of a multi-storied timber building that continues through the floor levels.

STRAINING BEAM-a horizontal beam between two posts, acting in compression.

STRUT-a secondary timber in a roof system that acts in compression.

STUD-the vertical common timber in a framed wall.

SUMMER BEAM-the principal floor timber that connects from tie beam to tie beam into which floor joists are joined.

SWEEP-the natural horizontal camber in a beam after milling.

TEASEL TENON-the tenon that protrudes from the sleeved face of the post in an English tying joint, which enters a mortise on the bottom of the tie beam.

TENSION BRACE-a brace joining from sill beam, or lower horizontal plate, to a post.

TIE BEAM-beam laid across a building to tie both walls together.

TIMBER-FRAMING-a method of construction in which walls are built of interlocking vertical and horizontal timbers.

TIMBER QUAKE-the loud, but harmless, sound of a timber checking in a frame often taking place several years after construction. The precursor to a 3 a.m. phone call to the builder.

TONGUE-a fillet worked along the edge of a plank to enter a groove in another; also the male tenon of tongue & fork joint.

TOP PLATE-a horizontal timber along the top of a framed wall.

TRANSOM-a cross beam acting as a support for the superstructure.

TRUSS-a number of timbers framed together to bridge a space, to be self-supporting, and to carry other timbers.

TURRET-a small and slender tower.

TUSK-the wooden key driven through the end of a protruding tenon.

TUSK TENON-a horizontal tenon that extends at some point between the top and bottom faces of a beam, usually in principal floor members and purlins.

TUNK-(vernacular) to strike wood with a mallet.

UISQEBEATHA-(gaelic) see IRISH WHISKEY.

VICE-a spiral stair winding around a central column.

VOISSOIR-a wedge-shaped stone forming one of the units of an arch.

WANEY-used to describe timber, the squared section of which is the greatest that can be cut from the rounded trunk. Any missing sharp arises are said to be 'waney' edges.

WAINSCOT-boards applied vertically to the inside of a wall, sometimes framed and panelled.

WEATHERBOARDING-overlapping horizontal boards covering a timber-framed wall, clapboards or beveled siding.

WINDING-in carpentry, the result of torque or twisting, or the result of drying a spirally-grained tree.

WIND BRACES-braces fitted into the angles of either roofs or walls to resist lateral forces due wind pressures.

Bibliography

The Mechanical Properties of Wood
By Frederick F. Wangaard
John Wiley & Sons, Inc., New York: 1950

Structural Engineering for Architects
By Kenneth R. Lauer
McGraw-Hill Book Company, New York: 1981

Simplified Engineering for Architects and Builders
By Harry S. Parker, M.S.
6th ed. rev., James Ambrose, M.S.
John Wiley & Sons, Inc., New York: 1984

Simplified Design of Structural Timber
By Harry S. Parker
John Wiley & Sons, Inc., New York

Timber Design and Construction Handbook
By Timber Engineering Co.
F.W. Dodge Corp., New York

The Encyclopedia of Wood
Sterling Publishing Co., New York: 1980

The Penguin Dictionary of Architecture
By John Flemming
Hugh Honour
Nikolas Pevsner
Penguin Books, New York

Audels Carpenters and Builders Guide #2
By Frank D. Graham
Thomas J. Emery
Theo. Audel & Co., Publishers, New York, 1939

Wood: A Manual for its Use as a Shipbuilding Material
Teaparty Books, Kingston, MA: 1983

Mechanics and Materials
By James M. Gere & Stephen P. Timoshenko
3rd ed. PWS Publishing Co., Boston: 1990

Wood Handbook: Wood as an Engineering Material
Forest Products Laboratory
Agricultural handbook 72, revised 1987
U.S. Dept. of Agriculture, Washington D.C,
1987

Sir Banister Fletcher's: A History of Architecture
Ed. John Musgrove, conslt ed., John Tarn,
Peter Willis,
asst ed. Jane Farrow. 19th ed.,
The Royal Institute of British Architects and the
University of London
The Butterworth Group, 1989

Index

Index

Fox Maple School of Traditional Building

The Fox Maple School of Traditional Building began as a series of timber framing workshops in the early 1980s. Today, with the campus site on the Corn Hill Road, in West Brownfield, Maine, it has grown to include a variety of courses, seminars and events that incorporate the full array of traditional and natural building venues. Traditional straw clay and straw bale enclosures, natural earth plaster finishes, thatch, and experimentation with new ways to utilize and build with traditional systems are underway. The campus buildings were all constructed by students in structured workshops as teaching models. The goal has been to utilize the materials that come directly from the site as much as possible to within a 100 mile radius of the site. For the most part, we have been successful.

In the initial phase, our plan was to construct four new buildings—a new office, a library/conference building, a dining hall, and a workshop. In the process of designing the site and structures we attempted to incorporate a variety of traditional designs and systems that could utilize locally available and natural materials as much possible. With these first four structures nearing completion, our waste piles have consisted of little more than timber and wood scraps, straw, reed and clay—these being the essential materials used in the construction to date.

The building systems that we chose incorporated both ancient methods and progressive modern approaches based on traditional systems. Timber framing is at the core of our building and educational focus, but straw bales, traditional wattle and daub, wood chip and clay, reed thatching and compressed wheat straw panels are all incorporated. Our motivation for working with natural materials—beyond that of creating comfortable and healthy working environments—is geared toward understanding, analyzing and developing systems that may increase speed and efficiency and the long-term reliability of these traditional systems for our modern building needs. Essentially, we are using our new site as a testing ground to assess the viability of a number of systems, with the overriding goal of determining if they can be adapted to any building site, by any builder, with consistent results. We believe that building should be undertaken in a professional way, with fine craftsmanship the primary goal. We hope that the results of our efforts can provide information that may allow the everyday building professional, architect, designer and engineer to incorporate these systems into their everyday building projects. At the same time, we embrace the opportunity to train individuals interested in pursuing these truly dynamic building approaches, for both personal or professional reasons.

Books & Publications by Fox Maple Press

Joiners' Quarterly

The Journal of Timber Framing & Traditional Building
Published from 1983 - 2000, JQ unwittingly chronicles the revival of timber
framing from the early days. Back issues are available.

A Timber Framer's Workshop

Joinery, Design & Construction of Traditional Timber Frames

Advanced Timber Framing
The Art & Design of
Timber Frame Roof Systems

*Joinery, Design & Construction of Hip & Valley
Timber Frame Roof Systems*

In the Works
The New Vernacular House

*Practical approaches to building timber frame houses using local natural
materials; timbers, stone, clay, wood chips, straw and reeds*
Includes scribing timbers to stone and working with curved timbers and
round logs, round to square and square to round.

For information about books and publications in the Corn Hill Book Series,
traditional building workshops, and events at
Fox Maple School of Traditional Building, please contact to us.

Fox Maple Press, Inc.
P.O. Box 249
65 Corn Hill Road
Brownfield, Maine 04010
207-935-3720
foxmaple@foxmaple.com
www.foxmaple.com